TURBO PASCAL TOOLBOX

TURBO PASCAL® TOOLBOX
SECOND EDITION

FRANK DUTTON

SYBEX®

SAN FRANCISCO · PARIS · DÜSSELDORF · LONDON

Cover art by Thomas Ingalls + Associates
Cover photography by David Bishop
Book design by Ingrid Owen

IBM PC, AT, and XT are registered trademarks of International Business Machines Corporation.
MS-DOS is a registered trademark of Microsoft Corporation.
Turbo Pascal is a registered trademark of Borland International Inc.

SYBEX is a registered trademark of SYBEX Inc.

SYBEX is not affiliated with any manufacturer.

Library of Congress Card Number: 88-63217
ISBN 0-89588-602-2
Manufactured in the United States of America
10 9 8 7 6 5 4 3 2 1

ACKNOWLEDGMENTS

A debt of appreciation is owed to my ex-wife, Margaret, who suggested this book.

I also believe that an acknowledgment is due Phillippe Kahn of Borland International for his pioneering step in marketing Turbo Pascal at a reasonable price. It has allowed thousands the opportunity to experiment with a compiled language, which they might otherwise not have tried.

Dianne King, acquisitions editor for Sybex, was extremely helpful in the early stages of this project, as well as being just a very nice person to deal with.

Marilyn Smith, the editor of this book, has been invaluable in her efforts to help put together the best book possible and continued to lend advice and support when the going got rough.

I would also like to thank Barbara Gordon, Managing Editor at Sybex, for her assistance, patience, and cooperation. Pat Wong and her staff, who handled the technical review of the book, were also of great assistance. Christian Crumlish handled the changes for the second edition with skill and efficiency.

Other contributors to the book include John Kadyk and Jocelyn Reynolds, word processors; Cheryl Vega, typesetter; Maria Mart and Chris Calder, proofreaders; Ingrid Owen, designer; and Paula Alston, indexer.

The calendar functions in Chapter 4 were adapted from an article by Michael A. Covington, which appeared in the *PC Tech Journal*.

TABLE OF CONTENTS

CHAPTER 4
HANDLING AND STORING DATES AND TIMES   129

CHAPTER 5
PROGRAMMING MENUS

CHAPTER 6
BIT MAPPING FOR EFFICIENT DATA STORAGE

CHAPTER 7
SCREEN HANDLING

CHAPTER 8
DESIGNING SCREENS WITH A SCREEN GENERATOR   215

INTRODUCTION

....
....
....
....
....
....
....
....
....
....
....
....
....
....
....
....
....

WHY THIS BOOK WAS WRITTEN

When I first began teaching myself to program microcomputers, I relied heavily on the manuals that accompanied them and on various books that I purchased. Since that time, computer manuals are no longer as difficult for the novice to understand, but they can still be somewhat daunting. However, there still seems to be a dearth of information about how to add some polishing to programs to make them truly effective and professional. Virtually all the books that I have bought are loaded with neat little programs that serve well to illustrate points about programming, but seem to be of only slight practical value. Trying to put together useful routines for everyday business programming from these books has required a great deal of searching and reconstruction and, even then, I found that many points were not covered.

Over a period of time, I have put together a library of various routines to make programming faster, easier, and more effective. Had this same information been available to me, I could have progressed much more rapidly in my programming efforts. Knowing that others must be having the same difficulties led me to want to share the truly useful routines I found or developed. To that end, I have tried to include in this book only procedures and functions that can immediately be transported to virtually any program and used as a building block for the construction of that program. Most of the programs in this book are of no practical value; they serve only to illustrate the use of the procedures and functions, which are the real subject of the book.

WHO SHOULD READ THIS BOOK

This book is directed toward three basic classes of programmers:

- The novice who has only a working knowledge of Turbo Pascal and wishes to be able to produce effective, professional programs quickly and who also would like to gradually learn the technical aspects that may be garnered from a closer inspection of the various procedures and functions
- Intermediate-level programmers who may need only some of the information presented here or who may simply find it expedient to use some of the procedures and functions to save the time and effort necessary to construct and test similar procedures for themselves
- Professional programmers who may be working with Turbo Pascal for the first time and want a rapid start with the language and a ready-made library of procedures and functions

WHAT KIND OF PROCEDURES AND FUNCTIONS ARE IN THE BOOK?

This book contains procedures and functions for use in virtually any programming effort. Among the many routines, you will find those that:

- Call the operating system functions provided by DOS
- Query RAM about the status of various components of the whole computer system
- Directly manipulate video RAM for faster, easier screen displays

- Provide a universal menu format, which is fast and easy to program as well as sophisticated and satisfying to the end user
- Allow faster programming of reliable data input and display routines
- Display screens with visual impact (e.g., "exploding" windows)

There is also a relatively simple screen-generator program and suggestions for custom enhancements. Producing screens with a generator can save great amounts of time and code and allow substantial screen changes in moments.

The procedures, functions, and some programs in this book are designed to facilitate the production of professional programs in less time. They are written with more emphasis on clarity than on absolute optimization of code, so that less experienced programmers can more easily follow and understand the code.

HARDWARE AND SOFTWARE REQUIREMENTS

All the procedures and functions in this book are designed for use with Turbo Pascal versions 3.xx, 4.0, or 5.0 on IBM PC, XT, AT, and compatible computers using DOS 2.xx or later versions. The routines for screen display are designed to work with monochrome monitors, with or without a color graphics display card, because these are the most common business systems.

HOW TO USE THIS BOOK

The procedures and functions in this book are ready to use in any program. This means that you can include the routine in a program without understanding its mechanics. You need only understand how the procedure is to be called and the results it will produce. Refer to the appropriate test program to see how the procedure is used in a program.

All the routines have been tested and proven to work on a number of IBM PC compatible systems. However, some of the procedures and functions that use specific memory addresses may not function properly on systems that are not fully compatible.

CONVENTIONS USED IN THIS BOOK

The procedures and functions are presented as *tools*. The purpose and operation of each one is described in detail, including a step-by-step explanation of how it works.

Most of the procedures and functions are demonstrated in a test program. The procedures are separated from the programs so that you can easily copy them from the book and incorporate them in your programs. A disk that contains all the listings is also available; see the disk offer at the back of the book.

The test programs use the Turbo Pascal compiler Include directive to include the appropriate procedure or function files. Each procedure or function, therefore, should be placed in its own include file (FName.INC), and when the example program is compiled, the appropriate files should be included ({$I FName.INC}).

Because the programs are primarily vehicles for demonstrating the various tools, they do not go to any special lengths themselves to guard data entry or provide more than the bare necessities for illustrating the procedures and functions.

Some of the procedures and functions require special global declarations in the host program. Appendix A gives specific information about the necessary global declarations and about including the files in your programs, as well as placing them in units (Turbo Pascal 4.0 or 5.0) or overlay files (earlier versions) to conserve the overall size of the program and stay within the limits of Turbo Pascal program size.

In the procedure, function, and program listings, the Turbo Pascal reserved words are in all uppercase letters. Standard identifiers and other names are in mixed uppercase and lowercase letters. These are just conventions; you can enter the code as you wish.

SUMMARY OF
THE CHAPTERS

Chapter 1 presents procedures that access functions available through DOS interrupt 33 that provide valuable services not handled through the Turbo Pascal language itself.

In Chapter 2, a group of DOS function calls related to directory searches is presented. The methods of searching for a file or producing an entire directory are illustrated.

Controlling the keyboard and user input through the keyboard is discussed in Chapter 3. The various keyboard return codes are examined, and a keyboard input procedure to allow only the desired data type to be input is presented. Programming for more efficient data input and display is discussed, and a method of handling data input and display by using templates is presented.

Chapter 4 deals with handling and storing dates and times. It also presents routines for verifying dates and changing invalid dates (e.g., February 31) to valid ones. Fiscal dates and elapsed times are also covered.

The single subject of Chapter 5 is menus. The menu procedures presented here will enable your programs to display menus from which the user makes a choice by simply pressing a cursor-movement key to position the highlighting over the proper selection.

Chapter 6 presents procedures to manipulate or read the various individual bits of a byte or integer that has been mapped to contain numerous data items. This technique (bit mapping) is widely used by DOS to store system information efficiently in RAM.

Chapter 7 deals with the video display. The greater part of the information presented here addresses itself to direct manipulation of video RAM. Windowing procedures are also presented.

The uses of a screen generator are examined in Chapter 8, and the basic components for a screen generator are presented in several procedures. The example programs in this chapter produce working screen generators and suggestions are made for further enhancements.

Chapter 9 contains procedures for giving your screen displays some visual interest. You will find routines for displaying large and "active" characters, changing the cursor's shape, and producing bar graphs.

Chapter 10 includes procedures and functions that do not fall into any specific category. This chapter covers a wide variety of topics, ranging from prompts and string handling to computer equipment information and data-integrity protection.

Appendix A supplies information to facilitate the inclusion of the procedures and functions in your programs. The few required global declarations are explained. Those procedures that require special placement within a program (because they call upon other procedures) are listed and discussed.

Appendix B is a quick reference and index to all of the procedures and functions in the book. It includes the primary purpose of the procedure and the syntax to be used with it.

CHAPTER 1
ACCESSING DOS FUNCTIONS

DOS functions are services performed by the operating system. You may use these functions many times without even realizing it. High-level languages, and even operating system commands such as CD or ChDir, employ DOS functions to accomplish their tasks. Whenever a file is opened, closed, written to, or read from, these functions come into play.

Most of the DOS functions are of no interest to us because the services that they provide are more easily accessible directly through the language. For example, there is no reason to use DOS functions 15 or 61 to open a file when you can use Turbo Pascal's Reset procedure to perform the same task. However, there are some DOS functions that are very valuable because they are not available in Turbo Pascal itself. In this chapter, you'll find routines for accessing the most useful DOS functions.

DOS VERSION COMPATIBILITY

The various functions available through DOS have grown and evolved with the evolution of DOS itself. DOS version 1.xx has the so-called *universal* DOS functions; version 2.xx has a number of additional functions that are quite valuable; and version 3.xx has a few more functions, primarily relating to networks. The DOS function calls are *upwardly compatible*, so function calls for earlier versions are generally supported by later DOS versions, but they are not *downwardly compatible;* that is, the earlier versions cannot process the function calls of the later versions.

If you are writing programs that will not run under all DOS versions, you can have the program itself check that the version in use can support the function calls made within it. You'll see how to use DOS function 48 to accomplish this task a little later in the chapter. Alternatively, you could alert the user through the documentation and/or a notice in the software that a certain DOS version is required for proper operation.

In this book, a DOS-specific symbol in the margin denotes a procedure or function that will not run on all versions of DOS.

DOS 2.xx

CALLING DOS FUNCTIONS FROM TURBO PASCAL PROGRAMS

We can access the various DOS functions through DOS interrupt 33 (hex $21). Table 1.1 lists the functions currently available through this interrupt.

Turbo Pascal's Intr and MsDos procedures both provide access to the DOS functions. The MsDos procedure is a bit simpler to use, so we will concentrate on it here. Before we get to the routines for calling the useful DOS functions, let's examine how the MsDos procedure works.

THE MSDOS PROCEDURE

The MsDos procedure requires passing a record as a parameter. This record duplicates the DOS registers. It relays the information necessary to implement the function and returns information that has become available through the execution of the function. Before Turbo Pascal makes the DOS

Table 1.1:
DOS Functions Accessible through Interrupt 33

UNIVERSAL FUNCTIONS

Decimal No.	Hex No.	Function
0	0	Program terminate
1	1	Keyboard input
2	2	Display output
3	3	Auxiliary input
4	4	Auxiliary output
5	5	Printer output
6	6	Direct console I/O
7	7	Direct console input without echo
8	8	Console input without echo
9	9	Print string
10	A	Buffered keyboard input
11	B	Check standard input status
12	C	Clear keyboard buffer and do KBD function
13	D	Reset disk
14	E	Select disk
15	F	Open file
16	10	Close file
17	11	Search for first entry
18	12	Search for next entry
19	13	Delete file
20	14	Sequential read
21	15	Sequential write
22	16	Create file
23	17	Rename file
24	18	
25	19	Current disk
26	1A	Set disk transfer address (DTA)

Table 1.1:
DOS Functions Accessible through Interrupt 33 (continued)

UNIVERSAL FUNCTIONS (continued)

Decimal No.	Hex No.	Function
27	1B	Get file attribute table (FAT) information, current drive
28	1C	Get FAT information, any drive
29	1D	
30	1E	
31	1F	
32	20	
33	21	Random read
34	22	Random write
35	23	File size
36	24	Set relative record field
37	25	Set interrupt vector
38	26	Create new program segment
39	27	Random block read
40	28	Random block write
41	29	Parse file name
42	2A	Get date
43	2B	Set date
44	2C	Get time
45	2D	Set time
46	2E	Set/reset verify switch

DOS 2.0 AND HIGHER FUNCTIONS

Decimal No.	Hex No.	Function
47	2F	Get disk transfer area (DTA) address
48	30	Get DOS version number
49	31	Terminate and stay resident
50	32	

Table 1.1:
DOS Functions Accessible through Interrupt 33 (continued)

DOS 2.0 AND HIGHER FUNCTIONS (continued)

Decimal No.	Hex No.	Function
51	33	Get/set Control-Break
52	34	
53	35	Get interrupt vector
54	36	Get disk free space
55	37	
56	38	Get country-dependent information
57	39	MkDir
58	3A	RmDir
59	3B	ChDir
60	3C	Create a file
61	3D	Open a file
62	3E	Close file handle
63	3F	Read from file or device
64	40	Write to file or device
65	41	Delete file
66	42	Move file pointer
67	43	Get/set file attributes
68	44	I/O control for devices
69	45	Duplicate file handle
70	46	Force handle duplication
71	47	Get current directory
72	48	Allocate memory
73	49	Free allocated memory
74	4A	Modify allocated memory block
75	4B	Load/execute program
76	4C	Terminate process
77	4D	Get return code of subprogram

Table 1.1:
DOS Functions Accessible through Interrupt 33 (continued)

DOS 2.0 AND HIGHER FUNCTIONS (continued)

Decimal No.	Hex No.	Function
78	4E	Start file search
79	4F	Continue file search
80	50	
81	51	
82	52	
83	53	
84	54	Get verify state
85	55	
86	56	Rename file
87	57	Get/set file date/time
88	58	

DOS 3.0 AND HIGHER FUNCTIONS

Decimal No.	Hex No.	Function
89	59	Get extended error code
90	5A	Create temporary file
91	5B	Create new file
92	5C	Lock/unlock file access
93	5D	
94	5E	Network functions
95	5F	Network redirection
96	60	
97	61	
98	62	Get program segment prefix (PSP) address

system call, certain registers (AX, BX, CX, DX, BP, SI, DI, and ES) are loaded with the values passed to the MsDos procedure in the record parameter; after the call, the procedure returns the new register values to the record to make the results of the DOS function available to the program.

Turbo Pascal 4.0 and 5.0 have a predefined record of type Registers, in the DOS unit, which duplicates the DOS registers. The tools presented here use a variable (Regs) of that type. If you have an earlier version of Turbo Pascal, you will have to define type Registers in your program or in the procedure, as noted in the individual tool listings.

The Registers

In the procedures presented later in this chapter, you may notice that the register information appears to be in two separate records. Actually, both records refer to the same information broken down in two different ways. As with the Turbo Pascal arrays Mem and MemW, the registers can be accessed as single bytes or as 2-byte words. Register AX is a 2-byte word; registers AH and AL refer to the two individual bytes—the high-order and low-order bytes—in that word.

Calling a Function

When you call a DOS function with the MsDos procedure, it does not matter if you use its decimal or hexadecimal (hex) function number. Hex numbers are preceded by a dollar sign ($), for example, $1A. Generally, the function number is loaded to register AH, and register AL is set to zero. Depending on the function being called, information may be loaded to various other registers as well, and upon return from the function, there may be information relayed to the calling program in one or more registers.

ASCIIZ Strings

Some DOS functions require that you pass information to them in the form of a string. For example, you may have to pass a file name. DOS requires an *ASCIIZ string*, which is slightly different than the typical strings used in Turbo Pascal. Both strings consist of ASCII characters, but the Turbo Pascal string begins with a byte indicating the length of the active string and the ASCIIZ string begins at the first actual character in the string. Instead of having a length indicator, an ASCIIZ string has a *zero byte* as its terminator; that is, the string continues until a zero byte (null character) is encountered.

STRING STRUCTURES

A Turbo Pascal string is structured like this:

Element[0]	Element[1]	Element[2] ...	Element[255]
String length	Any Character	Any Character	Any Character

An ASCIIZ string has this structure:

Element[0]	Element[1]	Element[2] ...	Element[255]
Any Character	Any Character	Any Character	CHR(0) (terminates the string wherever it is placed, to a maximum of position 255)

You can construct an ASCIIZ string as an array of characters with a zero byte, CHR(0), as the final character, or as an ordinary Turbo Pascal string with a zero byte added to the end (for example, String: = String + #0). You can obtain the address of an ASCIIZ string constructed as an array with the statement

```
DataSegment: = Seg(ByteArray[FirstElement]);
Offset: = Ofs(ByteArray[FirstElement]);
```

To obtain the address of an ASCIIZ string that is an ordinary Turbo Pascal string ended with a zero byte, you would use the statement

```
DataSegment: = Seg(String[1]);
Offset: = Ofs(String[1]);
```

Note that with the array, the actual data begin in the first element; in the ordinary string, the first element (String[0]) is the length of the string, and the actual data begin in the second element (String[1]). Keep this in mind when you are obtaining or providing the address of either type of Turbo Pascal ASCIIZ string.

USEFUL DOS FUNCTIONS

As I said at the beginning of the chapter, although most of the DOS functions are handled by Turbo Pascal or aren't necessary in most applications, some of them are very useful. The procedures that follow call upon DOS functions that can be quite handy in many programs and are not included in the language structure.

For more information about other DOS functions, refer to *The MS-DOS Handbook*, Second Edition, by Richard Allen King (SYBEX, 1986). Another excellent book for delving deeper into the operating system is *Programmer's Guide to the IBM PC*, by Peter Norton (Microsoft Press, 1985).

GETTING THE DOS VERSION NUMBER

Procedure GetVersion, shown as Tool 1.1, uses DOS function 48 (hex $30) to check to see which DOS version is being used. This procedure is useful in programs with operations or other DOS functions that are available only in certain versions of DOS. If there is a chance that someone would try to use your program under a different version, you will want to include this procedure at the beginning. If the program finds that an improper version is in use, it could activate an IF statement to clear the screen, display an informative message, and halt the program.

Although function 48 is not available in DOS version 1.xx, this procedure will work with that version, although not as precisely. For DOS versions 2.xx and later, the version number is returned in two registers. Register AL returns the major version number, and register AH returns the minor version number. For example, version 2.11 would return a 2 in register AL and an 11 in register AH. If you use the procedure under version 1.xx, nothing happens and the registers return zeroes. Therefore, if

```
PROCEDURE GetVersion(VAR DOSVersion:Real);

{If this procedure is to be used with Turbo Pascal versions
    prior to 4.0, the following declaration must be included:

    TYPE
        Registers = RECORD CASE Integer OF
            1: (AX,BX,CX,DX,BP,SI,DI,DS,ES,Flags :Integer);
            2: (AL,AH,BL,BH,CL,CH,DL,DH          :Byte);
        END;}

    VAR
        Regs        :Registers;
        Major,Minor :Integer;

    BEGIN  {get DOS version}
        Regs.AH:=48;
        Regs.AL:=0;
        MsDos(Regs);
        Major:=Regs.AL;
        Minor:=Regs.AH;
        IF Major=0 THEN DosVersion:=1.0
            ELSE
                BEGIN
                    DOSVersion:=Minor/100;
                    DOSVersion:=DOSVersion+Major;
                END;
    END;    {get DOS version}
```

Tool 1.1: Procedure GetVersion for getting the DOS version number.

zeroes are returned, you know that you are dealing with DOS version 1, but you cannot be sure of the minor release. The new OS/2 should return a major version number of 10. Turbo Pascal 5.0 includes the procedure Dos-Version which serves the same purpose as GetVersion.

When including the GetVersion procedure in a host program, use a variable of type Real as the parameter. Upon the return of the procedure, the Real variable parameter will contain the DOS version number.

Here's how the procedure works:

- Set registers AH and AL to function number 48.
- Call the MsDos procedure.
- Return the major and minor version numbers in registers AH and AL.
- Convert the two integers (major and minor version numbers) to a real number.

Test Program 1.1 demonstrates how the GetVersion procedure might be used in a program. The program simply displays a message relaying the DOS version obtained by the procedure.

```
PROGRAM TestGetVersion;

    {To use this program with Turbo Pascal versions prior to
        4.0, remove the Uses statement below.}

    Uses DOS;

    VAR
        VersionNumber :Real;

    {$I GetVers.Inc}

    BEGIN {program}
        GetVersion(VersionNumber);
        WriteLn('DOS Version on this computer is: ',
            VersionNumber:4:2);
    END.   {program}
```

Test Program 1.1: Using procedure GetVersion in a program.

REPORTING THE CURRENT DRIVE

Procedure CurrDrive, shown as Tool 1.2, uses DOS function 25 (hex $19) to report the current drive. This procedure is useful when you are not sure which computer drive your program will actually run on (i.e., the default drive).

Procedure CurrDrive returns the variable parameter Drive as a character indicating the current drive. The current drive code is 0 = A, 1 = B, 2 = C, and so on.

Here's how the procedure works:

- Set register AH to function number 25.
- Set register AL to zero.
- Call the MsDos procedure.
- Add 65 to the value returned in register AL to produce the ASCII value of the character representing the current drive. Assign the proper character value to the current drive parameter so it can be passed back to the program.

```
PROCEDURE CurrDrive(VAR Drive:Char);

{If this procedure is to be used with Turbo Pascal versions
    prior to 4.0, the following declaration must be included:

    TYPE
        Registers = RECORD CASE Integer OF
            1: (AX,BX,CX,DX,BP,SI,DI,DS,ES,Flags :Integer);
            2: (AL,AH,BL,BH,CL,CH,DL,DH          :Byte);
        END;}

    TYPE
        Str65 = STRING[65];

    VAR
        Regs :Registers;

    BEGIN {get current drive}
     Regs.AH:=25;
     Regs.AL:=00;
     MsDos(Regs);
     Drive:=CHR(65+Regs.AL);
    END;  {get current drive}
```

Tool 1.2: Procedure CurrDrive for getting the current drive.

Test Program 1.2 shows how this procedure might be used in a program. It simply calls the CurrDrive procedure to obtain the current drive and displays the information on the screen.

REPORTING THE CURRENT DIRECTORY

Procedure CurntPath, shown as Tool 1.3, uses DOS function 71 (hex $47) to report, in the form of an ASCIIZ string, the current directory and path for the given drive. The procedure is useful for programs that use multiple drives or directories. It returns the currently defined directory path on any given drive.

The procedure begins by setting register AH to the function number, register AL to zero, and register DL to the drive for which the current directory path is desired. Register DL is set with a code number representing the desired drive: 0 = default drive, 1 = A, 2 = B, and so on. After the MsDos procedure call, a value of 15 in register AL signals an error; an invalid drive was specified in register DL. Otherwise, registers DS and SI

```
PROGRAM TestCurrDrive;

    {To use this program with Turbo Pascal versions prior to
        4.0, remove the Uses statement below.}

    Uses DOS;

    VAR
        DriveName : Char;

    {$I CurDrive.Inc  }

    BEGIN {program}
        CurrDrive(DriveName);
        WriteLn('Current drive is: ',DriveName);
    END.  {program}
```

Test Program 1.2: Using procedure CurrDrive in a program.

will contain the segment and offset in memory where the ASCIIZ string with the current directory path has been returned. This string may be up to 65 bytes in length (64 bytes for the path plus the zero byte that ends an ASCIIZ string).

The CurntPath procedure must have the drive letter passed to it as a parameter. The drive letter can be any active drive on the computer, or it can be zero to indicate the default drive. Each available drive has a current path, regardless of the active, or default, drive.

The procedure returns the directory path of the desired drive in the variable parameter Path. Path is a generic string variable of type Str255. See Appendix A for the global declarations that should be made within the host program to use the procedures and functions presented in this book.

Here's how the procedure works:

- Place the drive identifier character in uppercase, in case it was not originally passed in that form.
- Set register AH to function number 71.
- Set register AL to zero.
- Set register DL to the drive identifier code, based on the parameter passed in the variable Drive.
- Call the MsDos procedure.

- Check register AL to see if an error occurred; if there was an error, halt the program.
- If there was no error, read the ASCIIZ string containing the directory path into the variable parameter Path and return it to the program.

See Test Program 1.3 for an example of the use of procedure CurntPath in a program. The program first checks the default drive and path and

```
PROCEDURE CurntPath(Drive:CHAR; VAR Path:Str255);

{If this procedure is to be used with Turbo Pascal versions
    prior to 4.0, the following declaration must be included:

    TYPE
        Registers = RECORD CASE Integer OF
            1: (AX,BX,CX,DX,BP,SI,DI,DS,ES,Flags :Integer);
            2: (AL,AH,BL,BH,CL,CH,DL,DH          :Byte);
        END;}

    TYPE
        Str65 = STRING[65];

    VAR
        Regs :Registers;
        ASCIIZ    :Str65;
        Error, X  :Integer;

    BEGIN {get current directory path}
        Path:='';
        Regs.AH:=71;
        Regs.AL:=00;
        X:=ORD(Drive)-64;
        {if '0' is passed for default drive, then X=-16}
        IF X<0 THEN X:=0;
        Regs.DL:=X;
        MsDos(Regs);
        Error:=Regs.AL;
        IF Error=15 THEN
            Begin {invalid drive specification}
                WriteLn(#7,'>>ERROR: Invalid drive <<');
                Halt;
            END;   {invalid drive specification}
        Move(Mem[Regs.DS:Regs.SI],ASCIIZ,65);
        X:=0;
        WHILE X<65 DO
            BEGIN
                IF ASCIIZ[X]<>#0 THEN Path:=Path+ASCIIZ[X]
                    ELSE X:=65;
                X:=X+1;
            END;
    END;  {get current directory path}
```

Tool 1.3: Procedure CurntPath for getting the current path.

```
PROGRAM TestCurntPath;

     {To use this program with Turbo Pascal versions prior to
         4.0, remove the Uses statement below.}

     Uses DOS,CRT;

     TYPE
         Str255 = STRING[255];

     VAR
         DriveToCheck   :Char;
         DirectoryPath  :Str255;

     {$I CurPath.Inc}

     BEGIN {program}
         {check default drive}
         DriveToCheck:='0';
         CurntPath(DriveToCheck,DirectoryPath);
         WriteLn('Default drive path is: ',DirectoryPath);
         WriteLn;
         Write('Enter drive to check ("0", "A" - "Z") : ');

         {To use this program with Turbo Pascal versions prior
             to 4.0, add the line below:}
         { Read(KBD,DriveToCheck); }

         {To use this program with Turbo Pascal versions prior
             to 4.0, remove the line below:}
         DriveToCheck:=ReadKey;
         WriteLn(DriveToCheck);
         DriveToCheck:=UpCase(DriveToCheck);
         CurntPath(DriveToCheck,DirectoryPath);
         WriteLn('Drive ',DriveToCheck,': path is: ',DirectoryPath);
     END.  {program}
```

Test Program 1.3: Using procedure CurntPath in a program.

displays this information on the screen. Next it requests a drive specifier, checks the default path for that drive, and reports it on the screen.

DOS 3.xx

GETTING THE EXTENDED ERROR CODE

Procedure GetError, shown as Tool 1.4, uses DOS function 89 (hex $59) to provide information about DOS errors. The procedure, which works only with DOS versions 3.xx, returns codes for extended errors, error classes, suggested actions, and locus (general area of the error). When a DOS version 3.xx function returns with an error, you could use this procedure to obtain additional information about the error and suggested action.

```
PROCEDURE GetError(VAR Extended,Class,Action,Loc:Integer);

     {This procedure is for DOS 3.00 through 3.10 only}

{If this procedure is to be used with Turbo Pascal versions
     prior to 4.0, the following declaration must be included:

     TYPE
          Registers = RECORD CASE Integer OF
               1: (AX,BX,CX,DX,BP,SI,DI,DS,ES,Flags :Integer);
               2: (AL,AH,BL,BH,CL,CH,DL,DH          :Byte);
          END;}


     VAR
          Regs                :Registers;

     BEGIN {get extended error code}
          Regs.AH:=89;
          Regs.AL:=00;
          Regs.BX:=0;
          MsDos(Regs);
          Extended:=Regs.AX;
          Class:=Regs.BH;
          Action:=Regs.BL;
          Loc:=Regs.CH;
     END;   {get extended error code}
```

Tool 1.4: Procedure GetError for getting extended DOS error codes.

Use the GetError procedure only when your program calls a DOS function and returns with an error code, and the carry flag was set to indicate an error. The procedure will call DOS function 89 for the extended error codes and return with the variable integer parameters Extended, Class, Action, and Loc, representing the extended code, error class, suggested action, and locus. The meanings of these codes could help you to pinpoint the problem and determine how to rectify it. Table 1.2 lists the error codes and their meanings, Table 1.3 shows the error classes, Table 1.4 lists the suggested actions and their codes, and Table 1.5 shows the locus codes.

Here's how the GetError procedure works:

- Set register AH to function number 89.

- Set register AL to zero.

- Set register BX to zero to indicate that DOS version 3.1 or 3.2 is being used. Currently, this is the only code for the version of

Table 1.2:
DOS Extended Error Codes

BASIC DOS EXTENDED ERROR CODE GROUPINGS

0	=	No error to report on
1–18	=	Function call errors (interrupt 33)
19–33	=	Critical error-handler errors (interrupt 36)
32–83	=	Errors new to DOS 3.xx services

ERROR CODES

1	Invalid function number
2	File not found
3	Path not found
4	Too many open files
5	Access denied
6	Invalid handle
7	Memory control blocks invalid
8	Insufficient memory
9	Invalid memory block address
10	Invalid environment
11	Invalid format
12	Invalid file access code
13	Invalid data
15	Invalid drive specification
16	Requested removing current directory
17	Not same device
18	No more files
19	Disk write protected
20	Unknown unit
21	Disk drive not ready
22	Unknown command
23	Disk data error (CRC)

Table 1.2:
DOS Extended Error Codes (continued)

ERROR CODES (continued)

24	Bad request structure length
25	Disk seek error
26	Unknown disk media type
27	Disk sector not found
28	Printer out of paper
29	Write error
30	Read error
31	General failure
32	File sharing violation
33	File locking violation
34	Improper disk change
35	No file control block (FCB) available
36	Sharing buffer overflow
50	Network request not supported
51	Remote computer not listening
52	Duplicate identifier on network
53	Network name not found
54	Network busy
55	Network device does not exist
56	Net BIOS command limit exceeded
57	Network adapter hardware error
58	Incorrect response from network
59	Unexpected network error
60	Incompatible remote adapter
61	Print queue full
62	Insufficient space for print file
63	Print file deleted
64	Network name deleted
65	Access denied

Table 1.2:
DOS Extended Error Codes (continued)

ERROR CODES (continued)

66   Network device type incorrect
67   Network name not found
68   Network name limit exceeded
69   Net BIOS session limit exceeded
70   Temporarily paused
71   Network request not accepted
72   Redirection paused
80   File already exists
82   Cannot make directory entry
83   Critical-error interrupt failure
84   Too many redirections
85   Duplicate redirection
86   Invalid password
87   Invalid parameter
88   Network device fault

DOS being used, but future versions of DOS may require a different setting for register BX.

- Call the MsDos procedure.
- After returning from the MsDos procedure, load the contents of registers AX, BH, BL, and CH into the variable parameters Extended, Class, Action, and Loc, respectively.

Test Program 1.4 demonstrates the use of the GetError procedure in a program. The program first calls another DOS function improperly to cause an error, and then calls the procedure to get the extended error codes. Remember, this demonstration program will operate correctly only on computers using DOS versions 3.1x and 3.2x.

Table 1.3:

Error Classes

1	Out of resource (space, channels, etc.)
2	Temporary situation (not an error condition—a situation such as file locked)
3	Authorization (permission problem)
4	Internal error in DOS (apparent bug in DOS)
5	Hardware failure (problem not fault of user program)
6	System software error (e.g., configuration files missing)
7	Application software error
8	Item requested not found (e.g., file not found)
9	Bad format
10	Item locked
11	Media error (e.g., CRC error, bad spot on disk)
12	Already exists
13	Error class unknown (no other appropriate class)

Table 1.4:

Suggested Actions for DOS Errors

1	Try again now (retry a few times)
2	Try later (retry a few times after pausing)
3	Retry after user action (reenter input; typically bad drive letter or file name)
4	Close files, stop program (application program cannot continue, but an orderly shutdown may be done)
5	Stop program immediately
6	Ignore
7	Retry after user action (user needs to do something such as insert a different diskette)

Table 1.5:
DOS Locus Codes

1   Unknown (nonspecific or inappropriate)

2   Block device error (random-access storage)

3   Network related

4   Serial device error

5   Memory error (random-access memory)

```
PROGRAM TestGetError;

     {To use this program with Turbo Pascal versions prior to
        4.0, remove the Uses statement below.}

     Uses DOS;

     TYPE
          Str255 = STRING[255];

     VAR
          Error, Extended, Class, Action, Loc,
              BPS, SPC, AC, TC                          :Integer;
              TS, TF                                    :Real;

     {$I GetError.Inc}
     {$I FreeSpc.Inc }

     BEGIN {program}
          DiskFreeSpc('Z',BPS,SPC,AC,TC,TS,TF);
          IF (TS>0.0) THEN Error:=0
              ELSE Error:=1;
          IF (Error<>0) THEN
              BEGIN
                   WriteLn('>> Function Error <<');
                   GetError(Extended,Class,Action,Loc);
                   WriteLn('Extended error code: ',Extended);
                   WriteLn('Error class: ',Class);
                   WriteLn('Suggested action: ',Action);
                   WriteLn('Locus code: ',Loc);
              END;
     END.   {program}
```

Test Program 1.4: Using procedure GetError in a program.

The program displays the error code number for the function error, and then:

Extended error code: 15
Error class: 8

Suggested action: 3
Locus code: 4

Looking up these codes in Tables 1.2 through 1.5 reveals that the extended error code signifies an invalid drive, the error class means that the item requested was not found, the suggested action is to retry after user action, and the locus code is for a serial device error.

DOS 2.xx

GETTING THE VERIFY STATE

Procedure GetVerify, shown as Tool 1.5, uses DOS function 84 (hex $54) to report the current state of the verify switch. This function is valid only in DOS versions 2.xx or greater. Turbo Pascal 5.0 includes a GetVerify procedure that operates similarly.

The verify switch controls whether write operations to the disk will be verified by DOS. When the verify switch is on, each write to disk will be followed by a read to check the CRC (cyclical redundancy check). The CRC is a complex parity check of the data which indicates whether or not the correct data were written. Note that the CRC only indicates whether the data are generally correct; it does not reread and compare the data to verify that each element is written properly.

```
PROCEDURE GetVerify(VAR Verify:Boolean);

{If this procedure is to be used with Turbo Pascal versions
     prior to 4.0, the following declaration must be included:

   TYPE
        Registers = RECORD CASE Integer OF
             1: (AX,BX,CX,DX,BP,SI,DI,DS,ES,Flags :Integer);
             2: (AL,AH,BL,BH,CL,CH,DL,DH           :Byte);
        END;}


   VAR
        Regs              :Registers;

   BEGIN {get verify state}
        Regs.AH:=84;
        Regs.AL:=0;
        MsDos(Regs);
        Verify:=(Regs.AL=1);
   END;   {get verify state}
```

Tool 1.5: Procedure GetVerify to get the current state of the verify switch.

When your program absolutely must have the highest possible data integrity, you could use the GetVerify procedure to determine if the verification process is in effect. If the verify switch is off, you could use the Set-Verify procedure (described next) to turn it on. The verification process does slow down the write process somewhat, and your program's speed will be reduced by the many disk writes.

DOS function 84, used in conjunction with function 46 (used in Set-Verify), is the same as the DOS commands Verify (to check the current status), Verify On (to set the verify switch on), and Verify Off (to set the verify switch off).

The GetVerify procedure returns the variable parameter Verify as either true or false, depending on the state of the verify switch. The parameter Verify is a Boolean value. Here's how the procedure works:

- Set register AH to function number 84.
- Set register AL to zero.
- Call the MsDos procedure.
- After returning from the MsDos procedure, if register AL is set to 1, the variable parameter Verify is true; otherwise, Verify is false.

The GetVerify procedure (along with SetVerify) is demonstrated in Test Program 1.5.

SETTING THE VERIFY STATE

Procedure SetVerify, shown as Tool 1.6, uses DOS function 46 (hex $2E) to set the verify state for disk-write operations. When it is critical that data be written correctly, you should turn on the verify switch to help ensure their accuracy, even though the write procedures will be a bit slower. See the previous discussion of the GetVerify procedure for more details. Turbo Pascal 5.0 includes a SetVerify procedure that operates similarly.

The procedure SetVerify requires the Boolean parameter Verify to be set to either true or false when it is called. The DOS verify switch will be set on or off, based on the setting of Verify.

- Set register AH to function number 46.
- Set register DL to zero.

- Set register AL to 1 if Verify is true, or to zero if Verify is false.
- Call the MsDos procedure to set the verify switch in the operating system.

Test Program 1.5 demonstrates the use of both the GetVerify and SetVerify procedures in a program. The program displays on the screen the appropriate use of the verify switch as a DOS command. Next it checks the current setting of the verify switch and reports the status on the screen. The program changes the verify switch to its opposite status (from on to off or vice versa). The current state of the verify switch, as changed, is checked again and reported on the screen. When the program ends, the status of the verify switch is the opposite of what it was when the program began.

GETTING THE DISK FREE SPACE

Although Turbo Pascal 4.0 and 5.0 provide (in the DOS unit) the predefined functions DiskFree and DiskSize for obtaining total disk size and free space, more detailed information about disk space is available from DOS. If you have version 4.0 or 5.0, you can use our next tool instead of or with those functions for a complete account of the space available. Users of earlier versions will find the procedure very valuable.

```
PROCEDURE SetVerify(Verify:Boolean);

{If this procedure is to be used with Turbo Pascal versions
    prior to 4.0, the following declaration must be included:

    TYPE
        Registers = RECORD CASE Integer OF
            1: (AX,BX,CX,DX,BP,SI,DI,DS,ES,Flags :Integer);
            2: (AL,AH,BL,BH,CL,CH,DL,DH          :Byte);
        END;}

    VAR
        Regs            :Registers;

    BEGIN {set verify state}
        Regs.AH:=46;
        IF Verify THEN Regs.AL:=1
            ELSE Regs.AL:=0;
        MsDos(Regs);
    END;  {set verify state}
```

Tool 1.6: Procedure SetVerify to set the verify state.

Tool 1.7 shows procedure DiskFreeSpc, which uses DOS function 54 (hex $36) to calculate the free space on a disk and, in the process, gives a great deal of other useful information. Use this procedure before you copy files to a floppy disk to ensure that there is enough space for them (of course, you may run out of space on a hard disk, but much less frequently).

In the DiskFreeSpc procedure, the logical drive number is loaded to register DL: 0 = the default drive, 1 = A, 2 = B, and so on. After returning from the MsDos procedure, this procedure sets register AX to hex FFFF if an error occurred. Otherwise, register AX contains the number of sectors per allocation unit (per cluster), register CX has the number of bytes per sector, register BX gives the number of available clusters, and register DX contains the total number of clusters available.

The procedure DiskFreeSpc is passed the Drive parameter, which indicates the drive to be checked. This parameter should be either a letter representing a valid drive name (A, B, C, etc.) or a zero for the default drive.

```
PROGRAM TestVerify;

     {To use this program with Turbo Pascal versions prior to
        4.0, remove the Uses statement below.}

     Uses DOS;

     VAR
        VerifyState :Boolean;

     {$I GetVerif.Inc  }
     {$I SetVerif.Inc  }

     BEGIN {program}
        WriteLn('Using the Verify Switch through DOS:');
        WriteLn('Check status:    VERIFY');
        WriteLn('Turn on:         VERIFY ON');
        WriteLn('Turn off:        VERIFY OFF');
        WriteLn;
        GetVerify(VerifyState);
        WriteLn('"Verify" is now : ',VerifyState);
        WriteLn('Changing verify state...');
        VerifyState:=NOT VerifyState;
        SetVerify(VerifyState);
        {now check it again}
        GetVerify(VerifyState);
        WriteLn('"Verify" is now : ',VerifyState);
     END.   {program}
```

Test Program 1.5: Using procedures GetVerify and SetVerify in a program.

```
PROCEDURE DiskFreeSpc(Drive:Char;
                      VAR BytesPerSect,SectorsPerClust,
                          AvailClust,TotClust :Integer;
                      VAR TotSpace,TotFree :Real);

{If this procedure is to be used with Turbo Pascal versions
    prior to 4.0, the following declaration must be included:

    TYPE
        Registers = RECORD CASE Integer OF
               1: (AX,BX,CX,DX,BP,SI,DI,DS,ES,Flags :Integer);
               2: (AL,AH,BL,BH,CL,CH,DL,DH           :Byte);
        END;}

    VAR
        Regs                :Registers;
        X                   :Integer;
        Error               :Boolean;

    BEGIN {get disk free space}
        {initialize}
        Drive:=UpCase(Drive);
        X:=ORD(Drive)-64;
        {if '0' is passed for default drive, then x=-16}
        IF X<0 THEN X:=0;
        BytesPerSect:=0; SectorsPerClust:=0;
        AvailClust:=0; TotClust:=0;
        TotSpace:=0.0; TotFree:=0.0;
        Regs.AH:=54;
        Regs.AL:=0;
        Regs.DL:=X;
        MsDos(Regs);
        Error:=(Regs.AX=$FFFF);
        IF NOT Error THEN
            BEGIN
                SectorsPerClust:=Regs.AX;
                BytesPerSect:=Regs.CX;
                AvailClust:=Regs.BX;
                TotClust:=Regs.DX;
                TotFree:=BytesPerSect*SectorsPerClust;
                TotFree:=TotFree*AvailClust;
                TotSpace:=BytesPerSect*SectorsPerClust;
                TotSpace:=TotSpace*TotClust;
            END;
    END;  {get disk free space}
```

Tool 1.7: Procedure DiskFreeSpc for getting the free space on a disk.

After completing its operations, the procedure loads the variable parameters with their respective values. The variable parameters and their data types and meanings are listed below:

Parameter	Type	Meaning
BytesPerSect	Integer	Bytes per sector

SectorsPerClust	Integer	Sectors per cluster
AvailClust	Integer	Available clusters
TotClust	Integer	Total clusters on disk
TotSpace	Real	Total bytes on disk
TotFree	Real	Total bytes free space

Here's how the procedure works:

- Place the drive identifier character in uppercase, in case it was not originally passed in that form.
- Determine the logical drive number from the drive letter. (If the drive character was 0, then the logical drive is the default drive.)
- Initialize variable parameters to zero.
- Set register AH to function number 54.
- Set register AL to zero.
- Set register DL to the logical drive number.
- Call the MsDos procedure.
- If there is no error, load the integer variable parameters with the values from the appropriate registers and calculate the real variable parameters from the integer parameters.
- If there is an error, return all values as zeroes.

Test Program 1.6 demonstrates the use of the DiskFreeSpc procedure in a program. It first asks you which disk is to be checked; then it displays the information obtained from this check on the screen. It reports the drive checked, bytes per sector, sectors per cluster, total clusters, free (unused) clusters, total disk space, and free disk space.

DOS FUNCTIONS FOR TURBO PASCAL VERSIONS PRIOR TO 4.0

Turbo Pascal 4.0 and 5.0 include predefined procedures for obtaining and setting the system date and time as well as file attributes. Users of earlier versions can employ the tools in this section to accomplish these tasks.

```
PROGRAM TestDiskFreeSpc;

     {To use this program with Turbo Pascal versions prior to
         4.0, remove the Uses statement below.}

     Uses DOS,CRT;

     VAR
          DriveName              :Char;
          B_S, S_C, AvailC, TotC  :Integer;
          TotBytes, FreeBytes     :Real;

     {$I FreeSpc.Inc}

     BEGIN {program}
          Write('Check space on which drive (0, A - Z) : ');

          {To use this program with Turbo Pascal versions prior
              to 4.0, add the line below:}
          { Read(KBD,DriveName); }

          {To use this program with Turbo Pascal versions prior
              to 4.0, remove the line below:}
          DriveName:=ReadKey;

          DriveName:=UpCase(DriveName);
          WriteLn(DriveName);
          DiskFreeSpc(DriveName,B_S,S_C,AvailC,TotC,
                     TotBytes,FreeBytes);
          WriteLn('Report on Drive ',DriveName,':');
          WriteLn('There are ',B_S,' bytes per sector.');
          WriteLn('There are ',S_C,' sectors per cluster.');
          WriteLn('There are ',TotC,' clusters, total.');
          WriteLn('There are ',AvailC,' free clusters.');
          WriteLn('There are ',TotBytes:8:0,
                    ' bytes disk space - total.');
          WriteLn('There are ',FreeBytes:8:0,
                    ' bytes disk space free.');
     END.   {program}
```

Test Program 1.6: Using procedure DiskFreeSpc in a program.

GETTING OR SETTING FILE ATTRIBUTES

DOS function 67 (hex $43) allows you to read and reset file attributes. Before we get to the procedure that uses this function, a little background is in order.

The Attribute Byte

Each file in DOS has an attribute byte maintained for it as a part of the directory entry. The purpose of this attribute byte is to allow the file to be marked for special handling by DOS. Each bit in the attribute byte indicates the presence or absence of a specific attribute. Table 1.6 shows the bit values of the attribute byte and corresponding attributes of the file.

Table 1.6:
Bit Values of the Attribute Byte

Bit Value	7	6	5	4	3	2	1	0	Bit Significance
128	1	-	-	-	-	-	-	-	Shareable
64	-	1	-	-	-	-	-	-	Unused
32	-	-	1	-	-	-	-	-	Archive
16	-	-	-	1	-	-	-	-	Directory entry containing a subdirectory
8	-	-	-	-	1	-	-	-	Root directory entry with volume label
4	-	-	-	-	-	1	-	-	System
2	-	-	-	-	-	-	1	-	Hidden
1	-	-	-	-	-	-	-	1	Read-only

Files can have the following attributes:

- **Read-only** will not allow write operations to take place.
- **Hidden** prevents listing of the file in normal directory searches.
- **System** indicates that this is a DOS file.
- **Root directory entry with volume label** is the volume label of the root directory itself. Although volume labels are sometimes placed in the root directory, they typically are not.
- **Directory entry containing a subdirectory** is the entry in the root or other directory that lists a subdirectory of the directory being searched or the DOS entries referring to the present and parent directories (the one and two dot entries that appear first in any subdirectory listing).
- **Archive** is used by the DOS Backup command and some software to denote files that have been copied.

• **Shareable** applies to files being used on network systems and tells the operating system whether two or more users may access a given file (i.e., have it open for read and write operations) at the same time.

Each bit in the attribute byte represents a specific attribute of the file. The attribute byte is passed as a decimal number in register CX. The file attributes that can be passed include the following:

$$
\begin{array}{rcl}
0 & = & \text{Normal read/write} \\
1 & = & \text{Read-only} \\
2 & = & \text{Hidden} \\
4 & = & \text{System} \\
7 & = & \text{Read-only + Hidden + System} \\
8 & = & \text{Volume label} \\
16 & = & \text{Subdirectory} \\
32 & = & \text{Archive} \\
128 & = & \text{Shareable}
\end{array}
$$

Some files may have more than one bit set. For example, DOS operating system files have an attribute of 7, indicating that they are read-only, system, and hidden files. You can use binary arithmetic to produce attribute combinations. See Chapter 6 for a more detailed explanation of binary arithmetic and bit-mapping combinations.

The Attribute Procedure

(PRIOR TO 4.0)

Procedure Attribute, listed as Tool 1.8, uses function 67 to read and/or reset file attribute codes. With this procedure, your program can hide files (from less sophisticated users—power users can find them!) or make a file read-only. But use the procedure carefully. Problems can arise if a program sets a file to a given attribute, and then is abnormally terminated before it resets the attribute to its normal, or expected, state.

In procedure Attribute, register AH is first set to the function number. The address of an ASCIIZ string containing the name of the file that you want to access is set in registers DS and DX. If an error occurs, the carry flag will be set and the error code will be returned in register AX. (For more information about DOS flags, see Chapter 6.) We'll review the possible error codes shortly.

If the present attribute is to be read, register AL is set to zero. The present file attribute is returned in register CX.

If you want to set the attribute, register AL is set to 1 and register CX is set to the desired attribute.

The procedure will either get or set the attribute associated with a disk file, depending on the character passed in the Get_Set parameter (G = get, S = set). The parameter FileName is a string containing the file name and, if applicable, path of the disk file that is being checked or changed. The FileAttribute parameter is an integer representing the desired file attribute

```
PROCEDURE Attribute(GetSet:Char;
                    FileName:Str255;
                    VAR FileAttribute, ErrorCode:Integer);

    TYPE
        Registers = RECORD CASE Integer OF
            1: (AX,BX,CX,DX,BP,SI,DI,DS,ES,Flags :Integer);
            2: (AL,AH,BL,BH,CL,CH,DL,DH          :Byte);
        END;

    VAR
        Regs                :Registers;
        ASCIIZ              :STRING[65];
        X                   :Integer;
        Carry               :Boolean;

    BEGIN {get/set file attribute}
        GetSet:=UpCase(GetSet);
        Regs.AH:=67;
        ASCIIZ:=FileName+CHR(0);
        IF GetSet='G' THEN Regs.AL:=0
            ELSE
                BEGIN {set}
                    Regs.AL:=1;
                    Regs.CX:=FileAttribute;
                END;  {set}
        Regs.DS:=Seg(ASCIIZ);
        Regs.DX:=Ofs(ASCIIZ)+1;
        MsDos(Regs);
        {check carry flag}
        X:=Regs.Flags;
        Carry:=(ODD(X));
        IF Carry THEN ErrorCode:=Regs.AX
            ELSE ErrorCode:=0;
        IF Carry THEN FileAttribute:=0
            ELSE FileAttribute:=Regs.CX;
    END;  {get/set file attribute}
```

Tool 1.8: Procedure Attribute for getting or setting file attributes (for versions prior to 4.0).

to be set. If you are just getting the present attribute, this parameter is returned with that value. The ErrorCode parameter is returned to indicate the success of the operation.

The following error codes might be returned:

0 = No error

2 = File not found

3 = Path not found

5 = Access denied

Here's how the procedure works:

- Set the parameter Get_Set to an uppercase character in case a lowercase character was inadvertently used in the host program when calling this procedure.
- Set register AH to 67 to tell DOS which function to perform.
- Convert the file name, which was passed as a parameter, to an ASCIIZ string by adding the null character, CHR(0), to the end of the file name (this DOS function requires the file name in that format.)
- Set register AL to either zero (to get the attribute) or 1 (to set the attribute).
- If the attribute is to be set, load register CX with the desired attribute value.
- Set registers DS and DX, which contain the address in memory of the ASCIIZ string denoting the name of the file to be operated upon.
- Upon return from the MsDos procedure, check the carry flag from the DOS registers to see if the function was carried out without error, and set the variable ErrorCode accordingly.
- If there was no error, obtain the present file attribute from register CX and return it to the host program through the parameter FileAttribute; if there was an error, set this parameter to zero.

Test Program 1.7 demonstrates how the Attribute procedure might be used in a program. The program begins by asking if an attribute is to be obtained or set, and then requests the name of the file. If you responded set, you next specify which attribute. If the operation proceeds successfully, the program displays a

```
PROGRAM TestAttribute;

    TYPE
        Str255 = STRING[255];

    VAR
        GetOrSet                :Char;
        FileName                :Str255;
        FileAttribute, Error :Integer;

    {$I Attribut.Inc  }

    BEGIN {program}
        Write('(G)et or (S)et an attribute ? ');
        Read(KBD, GetOrSet);
        GetOrSet := UpCase(GetOrSet);
        WriteLn(GetOrSet);
        Write('Enter filename: ');
        ReadLn(FileName);
        IF (GetOrSet='S') THEN
            BEGIN
                Write('Attribute number to set: ');
                ReadLn(FileAttribute);
            END;
        Attribute(GetOrSet,FileName,FileAttribute,Error);
        IF (Error=0) THEN
            BEGIN
                Write('File ',FileName);
                IF (GetOrSet='G') THEN Write(' has ')
                    ELSE Write(' set to ');
                WriteLn('attribute: ',FileAttribute);
            END
            ELSE
                WriteLn('>> Error = ',Error);
    END.   {program}
```

Test Program 1.7: Using procedure Attribute in a program.

message indicating the result and attribute. If the operation was unsuccessful, it displays an error number.

(PRIOR TO 4.0)

GETTING THE SYSTEM DATE

Procedure GetDate, shown as Tool 1.9, uses DOS function 42 (hex $2A) to return the present date according to the operating system clock. You can use this procedure to get a correct, current default date for use in screen entries and for putting a *date stamp* (the date a transaction record is created and entered into an inventory or accounting program) into records. Before invoking this procedure, your program should have already ascertained, at its inception, that the system date is correctly set. See Chapter 4, Tool 4.6, for a procedure to handle date and time verification at the inception of a program.

```
PROCEDURE GetDate(VAR Month,Day,Year,WeekDay:Integer);

    TYPE
        Registers = RECORD CASE Integer OF
            1: (AX,BX,CX,DX,BP,SI,DI,DS,ES,Flags :Integer);
            2: (AL,AH,BL,BH,CL,CH,DL,DH          :Byte);
        END;

    VAR
        Regs    :Registers;

    BEGIN {get system date}
        WITH Regs DO
            BEGIN
                AH:=42;
                AL:=0;
                MsDos(Regs);
                Year:=CX; Month:=DH;
                Day:=DL;  WeekDay:=AL;
            END;
    END;   {get system date}
```

Tool 1.9: Procedure GetDate for getting the current date (for versions prior to 4.0).

In procedure GetDate, register AH is first set to the function number, and register AL is set to zero. After the MsDos procedure is called and returns, the month, day, and year are contained in registers DH, DL, and CX, respectively. Beginning with DOS 2.xx, this function also returns a weekday number, where 0 = Sunday, 1 = Monday, and so on. The weekday number is returned in register AL.

The GetDate procedure will return with the variable parameters Month, Day, Year, and WeekDay set to the system date. Month, Day, Year, and WeekDay are all integers.

Here's how the procedure works:

- Set register AH to function number 42.

- Set register AL to zero.

- Call the MsDos procedure.

- Set the variable parameters Month, Day, Year, and WeekDay equal to registers DH, DL, CX, and AL, respectively, to return the system date to the program.

Test Program 1.8, presented a little later, illustrates how the GetDate (as well as the SetDate, GetTime, and SetTime procedures, described next) might be used in a program.

(PRIOR TO 4.0)

SETTING THE SYSTEM DATE

Procedure SetDate, shown as Tool 1.10, uses DOS function 43 (hex $2B) to set the operating system clock to the desired values for Month, Day, and Year. You can use this procedure to set a correct, current default date for use in screen entries and for putting a date stamp into records. If you used the GetDate procedure at the inception of a program, and it determined that the system date was not correct, you could use procedure SetDate to correct the date. Note that any date prior to 1/1/1980 is invalid, and the system will not accept it.

```
PROCEDURE SetDate(Month,Day,Year:Integer);

    TYPE
        Registers = RECORD CASE Integer OF
            1: (AX,BX,CX,DX,BP,SI,DI,DS,ES,Flags :Integer);
            2: (AL,AH,BL,BH,CL,CH,DL,DH             :Byte);
        END;

    VAR
        Regs :Registers;

    BEGIN {set system date}
        WITH Regs DO
            BEGIN
                AH:=43; AL:=0;
                CX:=Year; DH:=Month;
                DL:=Day;
                MsDos(Regs);
            END;
    END;  {set system date}
```

Tool 1.10: Procedure SetDate for setting the date (for versions prior to 4.0).

NOTE: Function 43 will set the operating system clock, which will continue keeping the time (and date) from this setting, but it will not set the real-time clock used in the IBM PC-AT and compatible computers. When that system is rebooted, the date and time will revert to whatever is stored in the AT clock.

The SetDate procedure will set the values of the parameters Month, Day, and Year to the system date. Month, Day, and Year are all integers. As a safety precaution, you should have your program call the GetDate procedure (Tool 1.9) after setting the date with SetDate to ensure that a correct date was set. Incomplete or improper error trapping could result in an invalid date (i.e., prior to 1/1/1980) being passed, and if this was the case, the date would not actually be set.

Here's how the procedure works:

- Set register AH to function number 43.
- Set register AL to zero.
- Set the variable parameters Month, Day, and Year to registers DH, DL, and CX, respectively, to set the system date.
- Call the MsDos procedure.

Test Program 1.8 shows how the SetDate procedure might be used in a program.

GETTING THE SYSTEM TIME

(PRIOR TO 4.0)

Procedure GetTime, shown as Tool 1.11, uses DOS function 44 (hex $2C) to return the present time according to the operating system clock. You can use this procedure to get a correct, current default time for use in

```
PROCEDURE GetTime(VAR Hour,Min,Sec:Integer);

    TYPE
        Registers = RECORD CASE Integer OF
            1: (AX,BX,CX,DX,BP,SI,DI,DS,ES,Flags :Integer);
            2: (AL,AH,BL,BH,CL,CH,DL,DH          :Byte);
        END;

    VAR
        Regs :Registers;

    BEGIN {get system time}
        WITH Regs DO
            BEGIN
                AH:=44; AL:=0;
                MsDos(Regs);
                Hour:=CH; Min:=CL;
                Sec:=DH;
                {100ths second = DL}
            END;
    END;  {get system time}
```

Tool 1.11: Procedure GetTime to get the current time (for versions prior to 4.0).

screen entries and for putting a *time stamp* (the time a transaction record is created and entered into an inventory or accounting program) into records. The program should have already ascertained, at its inception, that the system time is correctly set. See Chapter 4, Tool 4.6, for a procedure to handle date and time verification at the inception of a program.

Procedure GetTime will return with the variable parameters Hour, Min, and Sec set to the system time. Hour, Min, and Sec are all integers.

Here's how the procedure works:

- Set register AH to function number 44.
- Sct register AL to zero.
- Call the MsDos procedure.
- Set the variable parameters Hour, Min, and Sec to equal registers CH, CL, and DH, respectively, to return the system time to the program. (Register DL contains the hundredths of a second.)

See Test Program 1.8 for an illustration of how the GetTime procedure might be used in a program.

(PRIOR TO 4.0)

SETTING THE SYSTEM TIME

Tool 1.12, Procedure SetTime, uses DOS function 45 (hex $2D) to set the operating system clock to the desired values for the hour, minute, and second. You can use this procedure to set a correct, current default time for use in screen entries and/or for putting a time stamp into records. If you used the GetTime procedure at the inception of a program, and it determined that the system time was not correct, you can use procedure SetTime to set the correct time.

> **NOTE:** Function 45 will set the operating system clock, which will continue keeping time from this setting, but it will not set the real-time clock used in the IBM PC-AT and compatible computers. When that system is rebooted, the date and time will revert to whatever is stored in the AT clock.

The SetTime procedure will set the values of the parameters Hour, Min, and Sec to the system time. Hour, Min, and Sec are all integers.

```
PROCEDURE SetTime(Hour,Min,Sec:Integer);

    TYPE
        Registers = RECORD CASE Integer OF
            1: (AX,BX,CX,DX,BP,SI,DI,DS,ES,Flags :Integer);
            2: (AL,AH,BL,BH,CL,CH,DL,DH            :Byte);
        END;

    VAR
        Regs :Registers;

    BEGIN {set system time}
        WITH Regs DO
            BEGIN
                AH:=45; AL:=0;
                CH:=Hour; CL:=Min;
                DH:=Sec; DL:=0;
                {DL = 100ths second}
                MsDos(Regs);
            END;
    END;  {set system time}
```

Tool 1.12: Procedure SetTime for setting the current time (for versions prior to 4.0).

Here's how the procedure works:

- Set register AH to function number 45.
- Set register AL to zero.
- Set the variable parameters Hour, Min, and Sec to registers CH, CL, and DH, respectively, to set the system time. (Register DL contains the hundredths of a second. Set this register to zero to ensure that it does not contain a value outside the range of 0 of 99.)
- Call the MsDos procedure.

Test Program 1.8 illustrates how the GetDate, SetDate, GetTime, and SetTime procedures might be used in a program. After obtaining the current date and displaying it on the screen, the test program asks if you want to change the date. If you decide to do this, the program displays three individual prompts, one for the month, day, and year. It will redisplay the date and offer to change it until you respond with an N for no. Next the program obtains and displays the time, offering you the option to change it, just as it did with the date.

```
PROGRAM TestDateTime;

    VAR
        Hour,Min,Sec,Month,Day,Year,WeekDay :Integer;
        ChangeTime, ChangeDate              :Char;

    CONST
        Days :ARRAY[0..6] OF STRING[9] =
              ('Sunday', 'Monday', 'Tuesday', 'Wednesday',
               'Thursday', 'Friday', 'Saturday');

    {$I GetTime.Inc}
    {$I SetTime.Inc}
    {$I GetDate.Inc}
    {$I SetDate.Inc}

    BEGIN {program}
        REPEAT
            GetDate(Month,Day,Year,WeekDay);
            WriteLn('Today is: ',Days[WeekDay],Month:5,
                    '/',Day,'/',Year);
            Write('Change the date ? (Y/N) ');
            Read(KBD,ChangeDate);
            WriteLn(ChangeDate);
            ChangeDate:=UpCase(ChangeDate);
            IF (ChangeDate='Y') THEN
                BEGIN
                    Write('Enter new month (1-12) : ');
                    ReadLn(Month);
                    Write('Enter new date (1-31) : ');
                    ReadLn(Day);
                    Write('Enter new year (1980-2099) : ');
                    ReadLn(Year);
                    SetDate(Month,Day,Year);
                END;
        UNTIL (ChangeDate<>'Y');
        REPEAT
            GetTime(Hour,Min,Sec);
            WriteLn('The time is: ',Hour,':',Min,':',Sec);
            Write('Change the time ? (Y/N) ');
            Read(KBD,ChangeTime);
            WriteLn(ChangeTime);
            ChangeTime:=UpCase(ChangeTime);
            IF (ChangeTime='Y') THEN
                BEGIN
                    Write('Enter new hour: ');
                    ReadLn(Hour);
                    Write('Enter new minute: ');
                    ReadLn(Min);
                    Write('Enter new second: ');
                    ReadLn(Sec);
                    SetTime(Hour,Min,Sec);
                END;
           UNTIL (ChangeTime<>'Y');
        END.  {program}
```

Test Program 1.8: Using procedures GetDate, SetDate, GetTime, and SetTime in a
program.

CHAPTER 2
DIRECTORY SEARCHES

A search of a directory for a specified file takes place every time that a Turbo Pascal program executes a Reset (*FileName*) statement. This is probably the simplest form of a directory search—you attempt to open a file, and it is either there or not there. The statement is often guarded with the compiler directive {$I –} to prevent the program from crashing if the file is not found.

A directory search can produce some valuable information about specific files, including their size and title. However, Turbo Pascal versions prior to 4.0 did not provide directory-search capabilities. Turbo Pascal 4.0 and 5.0 offer four new procedures in its Dos unit—FindFirst, FindNext, GetFTime, and UnpackTime—for searching directories and decoding DOS file information, as well as a predefined record—SearchRec—for handling the information.

This chapter presents procedures and functions that allow you to conduct simple and complex directory searches by using the new features of Turbo Pascal 4.0 and 5.0 or, for earlier versions, by calling DOS directory-related functions. First we'll review the basic search method. Then we will progress from a very simple directory search procedure to one that can find any type of file on the disk and create an ASCII file detailing the file or files that it found.

THE DOS FILE
SEARCH METHOD

The first chapter presented many tools for accessing useful DOS functions. In a similar manner, users of Turbo Pascal versions earlier than 4.0 will access DOS directory-related functions through the MsDos procedure.

DOS has two function pairs that work for file searches: 17 and 18 and 78 and 79. The first function in each pair finds the first occurrence of a file specification, and the second function finds any additional occurrences. The file specification can be a particular file name and extension, or it can be a name containing wild-card characters, as described below.

DOS 2.xx

The procedures and functions presented in this chapter for versions of Turbo Pascal earlier than 4.0 use DOS function set 78 and 79, which was added with DOS version 2.xx. These correspond to the FindFirst and FindNext procedures in Turbo Pascal 4.0 and 5.0. These functions pass information about directory entries through the disk transfer area (DTA). Beginning with DOS 2.xx, a file search considers not only the file specification, but the attribute of the file as well. This means that even when DOS finds a directory entry that matches the file specification, if a specified attribute is incompatible, it will not report that file.

FILE SPECIFICATION

To initiate a file search, you must give the system a *mask*, or file specification, for the file or files that you want to find (the same sort of mask that is used with the DOS Dir command). You can use ordinary file name characters, as well as wild-card characters and the drive and directory path. If you do not include a drive and directory path, the search takes place on the default drive or directory.

The wild-card characters that can be used are the asterisk and question mark (just as when using DOS directly). The asterisk represents any remaining characters in a file name or extension. For example, the specification ST*.* will match any files beginning with the letters *ST*. The question mark represents a specific character position and allows any character to be present in that position. For example, if you specify an extension of A?A, the center character may be anything, but the first and last characters must be A for a match.

After a string is constructed to represent the file specification, it must be put into ASCIIZ string format so that the operating system can interpret it correctly (see the section about ASCIIZ strings in Chapter 1).

ATTRIBUTE SPECIFICATION

If you specify any combination of attributes, the file search will match normal files (read/write = attribute 0), as well as those with any of the specified attributes. For example, to search for all files on the computer, you would combine the attributes for normal/read write (0), read-only (1), hidden (2), and system (4) for an attribute of 7. If you specify the volume-label attribute (8), the search will only match entries with that attribute. The desired attribute will be passed to a procedure, and the procedure will handle it from there. See Chapter 1, Table 1.2, for a list of file attribute values.

The archive and read-only attributes need not be specified for search operations because they are not considered; the archive bit (5) and read-only bit (1) are two attributes that are included in any file search whether they are specified or not. For DOS versions prior to 2.xx, the directory, volume label, archive, and read-only attributes do not apply.

(PRIOR TO 4.0)

BEGINNING A FILE SEARCH

If you are using Turbo Pascal 4.0 or 5.0, your file searches will begin with the language's FindFirst procedure. Users of earlier versions can start a search with the BeginDirSearch procedure.

Procedure BeginDirSearch, shown as Tool 2.1, uses DOS function 78 (hex $4E) to begin the file search. It looks for the first occurrence of a file matching the file specification, which is the file name and path in the form of an ASCIIZ string. The file name can contain the wild-card characters ? and *. You could use the procedure simply to see if a particular file exists in the current directory, another directory, or even another drive. It could also serve as the beginning of a complete directory search of a disk, which will ultimately list all the files in all the directories on that disk (as the DOS Tree command does).

The BeginDirSearch procedure requires two parameters to be passed to it: the file name and path in the form of an ASCIIZ string and the desired attribute of the file as an integer. You can specify more than one attribute

```
PROCEDURE BeginDirSearch(ASCIIZString:Str255;
                         Attribute:Integer;
                         VAR Error:Integer);


    TYPE
        Registers = RECORD CASE Integer OF
            1:(AX,BX,CX,DX,BP,SI,DI,DS,ES,Flags :Integer);
            2:(AL,AH,BL,BH,CL,CH,DL,DH          :Byte);
        END;

    VAR
        Regs:Registers;

    BEGIN {begin directory search}
        IF (ASCIIZString[Length (ASCIIZString)]<>#0) THEN
          ASCIIZString:=ASCIIZString+CHR(0);
        Regs.AH:=78;
        Regs.AL:=00;
        Regs.DS:=Seg(ASCIIZString);
        Regs.DX:=Ofs(ASCIIZString)+1;
        Regs.CX:=Attribute;
        MsDos(Regs);
        Error:=Regs.AL;
    END;   {begin directory search}
```

Tool 2.1: Procedure BeginDirSearch to begin a directory search (for versions prior to 4.0).

(and, of course, search for more than one file). The procedure returns the error code resulting from the search in the Error parameter.

Here's how the procedure works:

- Check the string that was passed to be certain that it is an ASCIIZ string (ends in a zero byte); if necessary, add a zero byte to the string to convert it to an ASCIIZ string.

- Set register AH to function number 78.

- Set register AL to zero.

- Set registers DS and DX, which are pointers to the address in RAM of the ASCIIZ file specification string, to the segment and offset of that string. Note that the variable name used in the procedure for the string to be passed is ASCIIZ string. This string is passed to the procedure as a parameter in the form of a Turbo Pascal string, so it is not a true ASCIIZ string. Therefore, the offset is the address of ASCIIZ string plus 1 byte because the first byte of this Turbo Pascal string (ASCIIZ string[0]) indicates the length rather than the first character of the string.

- Set register CX to the attribute of the file to be searched for.
- Call the MsDos procedure.
- Return the error code in register AL and assign it to the variable parameter Error for return to the program.

The errors normally returned in register AX and passed to the program are 2, for file not found; 18, for no more files to be found; and 0, for no error.

A SIMPLE DIRECTORY SEARCH

The next step after beginning a directory search is obtaining its results. The Exist function, shown as Tool 2.2, conducts a simple directory search to determine if a given file is present. The function shown at the top of the listing is for versions of Turbo Pascal prior to 4.0; the second function (Exist4) is for versions 4.0 and 5.0.

The Exist function is passed a file specification and returns a value of true or false for the existence of the specified file. The file specification can contain a drive and path name, as well as wild-card characters. The file name to be passed is not an ASCIIZ string; it's just an ordinary file name with or without a drive and path. The function looks for only a single occurrence of the file specification.

Here's how the Exist function for Turbo Pascal versions prior to 4.0 works:

- Set register AH to function number 78.
- Set register CX to zero for the file attribute specification (only normal read/write files will be found).
- Create an ASCIIZ string from the file specification passed as a parameter by adding a zero byte to it.
- Set registers DS and DX to point to the data in the ASCIIZ string.
- If register AX is zero after returning from the MsDos procedure, there is no error; a file was found, so return a true for Exist.
- If register AX contains a value other than zero, an error occurred; a file was not found, so return a false for Exist.

```
FUNCTION Exist(FileName:Str255):Boolean;

     {This version of the Exist function is to be used with
         versions of Turbo Pascal prior to 4.0}

     TYPE
         Registers = RECORD CASE Integer OF
                 1: (AX,BX,CX,DX,BP,SI,DI,DS,ES,Flags :Integer);
                 2: (AL,AH,BL,BH,CL,CH,DL,DH          :Byte);
         END;
         Str65 = STRING[65];

     VAR
         Regs :Registers;
         ASCIIZ     :Str65;
         X          :Integer;

     BEGIN {find file}
         Regs.AH:=78;
         Regs.AL:=0;
         Regs.CX:=0;
         ASCIIZ:=FileName+CHR(0);
         Regs.DS:=Seg(ASCIIZ);
         Regs.DX:=Ofs(ASCIIZ)+1;
         MsDos(Regs);
         Exist:=(Regs.AX=0);
     END;  {find file}


FUNCTION Exist4(FileName:Str255):Boolean;

     {This version of the Exist function is to be used with
         Turbo Pascal 4.0}

     VAR
         S :SearchRec;

     BEGIN {find file}
         FindFirst(FileName,0,S);
         Exist4:=(DOSError=0);
     END;  {find file}
```

Tool 2.2: Function Exist for a simple directory search.

The Exist function for use with Turbo Pascal 4.0 and 5.0 calls the First-First procedure. If it returns with no error, as reported by DOSError, the file exists, and a true is returned. Otherwise, the function returns a false.

Exist, a Boolean function, is very simple to use in a program. Simply call the function and supply the file name parameter, as shown in Test Program 2.1. The program uses the Exist function to search for the file. If it finds the file, you'll see the message

IT IS HERE

If it doesn't find the file, you'll see

FILE NOT FOUND

```
    PROGRAM TestExist;

{To use this program with Turbo Pascal versions prior to
    4.0, remove the Uses statement below.}

Uses DOS;

        TYPE
            Str255 = STRING[255];

        VAR
            FName :STRING[65];

    {To use this program with Turbo Pascal versions prior
        to 4.0, add the line below:}
     (*    {$I Exist.Inc}   *)

    {To use this program with Turbo Pascal versions prior
        to 4.0, remove the line below:}
        {$I Exist4.Inc}

      BEGIN {program}
          Write('Enter file name:');
          ReadLn(FName);
          IF Exist4(FName) THEN WriteLn('IT IS HERE!')
              ELSE WriteLn('FILE NOT FOUND.');
      END.   {program}
```

Test Program 2.1: Using function Exist in a program.

(PRIOR TO 4.0)

CONTINUING A DIRECTORY SEARCH

If you are using Turbo Pascal 4.0 or 5.0, your file searches can continue to find more matches to your file specifications through the language's FindNext procedure. Users of earlier versions can continue with the Cont-DirSearch procedure.

The ContDirSearch procedure, shown as Tool 2.3, uses DOS function 79 (hex $4F) to continue the file search begun by DOS function 78. You will want to use this procedure when more than one file may match the file specification (usually when you've included wild-card characters in the file name).

When DOS function 78 finds a specified file, it places certain information in the first 21 bytes of the 43 bytes in the DTA reserved for data about

```
PROCEDURE ContDirSearch(VAR Error:Integer);

    TYPE
        Registers = RECORD CASE Integer OF
            1: (AX,BX,CX,DX,BP,SI,DI,DS,ES,Flags  :Integer);
            2: (AL,AH,BL,BH,CL,CH,DL,DH           :Byte);
        END;

    VAR
        Regs:Registers;

    BEGIN {continue directory search}
        Regs.AH:=79;
        Regs.AL:=00;
        MsDos(Regs);
        Error:=Regs.AL;
    END;   {continue directory search}
```

Tool 2.3: Procedure ContDirSearch to continue a directory search (for versions prior to 4.0).

that directory entry (we'll soon discuss that area in detail). Function 79 uses these 21 bytes of information to continue the directory search; for this reason, you should not alter the first 21 bytes of the directory-entry data in the DTA during the search process. Like DOS function 78, function 79 returns information about the files it finds by formatting 43 bytes of data and returning them in the DTA.

The ContDirSearch procedure does not require any parameters to be passed to it because it finds all the information it needs in the first 21 bytes of DTA data. This procedure returns the variable integer parameter Error each time it is called to indicate its success in finding another file to match the file specification originally given to function 78.

Generally, you will want to repeat the procedure in a loop until it returns with an error value of 18, indicating that no more files are to be found. In this continuing search loop, you can include procedures to decode and/or store the information that is being returned to the DTA during each pass through the loop. We'll discuss the techniques for storing and decoding the DTA information shortly, and you'll see how to put it all together in more complex directory search procedures at the end of this chapter.

Here's how the ContDirSearch procedure works:

- Set register AH to function number 79.
- Set register AL to zero.

- Call the MsDos procedure.
- Check register AL for the error code returned. If the error is 0, a file has been found, and the information about the file should be retrieved from the DTA before the next execution of ContDirSearch.

THE DISK TRANSFER AREA

As mentioned previously, when DOS function 78 finds a directory entry matching the file specification and attribute, DOS formats certain information about that file into a 43-byte data chunk and places that information in the DTA. Turbo Pascal 4.0 and 5.0 handle this information in a record defined as type SearchRec in the Dos unit. The FindFirst and FindNext procedures in versions 4.0 and 5.0 still obtain their information from the DTA, but they set the DTA to control where the data will be returned.

Initially, the DTA is, by default, a 128-byte buffer, established for those DOS function calls that need an area for passing and storing information. DOS provides a function for obtaining the address of the DTA and another function for relocating that area for a particular programming operation. We'll discuss both of these functions shortly.

After a file is found with function 78 or 79, DOS formats and returns the following data to the DTA:

- Information for continuing the directory search
- The attribute of the entry found
- Date and time stamps for the entry found
- The size of the file found, unless the entry has an attribute of 8 or 16, meaning that it is a volume label or directory (in which case, the size in bytes is not applicable, and this information is not passed)
- An ASCIIZ string containing the file name and extension, as well as the period separating them

Table 2.1 shows the format of the 43 bytes of information returned in the DTA by DOS functions 78 and 79.

Table 2.1:
Format of Data Returned by DOS Functions 78 and 79 in the DTA

Offset	Size	Bytes	Information
0	21	0–20	Used by DOS for function 79
21	1	21	Attribute of file found
22	2	22–23	Time stamp
24	2	24–25	Date stamp
26	4	26–29	File size in bytes
30	13	30–42	*Filename.Ext* (ASCIIZ string)

Although users of Turbo Pascal 4.0 and 5.0 do not have to worry about getting and setting the DTA for directory searches (FindFirst and FindNext do this for you), the capability to control the DTA can be very useful. You can use the following procedures in any of your programs that need to change the location of the DTA.

GETTING THE DTA

Procedure GetDTA, shown as Tool 2.4, uses DOS function 47 (hex $2F) to obtain the address of the current DTA. This could be the original DTA (from when the computer was booted up) or a different one subsequently set by your program. If you want to change the location of the DTA for a particular program, first use this procedure to get the original DTA address, then save those values. When you are finished working with the modified DTA, you should reset it to the original values.

The GetDTA procedure returns two variable integer parameters representing the address of the current DTA. The parameter DTASegment is the data segment, and DTAOffset is the offset.

Here's how the procedure works:

- Set register AH to function number 47.
- Set register AL to zero.

```
PROCEDURE GetDTA(VAR DTASegment,DTAOffset:Integer);

{If this procedure is to be used with Turbo Pascal versions
     prior to 4.0, the following declaration must be included:

     TYPE
          Registers = RECORD CASE Integer OF
               1: (AX,BX,CX,DX,BP,SI,DI,DS,ES,Flags :Integer);
               2: (AL,AH,BL,BH,CL,CH,DL,DH           :Byte);
          END;}

     VAR
          Regs:Registers;

     BEGIN {get current DTA}
          Regs.AH:=47;
          Regs.AL:=00;
          MsDos(Regs);
          DTASegment:=Regs.ES;
          DTAOffset:=Regs.BX;
     END;   {get current DTA}
```

Tool 2.4: Procedure GetDTA for getting the address of the DTA.

- After returning from the MsDos procedure, load DTASegment with the value returned by register ES and DTAOffset with the value returned by register BX, and return these values to the program.

SETTING THE DTA

Procedure SetDTA, shown as Tool 2.5, uses DOS function 26 (hex $1A) to reset the DTA to a new address. You could use this procedure to set the DTA to the address of a specific string or buffer to hold transferred information. For example, you may want to use several DTAs for a complex directory search. The program would use one at a time, preserving the information in the other DTAs for further use. The Directry procedure presented later in this chapter performs this type of operation. Before you change the DTA, you should determine the address of the original DTA (using procedure GetDTA), save it, and restore it when you're finished with the modified one.

The SetDTA procedure simply passes the address of the buffer being used as a receptor (easily done by using the Turbo Pascal Seg(*variable*) and Ofs(*variable*) functions) and puts the address into the DS and DX registers. When the

```
PROCEDURE SetDTA(DTASeg,DTAOfs:Integer);

{If this procedure is to be used with Turbo Pascal versions
    prior to 4.0, the following declaration must be included

    TYPE
        Registers = RECORD CASE Integer OF
            1: (AX,BX,CX,DX,BP,SI,DI,DS,ES,Flags :Integer)
            2: (AL,AH,BL,BH,CL,CH,DL,DH          :Byte);
        END;}

    VAR
        Regs:Registers;

    BEGIN {set DTA}
        Regs.AH:=26;
        Regs.AL:=00;
        Regs.DS:=DTASeg;
        Regs.DX:=DTAOfs;
        MsDos(Regs);
    END;  {set DTA}
```

Tool 2.5: Procedure SetDTA to reset the DTA.

procedure returns to the program, the DTA address has been changed.

Here's how the SetDTA procedure works:

- Set register AH to function number 26.
- Set register AL to zero.
- Set registers DS and DX to the segment and offset, respectively, that have been passed as parameters and will be the new DTA address.

DECODING THE INFORMATION IN THE DTA

So far, we've covered procedures that allow us to begin a directory search, find the first occurrence of a specified file, continue the search, and direct the information that DOS formats about that directory entry to a buffer area of our own choosing. These provide the basic foundation for obtaining a good deal of information about a specific file. For the returned data to have any real meaning, however, it must be broken down and decoded. (Table 2.1 shows how the data are formatted on a byte-by-byte basis, but we need to know more than the DTA's organization to learn anything from it.)

We can ignore the first 21 bytes (0 through 20) of the DTA because they are used by DOS function 79 to continue the file search.

Byte 21 holds the value of the attribute byte of the directory entry found by the search. Therefore, to assign the value of that directory entry to a variable in a program, you could use the statement

FileAttributeValue: = DTAString[21];

where FileAttributeValue is an integer or byte variable and DTAString is the buffer to which the DTA has been assigned.

(PRIOR TO 4.0)

DECODING THE TIME

Bytes 22 and 23 give the time that the file was created. The time is kept in a formula that allows the hour, minute, and second to be stored in 2 bytes. These 2 bytes form an integer word, and various bits of the word denote certain aspects of the time: bits 11 through 15 give the hour, bits 5 through 11 give the minute, and bits 0 through 4 give the second (actually, the number of 2-second increments from which the second is computed).

DTA TIME FORMAT

Graphically, the DOS time format for directory entries looks like this
(h = hour, m = minute, and s = second):

Byte 23								Byte 22							
15	14	13	12	11	10	9	8	7	6	5	4	3	2	1	0
h	h	h	h	h	m	m	m	m	m	m	s	s	s	s	s

Turbo Pascal 4.0 and 5.0 provide the procedures GetFTime and UnpackTime to obtain and decode the time and date information. For users of earlier versions, one method of interpreting the 2-byte integer carrying the time is by using the InterpretTime procedure, shown as Tool 2.6. This method incorporates two other procedures, which are presented later in this book as Tools 6.1 and 6.3, as a portion of the interpretation process.

The ReadBits procedure returns a string of ones and zeroes, indicating just which bits are set and which are not. The SetBits procedure sets a selected bit of an integer to a desired state (1 or 0). (We'll discuss the uses of bit manipulation in Chapter 6.)

```
PROCEDURE InterpretTime(DTASegment,DTAOffset:Integer;
                        VAR Hour,Min,Sec:Integer);
    VAR
        BitString   :STRING[16];
        TimeCode,X  :Integer;

    BEGIN {interpret time}
        Move(Mem[DTASegment:DTAOffset+22],TimeCode,2);
        ReadBits(TimeCode,BitString);
        {hour}
        Hour:=0;
        FOR X:=12 TO 16 DO
            IF (BitString[X]='1') THEN
                SetBits('S',X-12,Hour);
        {minute}
        Min:=0;
        FOR X:=6 TO 11 DO
            IF BitString[X]='1' THEN
                SetBits('S',X-6,Min);
        {seconds}
        FOR X:=1 TO 5 DO
            IF BitString[X]='1' THEN
                SetBits('S',X-1,Sec);
        Sec:=Sec*2;
    END;  {interpret time}
```

Tool 2.6: Procedure InterpretTime to decode the DTA time (for versions prior to 4.0).

The InterpretTime procedure is passed the DTA address in the integers DTASegment and DTAOffset. You can pass these parameters easily by using the Turbo Pascal functions Seg(*DTAVariable*) and Ofs(*DTAVariable*). The variable integer parameters Hour, Min, and Sec are returned to the program with the decoded values set.

Here's how the InterpretTime procedure works:

- Move 2 bytes from offset 22 (bytes 22 and 23) to the integer, TimeCode.
- Call the ReadBits procedure, which returns with the string Bit-String set to a series of ones and zeroes representing the values of the 16 bits in TimeCode.

- Process the hour, minute, and second individually. Read the appropriate element of BitString and, if that element is set, set the corresponding bit in the integer variable Hour, Min, or Sec. When these bits are set, Hour, Min, and Sec have the correct values, which are returned as the parameters to the program.

(PRIOR TO 4.0)

DECODING THE DATE

Bytes 24 and 25 give the date that the file was created. Like the time, the date is kept in a formula that allows the month, day, and year to be stored in 2 bytes. These 2 bytes form an integer word, and various bits denote certain aspects of the date: bits 9 through 15 give the year, bits 5 through 8 give the month, and bits 0 through 4 give the day.

DTA DATE FORMAT

Graphically, the DOS date format for directory entries looks like this (y = year, m = month, d = day):

Byte 25								Byte 24							
15	14	13	12	11	10	9	8	7	6	5	4	3	2	1	0
y	y	y	y	y	y	y	m	m	m	m	d	d	d	d	d

NOTE: DOS keeps the year as a Julian date from 1980; therefore, the year obtained is only the number of years elapsed since 1980. To obtain an actual year, add 1980 to the result obtained from the year calculation.

As mentioned previously, Turbo Pascal 4.0 and 5.0 have the GetFTime and UnpackTime procedures for obtaining and decoding the file creation date and time. For users of earlier versions, a procedure for interpreting the date is presented as Tool 2.7.

The InterpretDate procedure operates in the same manner as the time-interpretation procedure. It also uses the ReadBits and SetBits procedures from Chapter 6 and is passed the DTA address in the integers DTASegment and DTAOffset, using the Turbo Pascal functions Seg(*DTAVariable*) and Ofs(*DTAVariable*). The variable integer parameters Month, Day, and Year are returned to the program with the decoded values set. After the year is obtained, 1980 is added to the value that was stored.

```
PROCEDURE  InterpretDate(DTASegment,DTAOffset:Integer;
                         VAR Month,Day,Year:Integer);
    VAR
        BitString    :STRING[16];
        DateCode,X   :Integer;

    BEGIN {interpret date}
        Move(Mem[DTASegment:DTAOffset+24],DateCode,2);
        ReadBits(DateCode,BitString);
        {year}
        Year:=0;
        FOR X:=10 TO 16 DO
            IF (BitString[X]='1') THEN
                SetBits('S',X-10,Year);
        {month}
        Year:=Year+1980;
        Month:=0;
        FOR X:=6 TO 9 DO
            IF BitString[X]='1' THEN
                SetBits('S',X-6,Month);
        {day}
        Day:=0;
        FOR X:=1 TO 5 DO
            IF BitString[X]='1' THEN
                SetBits('S',X-1,Day);
    END;   {interpret date}
```

Tool 2.7: Procedure InterpretDate to decode the DTA date (for versions prior to 4.0).

Here's how the InterpretDate procedure works:

- Move 2 bytes from offset 24 (bytes 24 and 25) to the integer DateCode.
- Call the ReadBits procedure, which returns with the string BitString set to a series of ones and zeroes representing the values of the 16 bits in DateCode.
- Process the year, month, and day individually. Read the appropriate element of BitString and, if that element is set, set the corresponding bit in the integer variable Month, Day, or Year. When these bits are set, Month, Day, and Year have the correct values, which are returned as the parameters to the program.

GETTING THE FILE SIZE

Bytes 26, 27, 28, and 29 of the DTA form 2 integer words denoting the size of the file in bytes. We can convert these words to a real number representing the number of bytes in the file (we don't convert them to an integer because the file size may be larger than the maximum allowable integer in Turbo Pascal versions prior to 4.0). The ConvertWords procedure, shown as Tool 2.8, is one way of accomplishing this word conversion.

If you have Turbo Pascal 4.0 or 5.0, you can use the SearchRec record (defined in the Dos unit) to obtain the file size through the LongInt field named Size, as in the statement

LongIntVar: = SearchRec.Size;

```
PROCEDURE ConvertWords(DTASegment,DTAOffset:Integer;
                       VAR Size:Real);
     VAR
     X,Y :Integer;
     Z   :Real;

     BEGIN {convert words}
         Move(Mem[DTASegment:DTAOffset+26],X,2);
         Move(Mem[DTASegment:DTAOffset+28],Y,2);
         {calculate file size from two integer words X and Y}
         IF Y>0 THEN Size:=(65535.0*Y)
             ELSE Size:=0.0;
         IF X<0 THEN Z:=X+65535.0+1
             ELSE Z:=X;
         Size:=Size+Z+Y;
     END;  {convert words}
```

Tool 2.8: Procedure ConvertWords to get the file size from the DTA (for versions prior to 4.0).

The ConvertWords procedure is passed the DTA address through the integer parameters DTASegment and DTAOffset. After converting the 2 integer words to a real value, the procedure returns to the program with the variable parameter Size containing a real number that is the number of bytes in the file.

Here's how the ConvertWords procedure works:

- Move 2 bytes of data from offset 26 (bytes 26 and 27) to the integer X.

- Move the next 2 bytes from offset 28 (bytes 28 and 29) to the integer Y.
- Calculate the real variable parameter Size from the integer words X and Y and return it to the program.

GETTING THE FILE NAME

Bytes 30 through 42 of the DTA contain an ASCIIZ string with the name of the directory entry. If you have a version of Turbo Pascal earlier than 4.0, you can use the GetFileName procedure, shown as Tool 2.9, to move the information from the DTA to a proper file name string.

```
PROCEDURE GetFileName(DTASegment,DTAOffset:Integer;
                      VAR FileName:Str255);
    VAR
        X:Integer;

    BEGIN {get file name}
        Move(Mem[DTASegment:DTAOffset+30],FileName[1],13);
        X:=1;
        WHILE X<13 DO
            BEGIN
                IF FileName[X]<>#0 THEN FileName[0]:=CHR(X)
                    ELSE
                            X:=12;
                X:=X+1;
            END;
    END;  {get file name}
```

Tool 2.9: Procedure GetFileName to get the file name from the DTA (for versions prior to 4.0).

In Turbo Pascal 4.0, this information is available through the SearchRec record defined in the Dos unit. You can get the file name with a statement such as

FileName: = SearchRec.Name;

The GetFileName procedure is passed the DTA address through the integers DTASegment and DTAOffset. The file name is returned to the program through the variable parameter FileName, which is of type Str255. For this procedure to work, you must declare Str255 previously in the program as

Str255 = STRING[255])

Here's how the GetFileName procedure works:

- Move 13 bytes from the DTA to the FileName string.
- Check the FileName string to determine where the end of the file name is (as determined by the zero byte).
- Set the length of the string (FileName[0]) to the last valid character of the file name.

PUTTING IT ALL TOGETHER: SEARCHING A DIRECTORY AND RETRIEVING INFORMATION

The basic tools that we've discussed can be combined in another procedure to actually search the directory and return the findings. First we will look at a procedure that searches only the current directory. Our final procedure conducts a more complex search, which can include all disk directories and subdirectories, and produces a list of the directory entries in an ASCII text file.

A DEFAULT DIRECTORY SEARCH

The GetDirectory procedure, shown as Tool 2.10, will produce a quick, simple directory search of the currently active directory and display each entry on the screen. This directory search demonstrates the use of the procedures GetDTA, SetDTA, BeginDirSearch, GetFileName, and ContDirSearch, presented earlier in this chapter.

GetDirectory is called without parameters. It displays the directory listings on the screen, and then returns to the program. It could be modified to operate differently, depending on the needs of your program. For example, you may want to change the on-screen display to a specific screen area or window, or you may want to have the directory entries written to an ASCII file.

Here's how the GetDirectory procedure works:

- Establish an area for the directory entries returned by DOS in the variable DTA, an array of 43 bytes.
- Define the mask to be searched for as *.* to find all files in the directory.

```
PROCEDURE GetDirectory;

      VAR
            DTA                           :ARRAY[1..43] OF Byte;
            SysDTASeg, SysDTAOfs, Error   :Integer;
            Entry, Mask                   :STRING[65];

            {To use this procedure with Turbo Pascal versions prior
                 to 4.0, remove the line below:}
            S                             :SearchRec;

      BEGIN {get directory}
            Mask:='*.*'+CHR(0);
            GetDTA(SysDTASeg,SysDTAOfs);
            SetDTA(Seg(DTA),Ofs(DTA));

            {To use this program with Turbo Pascal versions prior
                 to 4.0, add the 2 lines below:}
            { BeginDirSearch(Mask,0,Error);
            IF (Error=0) THEN }

            {To use this procedure with Turbo Pascal versions prior
                 to 4.0, remove the 2 lines below:}
            FindFirst(Mask,0,S);
            IF (DOSError=0) THEN

                  BEGIN

            {To use this program with Turbo Pascal versions prior
                 to 4.0, add the 2 lines below:}
                  { GetFileName(Seg(DTA),Ofs(DTA),Entry);
                  WriteLn(Entry); }

            {To use this procedure with Turbo Pascal versions prior
                 to 4.0, remove the line below:}
                  WriteLn(S.Name);

                  REPEAT

            {To use this program with Turbo Pascal versions prior
                 to 4.0, add the 2 lines below:}
                        { ContDirSearch(Error);
                        IF (Error=0) THEN }

            {To use this procedure with Turbo Pascal versions prior
                 to 4.0, remove the 2 lines below:}
                        FindNext(S);
                        IF (DOSError=0) THEN

                              BEGIN

            {To use this program with Turbo Pascal versions prior
                 to 4.0, add the 2 lineS below:}
                              { GetFileName(Seg(DTA),
                                       Ofs(DTA),Entry);
                              WriteLn(Entry); }
```

Tool 2.10: Procedure GetDirectory to search the current directory.

```
            {To use this procedure with Turbo Pascal versions prior
               to 4.0, remove the line below:}
                                  WriteLn(S.Name);

                         END;
            {To use this program with Turbo Pascal versions prior
               to 4.0, add the line below:}
                   { UNTIL (Error<>0); }

            {To use this procedure with Turbo Pascal versions prior
               to 4.0, remove the line below:}
                    UNTIL (DOSError<>0);

                END;
           SetDTA(SysDTASeg,SysDTAOfs);
     END;   {get directory}
```

Tool 2.10: Procedure GetDirectory to search the current directory. (continued)

- Obtain the DTA address at the inception of the program and save the values in the variables SysDTASeg and SysDTAOfs so they can be restored later.
- Establish the new DTA at the address of the variable named DTA.
- Begin the directory search. Set the file attribute to zero so only standard files are reported.
- If a file is found, obtain the file name from the SearchRec record (with version 4.0 or 5.0), or decode the entry partially with Get-FileName (with earlier versions), and then write it to the screen.
- Continue the search until no more files are found.
- Use the file name found in SearchRec, or the GetFileName procedure, to read and format the data returned from successful continuing searches.
- Before exiting, restore the original DTA by setting it to the values obtained at the inception of the procedure.

You can use the GetDirectory procedure anywhere in a program by simply making a statement using the procedure name. Test Program 2.2

```
Program TestGetDirectory;

{To use this program with Turbo Pascal versions prior to
    4.0, remove the Uses statement below.}

Uses DOS;

    {$V-} {set compiler for relaxed parameter checking}

    TYPE
        Str255=STRING[255];

    {$I GetDTA.Inc}
    {$I SetDTA.Inc}

{To use this program with Turbo Pascal versions prior
    to 4.0, add the 3 lines below:}
    (* {$I BegSrch.Inc} *)
    (* {$I ContSrch.Inc} *)
    (* {$I GetFName.Inc} *)


    {$I GetDir.Inc}

    BEGIN {program}
        GetDirectory;
    END.  {program}
```

Test Program 2.2: Using procedure GetDirectory in a program.

demonstrates how the procedure could be used in a program. It calls the Get-Directory procedure, which writes the directory entries to the screen.

A COMPLEX, VARIABLE DIRECTORY SEARCH

The Directry procedure, shown as Tool 2.11, is our most complex directory search. It is called by supplying parameters for Mask and Level. The procedure can find any type of files, searching a single directory or all the directories on the disk. It creates an ASCII text file for the directory (or subdirectory) specified to the level indicated. Your program can use the information in the ASCII file in a number of ways. You could have a program find files with specified file name extensions and then calculate the total number of bytes occupied by these files. You could sort the files by type, indicated by extension, and produce a grouped list for display or printing. In general, a program can retrieve specific information about files more quickly and easily from an ASCII file than by dealing directly with the DOS directory every time that it needs to access the data.

```
PROCEDURE Directry(Level:Integer; Mask:Str255);

    TYPE
          Pointr = ^Integer;
          DTAPtr = ^DTAs;
          DTAs = RECORD
                  AZ                        :STRING[80];
                  DTASegment, DTAOffset     :Integer;
                  Last, Next                :DTAPtr;
          END;

    VAR
          FirstDTA,FinalDTA,CurrentDTA              :DTAPtr;
          PathName,FileMask,DirEntry,TempString     :STRING[80];
          SubLevel,Attribute,SrchAttribute,Error,
              Position,SysDTASegment, SysDTAOffset  :Integer;
          DayTime                                   :Char;
          TopHeap                                   :Pointr;
          FoundFirst                                :Boolean;
          DirFile                                   :Text;

          {To use this program with Turbo Pascal versions prior
              to 4.0, remove the line below:}
          S                                         :SearchRec;


    PROCEDURE SetSubDirectory;
        VAR
              Temp1,Temp2  :STRING[80];
              Position1    :Integer;

          BEGIN {set subdirectory mask}

    {when entering this procedure, if error = 18 = no more files,}
    {then... if sublevel>0 = if working in a subdirectory        }
    {then... reduce the sublevel and discard that record from    }
    {RAM and remove the subdirectory name from                   }
    {TempString - then revert to former DTA to continue search   }

            IF ((Error=18) AND (SubLevel>0)) THEN
                BEGIN {move up to parent directory}
                    SubLevel:=SubLevel-1;
                    Error:=0;
                    IF SubLevel>=0 THEN
                        BEGIN {strip off 1 subdirectory}
                            Temp1:=TempString;
                            Delete(Temp1,Length(Temp1),1);
                            REPEAT
                                Position1:=Pos('\',Temp1);
                                IF Position1>0 THEN
                                Temp1:=Copy(Temp1,
                                            Position1+1,
                                            Length(Temp1)
                                            -(Position1));
                            UNTIL Position1=0;
                            Position1:=Length(TempString)-
                                        Length(Temp1)-1;
                            Temp2:=COPY(TempString,1,
                                        Position1);
                            TempString:=Temp2;
                END;   {strip off 1 subdirectory}
```

Tool 2.11: Procedure Directry to conduct a complex directory search.

```
                        CurrentDTA:=CurrentDTA^.Last;
                        Release(CurrentDTA^.Next);
                        CurrentDTA^.Next:=NIL;
                        FinalDTa:=CurrentDtA;

        {To use this program with Turbo Pascal versions prior
           to 4.0, remove the line below:}
                        Move(CurrentDTA^.AZ,S,21);


        {To use this program with Turbo Pascal versions prior
           to 4.0, add the line below:}
                        { SetDTA(CurrentDTA^.DTASegment,
                            CurrentDTA^.DTAOffset); }

       END;   {move up to parent directory}
{when entering this procedure, if the last entry's }
{attribute = 8,16 = volume or subdirectory, then...}
{increase sublevel by 1 and put new DTA record into}
{RAM to begin a search of this newly found          }
{subdirectory.  Add the subdirectory name to        }
{TempString and make an ASCIIZ string for the new   }
{file search about to begin on this new             }
{directory.  Set Boolean FoundFirst to false to     }
{look for first entry in new subdirectory.          }

          IF (Attribute>=0) THEN
          IF ((Attribute IN[8,16]) AND (Level IN[2,4])) THEN
             IF (DirEntry[1]<>'.') THEN
                BEGIN {search subdirectory}
                    SubLevel:=SubLevel+1;
                    New(CurrentDTA);
                    CurrentDTA^.Last:=FinalDTA;
                    CurrentDTA^.Next:=NIL;
                    FinalDTA^.Next:=CurrentDTA;
                    FinalDTA:=CurrentDTA;
                    CurrentDTA^.DTASegment:=
                        Seg(CurrentDTA^.AZ);
                    CurrentDTA^.DTAOffset:=
                        Ofs(CurrentDTA^.AZ);
                    {make new mask for subdirectory}
                    Position:=Pos(' ',DirEntry);
                    IF SubLevel>1 THEN
                        TempString:=TempString+
                            Copy(DirEntry,1,
                                Position-1)+'\'

                               ELSE
                                  TempString:=
                                      Copy(DirEntry,1,
                                         Position-1)+'\';
                    CurrentDTA^.AZ:=PathName+TempString+
                        FileMask+CHR(0);

        {To use this program with Turbo Pascal versions prior
            to 4.0, add the line below:}
                        { SetDTA(CurrentDTA^.DTASegment,
                            CurrentDTA^.DTAOffset); }

                    FoundFirst:=False;
                END;   {search subdirectory}
       END;   {set subdirectory mask}
```

Tool 2.11: Procedure Directry to conduct a complex directory search. (continued)

```
PROCEDURE FormatItem;
    VAR
        Temp                                    :STRING[80];
        Temp1,Temp2,Temp3,Temp4,Temp5           :STRING[10];
        FileSize                                :Real;
        Month,Day,Year,Hour,Min,Sec,X           :Integer;

    {To use this program with Turbo Pascal versions prior
        to 4.0, remove the line below:}
        D                                       :DateTime;

    BEGIN {format item}
        {get the entry's attribute from the DTA}

    {To use this program with Turbo Pascal versions prior
        to 4.0, add the 2 lines below:}
        { Attribute:=ORD(CurrentDTA^.AZ[21]);
        GetFileName(CurrentDTA^.DTASegment,
            CurrentDTA^.DTAOffset,DirEntry); }

    {To use this program with Turbo Pascal versions prior
        to 4.0, remove the 2 lines below:}
        Attribute:=S.Attr;
        DirEntry:=S.Name;

        {pad directory entry to 12 places}
        WHILE (Length(DirEntry)<12) DO
            DirEntry:=DirEntry+' ';
        {if the entry found is not a directory, then...      }
        {get information about file and build directory string}
        IF NOT (Attribute IN[8,16]) THEN
            BEGIN {if attribute not in[8,16]}

    {To use this program with Turbo Pascal versions prior
        to 4.0, add the 2 lines below:}
                { ConvertWords(CurrentDTA^.DTASegment,
                    CurrentDTA^.DTAOffset,FileSize);
                InterpretDate(CurrentDTA^.DTASegment,
                    CurrentDTA^.DTAOffset,Month,
                    Day,Year); }

    {To use this program with Turbo Pascal versions prior
        to 4.0, remove the 5 lines below:}
                FileSize:=S.Size;
                UnpackTime(S.Time,D);
                Month:=D.Month;
                Day:=D.Day;
                Year:=D.Year;

                Str(FileSize:8:0,Temp);
                Temp:=Temp+' ';
                Str(Month:2,Temp1); Temp1:=Temp1+'/';
                Str(Day:2,Temp2); Temp2:=Temp2+'/';
                Str(Year:4,Temp3); Temp3:=Temp3+'  ';

    {To use this program with Turbo Pascal versions prior
        to 4.0, add the line below:}
                { InterpretTime(CurrentDTA^.DTASegment,
                    CurrentDTA^.DTAOffset,Hour,Min,Sec); }
```

Tool 2.11: Procedure Directry to conduct a complex directory search. (continued)

```
        {To use this program with Turbo Pascal versions prior
            to 4.0, remove the 3 lines below:}
                        Hour:=D.Hour;
                        Min:=D.Min;
                        Sec:=D.Sec;

                IF Hour>12 THEN
                        BEGIN
                                DayTime:='p'; Hour:=Hour-12;
                        END
                                ELSE DayTime:='a';
                Str(Hour:2,Temp4); Temp4:=Temp4+':';
                Str(Min:2,Temp5);
                FOR X:=1 TO 2 DO
                                IF NOT (Temp5[X] IN['0'..'9'])
                                        THEN Temp5[X]:='0';

                DirEntry:=Direntry+Temp+Temp1+Temp2+
                        Temp3+Temp4+Temp5+DayTime+'   ';
                Temp:='';
            END   {if attribute not in[8,16]}
                        ELSE
            {if the entry is a directory, note it as such}
                        Temp:='     <DIR>                    ';
        DirEntry:=DirEntry+Temp;
        Str(Attribute:3,Temp1);
        Temp:=PathName+TempString;
        WHILE (Length(Temp)<65) DO Temp:=Temp+' ';
        {if the entry is not either . or .., write it}
        IF ((Error=0) AND (DirEntry[1]<>'.'))
                THEN WriteLn(DirFile,Temp1,Temp,DirEntry);
    END;   {format item}


BEGIN {get disk directory}
    {initialize}
    SubLevel:=0; FoundFirst:=FALSE; TempString:='';
    FileMask:=Mask; PathName:='';
    {check the mask and separate the file specification from path}
    REPEAT
            Position:=Pos('\',FileMask);
            PathName:=PathName+Copy(FileMask,1,Position);
            FileMask:=Copy(FileMask,Position+1,
                    Length(FileMask)-Position+1);
    UNTIL Position=0;
    Mark(TopHeap);
    {depending on search level, set file search attribute}
    CASE Level OF
            1: SrchAttribute:=1;   {read only or read/write          }
            2: SrchAttribute:=17; {as above + subdirectories         }
            3: SrchAttribute:=7;  {standard, hidden, and system files}
            4: SrchAttribute:=23; {as above + subdirectories         }
    END;   {case level of}
    GetDTA(SysDTASegment,SysDTAOffset);
    {put first DTA record into RAM}
    New(FirstDTA);
    FirstDTA^.AZ:=Mask+CHR(0);
    FirstDTA^.DTASegment:=Seg(FirstDTA^.AZ);
    FirstDTA^.DTAOffset:=Ofs(FirstDTA^.AZ);
    FirstDTA^.Last:=NIL;
    FirstDTA^.Next:=NIL;
    FinalDTA:=FirstDTA;
    CurrentDTA:=FirstDTA;
```

Tool 2.11: Procedure Directry to conduct a complex directory search. (continued)

```
            {To use this program with Turbo Pascal versions prior
               to 4.0, add the line below:}
            { SetDTA(CurrentDTA^.DTASegment,CurrentDTA^.DTAOffset); }
            {open directory text file}
            Assign(DirFile,'DIR.$$$');
            Rewrite(DirFile);
            {if there was no error setting DTA, then...}
            {search until there is an error}
            REPEAT
            {if an entry has already been found, continue search}
                IF FoundFirst THEN
                     BEGIN {continue directory search # 79}

            {To use this program with Turbo Pascal versions prior
               to 4.0, add the line below:}
                          { ContDirSearch(Error); }

            {To use this program with Turbo Pascal versions prior
               to 4.0, remove the 3 lines below:}
                          FindNext(S);
                          Error:=DOSError;
                          Move(S,CurrentDTA^.AZ,21);


                          FormatItem;
                     END;   {continue directory search # 79}
            {if no entry found yet, begin search}
                IF NOT FoundFirst THEN
                     BEGIN {start directory search}

            {To use this program with Turbo Pascal versions prior
               to 4.0, add the line below:}
                          { BeginDirSearch(CurrentDTA^.AZ,
                                   SrchAttribute,Error); }

            {To use this program with Turbo Pascal versions prior
               to 4.0, remove the 3 lines below:}
                          FindFirst(CurrentDTA^.AZ,SrchAttribute,S);
                          Error:=DOSError;
                          Move(S,CurrentDTA^.AZ,21);

                          FormatItem;
                          FoundFirst:=True;
                     END;   {start directory search}
                IF Error<>0 THEN Attribute:=-1;
                SetSubDirectory;
            UNTIL Error<>0;
            {close directory text file}
            Close(DirFile);
            Release(TopHeap);
            {reset original DTA, set DTA #26}

            {To use this program with Turbo Pascal versions prior
               to 4.0, add the line below:}
            { SetDTA(SysDTASegment,SysDTAOffset); }

  END;   {get disk directory}
```

Tool 2.11: Procedure Directry to conduct a complex directory search. (continued)

The extent of the search is determined by the parameter Level. Level is an integer with a range of 1 through 4, as follows:

1 = Directory only

2 = Directory and its subdirectories

3 = Directory only; show hidden and system files, too

4 = Directory and its subdirectories; show hidden and system files, too

The parameter Mask indicates the drive, directory, and files for the search. Mask is of type string. When more than just the current subdirectory is to be displayed, the Mask should include a drive specifier as well as a directory specifier.

EXAMPLES OF MASK PARAMETERS FOR THE DIRECTRY PROCEDURE

Complete directory of C drive	**Directry(4,'C:*.*');**
Complete directory of C drive; do not show hidden or system files	**Directry(2,'C:*.*');**
Directory of current subdirectory only	**Directry(1,'*.*');**
Directory of current subdirectory only, showing hidden and system files, also	**Directry(3,'*.*');**
Complete directory of A drive showing all .PAS files	**Directry(2,'A:*.PAS');**
Directory of subdirectory PASCAL (on current drive), showing all files starting with TURBO	**Directry(1,'\PASCAL\TURBO???.*');**

The ASCII text file created by the Directry procedure is formatted as follows:

- The file is named DIR.$$$.

Assign(ASCIIFile,'DIR.$$$');

- Each line is a directory item.

    ReadLn(ASCIIFile,DirectoryItem);

- Each directory item is a string of 110 characters, in the format illustrated in Table 2.2.

Table 2.2:

Format of Directory Entries in the ASCII File Produced by the Directry Procedure

Characters	Information
1–3	File attribute (e.g., 032)
4–68	Path (to directory item)
69–81	*Filename.Ext*
82–89	File size (bytes)
90	Space (CHR(32))
91–100	File date (mm/dd/yyyy)
101–102	Spaces (CHR(32))
103–107	File time (hh:mm)
108	AM or PM time (a or p)
109–110	Spaces (CHR(32))

Note: Subdirectory entries use only characters 1 through 81, with the notation <DIR> beginning at character 82.

Before we discuss how the Directry procedure itself works, let's examine two of its subprocedures: SetSubDirectory and FormatItem.

The SetSubdirectory Procedure

In a search including subdirectories, each time a subdirectory is encountered, new memory is allocated and a directory search begins anew on that subdirectory. When a subdirectory is completely read (returns an error of 18), the search moves back up to the previous directory that was being read. The search continues until all the entries for files and subdirectories have been exhausted and written to the text file.

The SetSubDirectory procedure is called at the end of each directory search pass to determine what action to take next. The following are the possible conditions and the actions taken for each:

- Error other than 18; no action—loop will end.

- No error, attribute not 8 or 16; no action—loop will continue.

- Error is 18 and sublevel is 0 (the procedure is searching the basic directory and no more files are to be found); no action—loop will end.

- No error, attribute is 8 or 16, level is not 2 or 4; no action—subdirectories are not to be searched.

- Other combinations that duplicate some of the conditions above; no action—loop will end if error is not 0.

- Error is 18 and sublevel is more than 0 (if a subdirectory is being searched and there are no more files to be found in it); take the following actions to end the search of this subdirectory:

  1. Decrement the sublevel by one.
  2. Remove the name of the subdirectory presently being searched from TempString, which is always the path currently being used.
  3. Change the current DTA to the previously used DTA and release the RAM allocated to the DTA for this particular subdirectory.
  4. For Turbo Pascal 4.0 or 5.0, change the first 21 bytes of the SearchRec record to the information for the parent directory (we can't change the DTA used by FindNext, so we change the data in SearchRec). For versions prior to 4.0, reset the DTA to the next higher level (to the directory that was being searched prior to searching this subdirectory).

- No error, attribute is 8 or 16, level is 2 or 4, and the directory entry is . or ..; no action—loop will continue.

- No error, attribute is 8 or 16, level is 2 or 4, and the directory entry is a subdirectory name; take the following actions to begin a search of the new subdirectory:

  1. Increment the sublevel count.
  2. Allocate RAM for a new DTA.
  3. Make the new DTA the current DTA.
  4. Add the new directory entry, which is the name of the subdirectory to be searched now, to TempString, which is the current directory path.
  5. Set the new mask to an ASCIIZ string.
  6. Set the DTA to the new area.
  7. Set FoundFirst to false so the directory search may begin in the new directory.

The FormatItem Procedure

The purpose of the FormatItem procedure is to format the data returned in the DTA for writing to the ASCII file being created by the Directry procedure. Here's how it works:

- Ascertain the attribute of the entry just found.
- Obtain the file name from the SearchRec record (version 4.0 or 5.0) or call the GetFileName procedure (earlier versions) to get the name of the directory entry just found.
- Pad the directory entry (file name) to 12 spaces.
- If the attribute is not 8 or 16 (the entry is not a subdirectory), get the file size and creation time and date information from the SearchRec record and through the UnpackTime procedure (for version 4.0 or 5.0), or use the ConvertWords, InterpretDate, and InterpretTime procedures (earlier versions), and build a formatted string containing this information for writing to the ASCII file.
- If the attribute is 8 or 16, add a string indicating that this is a directory.
- If this is a regular directory or file (not a DOS parent directory entry of . or ..), write the entry to the ASCII file.

The Directry Procedure

The Directry procedure begins with initialization statements. The drive and pathname are separated from the actual directory specification in the parameter Mask. Then the heap top is marked because the procedure will be allocating RAM as necessary to track the various subdirectories that may be encountered. RAM will be cleared to the original heap-top marking when the procedure ends. The procedure continues as follows:

- Based on the Level parameter that was passed, set the attribute for the search.
- Determine the address of the original DTA and mark it for resetting prior to exiting the procedure.
- Allocate memory and create a record for the first DTA that will be used by the Directry procedure.
- Because the current DTA is always used, also assign the newly created first DTA as the current DTA.
- For versions prior to 4.0, call the SetDTA procedure to set the DTA to the desired address (the newly created record).
- To get ready to receive directory entries, open a text file to store them.
- Begin a repeat loop for the actual directory search; the loop will continue until an error is present at the completion of the loop operations.
- Change the value of FoundFirst, as necessary. When the loop is originally entered, FoundFirst is false; depending on search results, and subdirectories encountered, the value will change.
- If there is an error, reset the attribute to guard against infinite loop conditions.
- As the last operation in the loop, call the SetSubDirectory procedure, which changes directories as necessary and maintains the proper error code (as described above).
- After exiting the loop, close the ASCII file created for directory entries, release the RAM allocated, and restore the DTA to its original address.

Test Program 2.3 shows how the Directry procedure can be used in a program. The program requests the drive name to be searched, the path to be searched, the file name specification, and the search level. The drive name must be entered, but if no entries are made for the path and file specification, the program will default to the root directory and a global (*.*) file specification. If a search level is not entered, a default level of 1 will be assumed by the program. As the program is assembling the directory and writing the ASCII file, it displays a status message. When the ASCII directory file has been completed, all the entries in it will be displayed on the screen in sequence.

```
Program TestDirectry;

     {To use this program with Turbo Pascal versions prior to
        4.0, remove the Uses statement below.}

     Uses DOS,CRT;

     {$V-}   {set compiler for relaxed parameter checking}

     TYPE
         Str255  = STRING[255];

     VAR
         DirFile     :Text;
         DirEntry    :Str255;
         SetLevel,X  :Integer;
         SetMask     :STRING[65];
         Ch          :Char;


             {To use this program with Turbo Pascal versions prior
                to 4.0, add the 8 lines below:}
     (*
     {$I ReadBits.Inc}
     {$I SetBits.Inc}
     {$I BegSrch.Inc}
     {$I ContSrch.Inc}
     {$I IntTime.Inc}
     {$I IntDate.Inc}
     {$I ConvWord.Inc}
     {$I GetFName.Inc}
     *)

     {$I GetDTA.Inc}
     {$I SetDTA.Inc}
     {$I Directry.Inc}

     BEGIN {program}
         ClrScr;
         Write('Drive name for directory search: (A-Z)   ');
```

Test Program 2.3: Using procedure Directry in a program.

```
        {To use this program with Turbo Pascal versions prior
            to 4.0, add the line below:}
        { Read(KBD,Ch); }

        {To use this program with Turbo Pascal versions prior
            to 4.0, remove the line below:}
        Ch:=ReadKey;
        Ch:=UpCase(Ch);
        WriteLn(Ch,':');
        Write('Enter path (or press Return for root directory)to search:');
        ReadLn(SetMask);
        IF (Length(SetMask)<1) THEN SetMask:='\'
            ELSE SetMask:=SetMask+'\';
        GotoXY(45,WhereY-1);
        ClrEol;
        WriteLn(SetMask);
        Write('Enter file specification: ');
        ReadLn(DirEntry);
        GotoXY(27,WhereY-1);
        ClrEol;
        IF (Length(DirEntry)<1) THEN DirEntry:='*.*';
        WriteLn(DirEntry);
        SetMask:=Ch+':'+SetMask+DirEntry;
        Write('Enter search level (1-4) : ');
        ReadLn(SetLevel);
        IF NOT (SetLevel IN[1..4]) THEN SetLevel:=1;
        WriteLn;
        WriteLn('Directory search at level ',SetLevel,' for');
        WriteLn('mask: ',SetMask);
        WriteLn;
        WriteLn('      Assembling directory file...');
        Write('     Just a moment, please...');
        Directry(SetLevel,SetMask);
        Assign(DirFile,'DIR.$$$');
        Reset(DirFile);
        ClrScr;
        WriteLn(' Path');
        WriteLn('                    Attribute  FileName.Ext',
            ' --Bytes-  ---Date--- Time    ');
        Window(1,4,80,25);
        GotoXY(1,1);
        WHILE NOT EOF(DirFile) DO
            BEGIN
                ReadLn(DirFile,DirEntry);
                FOR X:=4 TO 68 DO Write(DirEntry[X]);
                WriteLn;
                Write('                        ');
                FOR X:=1 TO 3 DO Write(DirEntry[X]);
                Write('      ');
                FOR X:=69 TO 81 DO Write(DirEntry[X]);
                Write('  ');
                FOR X:=82 TO 89 DO Write(DirEntry[X]);
                Write('  ');
                FOR X:=90 TO 108 DO Write(DirEntry[X]);
                WriteLn; WriteLn;
                Delay(250);
            END;
    Close(DirFile);
END.   {program}
```

Test Program 2.3: Using procedure Directry in a program. (continued)

CHAPTER 3
THE KEYBOARD AND USER INPUT

For many programmers, user input is a necessary evil. The bright side is that it makes programming a continuing challenge—can we find a way to let users interface with our programs without wrecking them? One good starting point is a procedure that will, at least, force the user to enter exactly the type of data required by the program. At the same time that we are protecting our programs, we must make the data-entry process as easy as possible for the user.

In this chapter, you'll find procedures that greatly simplify keyboard data entry—for both the programmer and the user. First we'll consider how to control some crucial keys and interpret keyboard return codes. Then you'll see some procedures that can handle the entire data-entry process. Finally, you'll learn how to use templates to reduce the time required for programming data entry and display.

EASING
DATA ENTRY

Actually, controlling keyboard input not only protects your program, but promotes user friendliness as well. When you write programs that are secure from improper keyboard entries, you also make them easier for people to use; there is far less chance that a user's error will crash a program.

Those using our programs are generally fully involved with concentrating on what they are supposed to do next; we can make the experience much easier and more pleasant by handling certain small tasks within our programming and, at the same time, assure better performance from the software itself. For example, if your program presents a menu that requires the use of the cursor keys, it should ensure that those keys are activated by switching Num Lock off. Here are some other services your program can provide:

- Make it easy for users to change their minds and stop the data-entry process at any reasonable time or back up to a previous data-entry field without having to start all over again.

- Provide help screens that can be accessed during the data-entry process.

- Be certain that when a specific data type is called for, no other data types can be entered.

- Make sure that numbers entered fall within the allowed ranges of their data types (such as the byte range of 0 to 255).

- Make certain that the keyboard will respond as expected (for example, when the user presses a number pad key to enter numeric input, force the Num Lock status to be active).

CONTROLLING
KEY STATUS

The keyboard operations in IBM PC, XT, and AT (and compatible computers) are supervised by the read-only memory basic input/output system (ROM BIOS) and make use of a data area in low memory. We can control certain aspects of the keyboard functioning through the keyboard status bytes at memory addresses hex 417 and hex 418.

Table 3.1 shows the layout of the two keyboard status bytes and the meanings of each bit flag. We can use these memory locations to determine or alter certain keyboard states. Generally, you will only want to alter the states of the Caps Lock and Num Lock keys.

Table 3.1:
The Keyboard Status Bytes

FIRST KEYBOARD STATUS BYTE AT HEX 417

Bit	7	6	5	4	3	2	1	0	Meaning
	1	—	—	—	—	—	—	—	Insert state active
	—	1	—	—	—	—	—	—	Caps Lock active
	—	—	1	—	—	—	—	—	Num Lock active
	—	—	—	1	—	—	—	—	Scroll Lock active
	—	—	—	—	1	—	—	—	Alt-Shift active
	—	—	—	—	—	1	—	—	Ctrl-Shift active
	—	—	—	—	—	—	1	—	Left Shift key active
	—	—	—	—	—	—	—	1	Right Shift key active

SECOND KEYBOARD STATUS BYTE AT HEX 418

Bit	7	6	5	4	3	2	1	0	Meaning
	1	—	—	—	—	—	—	—	Insert key depressed
	—	1	—	—	—	—	—	—	Caps Lock depressed
	—	—	1	—	—	—	—	—	Num Lock depressed
	—	—	—	1	—	—	—	—	Scroll Lock depressed
	—	—	—	—	1	—	—	—	Hold state active
	—	—	—	—	—	1	—	—	Used in PC Jr
	—	—	—	—	—	—	1	—	Not used
	—	—	—	—	—	—	—	1	Not used

GETTING AND SETTING THE STATUS OF THE
CAPS LOCK, NUM LOCK, SCROLL LOCK, AND INSERT KEYS

The KbdCtrl procedure, shown as Tool 3.1, uses the keyboard status bytes to get and set the status of the Caps Lock, Num Lock, Scroll Lock, and Insert keys. This procedure is useful in programs that require input to be entered in a certain form, such as in all uppercase letters or as numbers. Although the Scroll Lock and Insert keys are not usually used in the data-entry process, there may be some occasions when their status is important.

```
PROCEDURE KbdCtrl(Get_Set:Char;
                  VAR Control,Setting:Str255;
                  VAR Result:Integer);

     VAR
           X,BitNo,Flag  :Integer;
           Operation     :Char;
           InControl     :STRING[3];
           InSetting     :STRING[2];
           IsSet         :Boolean;

     BEGIN {kbdctrl}
           Get_Set:=UpCase(Get_Set);
           IF (Get_Set IN['G','S']) THEN Result:=0
                ELSE Result:=1;
           IF Result<>0 THEN Exit;
           FOR X:=1 TO 3 DO Control[X]:=UpCase(Control[X]);
           FOR X:=1 TO 2 DO Setting[X]:=UpCase(Setting[X]);
           InControl:=Copy(Control,1,3);
           InSetting:=Copy(Setting,1,2);
           IF (InControl='INS') THEN BitNo:=7 ELSE
                IF (InControl='CAP') THEN BitNo:=6 ELSE
                     IF (InControl='NUM') THEN BitNo:=5 ELSE
                          IF (InControl='SCR') THEN BitNo:=4
                               ELSE Result:=2;
           IF Result<>0 THEN Exit;
           IF (InSetting='ON') THEN Operation:='S' ELSE
                IF (InSetting='OF') THEN Operation:='U'
                     ELSE Result:=2;
           IF ((Get_Set='G') AND (Result=2)) THEN Result:=0;
           IF Result<>0 THEN Exit;
           Move(Mem[0000:$0417],Flag,2);
           IF Get_Set='S' THEN
                BEGIN {set}
                     SetBits(Operation,BitNo,Flag);
                     Move(Flag,Mem[0000:$0417],2);
                END;  {set}
           IF Get_Set='G' THEN
                BEGIN {get}
                     IsSet:=BitSet(BitNo,Flag);
                     IF IsSet THEN Setting:='ON'
                          ELSE Setting:='OFF';
                END;  {get}
     END;  {kbdctrl}
```

Tool 3.1: Procedure KbdCtrl to get and set the status of the Caps Lock, Num Lock, Scroll Lock, and Insert keys.

NOTE: The KbdCtrl procedure uses specific memory addresses that may not be appropriate for computers that are not fully IBM-compatible.

The KbdCtrl procedure requires the passing of four parameters, as described below:

- The Get_Set parameter is a character; G signals the procedure to determine the present state of a given attribute bit, and S tells the procedure to set that bit to a given state.
- The Control parameter is a string telling the procedure which control attribute is to be checked or changed. INS indicates the insert state, CAP specifies the Caps Lock state, NUM denotes the Num Lock attribute, and SCR indicates the Scroll Lock attribute.
- The Setting parameter is another string that contains either ON or OFF to indicate the desired setting if the Get_Set parameter is S; if the Get_Set parameter is G, the value of Setting is ascertained by the procedure and returned to the program in the Setting parameter.
- The Result parameter is a variable integer. It is returned to the program with a value of 1 if Get_Set is not properly specified, 2 if Control is not properly specified, or 3 if Setting is not properly specified. A result of 0 indicates success. If your keyboard has lights that are lit when the Caps Lock, Num Lock, and Scroll Lock keys are on, the success of the operation will be apparent immediately.

This procedure employs two other procedures to work with the bit map: BitSet and SetBits. These are presented as Tools 6.1 and 6.2 in Chapter 6, where bit manipulation is discussed in more detail.

Here's how the KbdCtrl procedure works:

- Check all parameters to ensure that they are satisfactory.
- Convert the character in the Get_Set parameter to uppercase, in the event it was not passed in this form.

- If the Get_Set parameter is not G or S, set the error code to the Result parameter and end the procedure.
- Convert the applicable portion of the Control and Setting strings to uppercase characters.
- Set the appropriate bit number to be operated upon according to the parameter Control. If Control is not valid, set the error code to the Result parameter and end the procedure.
- Set the appropriate operation code according to the Setting parameter. If the Setting parameter is not valid, load the error value to the Result parameter and end the procedure.
- Even though the procedure actually only operates on the single byte at hex 417, move 2 bytes to the integer variable Flag (the bits in Flag will be manipulated by either the SetBits or BitSet procedures, which require an integer rather than a single byte).
- If the desired operation is to set the attribute bit, call the SetBits procedure to handle the setting and move the 2 bytes comprising Flag back to their memory location in their altered state.
- If the desired operation is to determine the present setting of a bit, call the BitSet function and load a value to the variable parameter Setting, which is returned to the program.

Test Program 3.1 illustrates the use of the KbdCtrl procedure in a program. As the program operates, if there are lighted Caps Lock, Num Lock, and Scroll Lock keys on your keyboard, you will be able to see them being turned on and off.

The program first obtains the status of the Num Lock key and displays it on the screen, and then the program sets it to its opposite state. The status is again obtained and displayed. After you press a key to continue the program, the status is returned to its original state. The program repeats the same process for the Caps Lock, Scroll Lock, and Insert keys.

FILTERING KEYSTROKES

With the various combinations of Shift, Control, Alternate, standard keyboard, cursor pad, number pad, and function keys, there is quite an array

```
PROGRAM TestKbdCtrl;


     {To use this program with Turbo Pascal versions prior to
        4.0, remove the Uses statement below.}

     Uses DOS,CRT;


     TYPE
          Str255 = STRING[255];

     VAR
          Ch                 :Char;
          Control, Setting :Str255;
          Result, X          :Integer;

     {$I BitSet.Inc}
     {$I SetBits.Inc}
     {$I KbdCtrl.Inc}

     BEGIN {program}
          ClrScr;
          WriteLn('Testing KbdCtrl procedure.');
          FOR X:=1 TO 4 DO
               BEGIN {x}
                    Setting:='';
                    CASE X OF
                         1: Control:='NUM';
                         2: Control:='CAP';
                         3: Control:='SCR';
                         4: Control:='INS';
                    END;
                    KbdCtrl('G',Control,Setting,Result);
                    IF Result<>0 THEN
                         BEGIN {error}
                              WriteLn(#7,'>>ERROR: ',Result);
                              Halt;
                         END;   {error}
                    WriteLn(Control,' key is now ',Setting,
                         '. Now switching.');
                    IF Setting='OFF' THEN Setting:='ON'
                         ELSE Setting:='OFF';
                    KbdCtrl('S',Control,Setting,Result);
                    KbdCtrl('G',Control,Setting,Result);
                    WriteLn(Control,' key is now ',Setting,
                         '.  Will switch.');
                    Write('Press any key...');

     {To use this program with Turbo Pascal versions prior
        to 4.0, add the line below:}
               { Read(KBD,Ch); }
     {To use this program with Turbo Pascal versions prior
        to 4.0, remove the line below:}
                    Ch:=ReadKey;

                    WriteLn(Ch);
                    IF Setting='OFF' THEN Setting:='ON'
                         ELSE Setting:='OFF';
                    KbdCtrl('S',Control,Setting,Result);
                    WriteLn(Control,' key is now ',Setting,'.');
               END;   {x}
     END.   {program}
```

Test Program 3.1: Using procedure KbdCtrl in a program.

of keystrokes that a user can submit to a program. While a program should not penalize a user for an improper keystroke or combination, neither should it allow the errant stroke to affect it. For this reason, a well-designed program will include some sort of routine that filters all incoming keystrokes and allows only the proper ones to get through. If, at a given time, a program needs numeric input, it should not recognize any character keys; if the numeric input is to be of type byte, decimals and minus signs should not be recognized or should be acknowledged only with a scolding beep from the computer. Similarly, control characters, function keys, and cursor keys should be recognized only when, and if, the program has been designed to respond to these signals with specific functions.

NONPRINTABLE CHARACTERS

Nonprintable characters are those entered by pressing function keys, cursor keys, or combinations involving the Control (Ctrl) or Alternate (Alt) keys. Our programs recognize them through the codes they generate as they pass through Turbo Pascal, which takes the extended scan codes and turns most of them into escape sequences. Table 3.2 lists the various keyboard return codes for Turbo Pascal versions prior to 4.0, and Table 3.3 lists those for versions 4.0 and 5.0.

All nonprintable characters have one of two basic characteristics. Keystrokes for standard printable characters have a return code in the range of 32 through 126. When a control sequence is entered (that is, the Ctrl key is held down while another key is pressed), the return code is either in the range of 1 through 31, or it is a special sequence. In Turbo Pascal 4.0 and 5.0, the ReadKey function returns extended scan codes that begin with a null character (0) for some Ctrl-key combinations and for the function keys, cursor pad keys, and Alt-key combinations. Versions earlier than 4.0 return an escape sequence beginning with the number 27 for these special keys.

The program ShowCode, shown below, allows any key combination to be pressed and reports the key return codes by displaying them on the screen.

For Turbo Pascal programs prior to 4.0, the program begins with a compiler directive that disables Ctrl-C so that it cannot be used to interrupt the program (by default, Turbo Pascal allows you to abort a program by pressing Ctrl-C). For 4.0 and 5.0, Ctrl-C and Ctrl-Break are disabled by setting

Table 3.2:
Keyboard Return Codes for Turbo Pascal Versions prior to 4.0

Key	+ Ctrl	+ Alt	Shifted	Unshifted
A	1	27 30	65	97
B	2	27 48	66	98
C	3	27 46	67	99
D	4	27 32	68	100
E	5	27 18	69	101
F	6	27 33	70	102
G	7	27 34	71	103
H	8	27 35	72	104
I	9	27 23	73	105
J	10	27 36	74	106
K	11	27 37	75	107
L	12	27 38	76	108
M	13	27 50	77	109
N	14	27 49	78	110
O	15	27 24	79	111
P	16	27 25	80	112
Q	17	27 16	81	113
R	18	27 19	82	114
S	19	27 31	83	115
T	20	27 20	84	116
U	21	27 22	85	117
V	22	27 47	86	118
W	23	27 17	87	119
X	24	27 45	88	120
Y	25	27 21	89	121
Z	26	27 44	90	122
[{	27		123	91
\ ¦	28		124	92
] }	29		125	93

Table 3.2:
Keyboard Return Codes for Turbo Pascal Versions prior to 4.0 (continued)

Key	+ Ctrl	+ Alt	Shifted	Unshifted
` ~			126	96
0)		27 129	41	48
1 !		27 120	33	49
2 @	27 3	27 121	64	50
3 #		27 122	35	51
4 $		27 123	36	52
5 %		27 124	37	53
6 ^	30	27 125	94	54
7 &		27 126	38	55
8 ★		27 127	42	56
9 (		27 128	40	57
★	27 114			42
+			43	43
- _	31	27 130	95	45
= +		27 131	43	61
, <			60	44
. >			62	46
/ ?			63	47
; :			58	59
' "			34	39
←	27 115	27 178	52	27 75
→	27 116	27 180	54	27 77
↑		27 175	56	27 72
↓		27 183	50	27 80
Home	27 119	27 174	55	27 71
End	27 117	27 182	49	27 79
PgUp	27 132	27 176	57	27 73
PgDn	27 118	27 184	51	27 81
Ins	27 182	27 185	48	27 82

Table 3.2:
Keyboard Return Codes for Turbo Pascal Versions prior to 4.0 (continued)

Key	+ Ctrl	+ Alt	Shifted	Unshifted
Del			46	27 83
Esc	27		27	27
Backsp	127		8	8
Tab			27 15	9
Return	10		13	13
Space	32	32	32	32
F1	27 94	27 104	27 84	27 59
F2	27 95	27 105	27 85	27 60
F3	27 96	27 106	27 86	27 61
F4	27 97	27 107	27 87	27 62
F5	27 98	27 108	27 88	27 63
F6	27 99	27 109	27 89	27 64
F7	27 100	27 110	27 90	27 65
F8	27 101	27 111	27 91	27 66
F9	27 102	27 112	27 92	27 67
F10	27 103	27 113	27 93	27 68

Note: The return codes of the numeric keypad and Ctrl or Alt key combinations may vary among different compatible computers.

Table 3.3:
Keyboard Return Codes for Turbo Pascal Version 4.0 and 5.0

Key	+ Ctrl	+ Alt	Shifted	Unshifted
A	1	0 30	65	97
B	2	0 48	66	98
C	3	0 46	67	99
D	4	0 32	68	100

Table 3.3:
Keyboard Return Codes for Turbo Pascal Version 4.0 and 5.0 (continued)

Key	+ Ctrl	+ Alt	Shifted	Unshifted
E	5	0 18	69	101
F	6	0 33	70	102
G	7	0 34	71	103
H	8	0 35	72	104
I	9	0 23	73	105
J	10	0 36	74	106
K	11	0 37	75	107
L	12	0 38	76	108
M	13	0 50	77	109
N	14	0 49	78	110
O	15	0 24	79	111
P	16	0 25	80	112
Q	17	0 16	81	113
R	18	0 19	82	114
S	19	0 31	83	115
T	20	0 20	84	116
U	21	0 22	85	117
V	22	0 47	86	118
W	23	0 17	87	119
X	24	0 45	88	120
Y	25	0 21	89	121
Z	26	0 44	90	122
[{	27		123	91
\		28		124	92
] }	29		125	93
` ~			126	96
0)		0 129	41	48
1 !		0 120	33	49
2 @	0 3	0 121	64	50

Table 3.3:
Keyboard Return Codes for Turbo Pascal Version 4.0 and 5.0 (continued)

Key	+ Ctrl	+ Alt	Shifted	Unshifted
3 #		0 122	35	51
4 $		0 123	36	52
5 %		0 124	37	53
6 ^	30	0 125	94	54
7 &		0 126	38	55
8 ★		0 127	42	56
9 (		0 128	40	57
★	0 114			42
+			43	43
- _	31	0 130	95	45
= +		131	43	61
, <			60	44
. >			62	46
/ ?			63	47
; :			58	59
, "			34	39
←	0 115	4	52	0 75
→	0 116	6	54	0 77
↑		8	56	0 72
↓		2	50	0 80
Home	0 119	7	55	0 71
End	0 117	1	49	0 79
PgUp	0 132	9	57	0 73
PgDn	0 118	3	51	0 81
Ins	0 82		48	0 82
Del			46	0 83
Esc	27		27	27
Backsp	127		8	8
Tab			0 15	9

Table 3.3:
Keyboard Return Codes for Turbo Pascal Version 4.0 and 5.0 (continued)

Key	+ Ctrl	+ Alt	Shifted	Unshifted
Return	10		13	13
Space	32	32	32	32
F1	0 94	0 104	0 84	0 59
F2	0 95	0 105	0 85	0 60
F3	0 96	0 106	0 86	0 61
F4	0 97	0 107	0 87	0 62
F5	0 98	0 108	0 88	0 63
F6	0 99	0 109	0 89	0 64
F7	0 100	0 110	0 90	0 65
F8	0 101	0 111	0 91	0 66
F9	0 102	0 112	0 92	0 67
F10	0 103	0 113	0 93	0 68

Note: The return codes of the numeric keypad and Ctrl or Alt key combinations may vary among different compatible computers.

```
Program ShowCode;
     {To use this program with Turbo Pascal versions prior
        to 4.0, remove the Uses statement below.}
Uses DOS,CRT;
     {To use this program with Turbo Pascal versions prior
        to 4.0, add the line below:}
(* {$C-} {defeat ^C from interrupting program} *)
VAR
     Ch        :Char;
     Special   :Boolean;
     Times,X :Integer;
BEGIN {program showcode}
     {To use this program with Turbo Pascal versions prior
        to 4.0, remove the line below:}
```

```
        CheckBreak: = False; {defeat ^ C from interrupting program}
ClrScr;
Write('How many key strokes do you wish to check? ');
ReadLn(Times);
FOR X: = 1 TO Times DO
    BEGIN
{To use this program with Turbo Pascal versions prior
    to 4.0, add the line below:}
        { Read(KBD,Ch); }
{To use this program with Turbo Pascal versions prior
    to 4.0, remove the line below:}
        Ch: = ReadKey;

        Special: = ((Ch < #32) OR (Ch > #126));
        IF Special THEN
{To use this program with Turbo Pascal versions prior
    to 4.0, add the line below:}
        { IF ((Ch = #27) AND (KeyPressed)) THEN }
{To use this program with Turbo Pascal versions prior
    to 4.0, remove the line below:}
        IF ((Ch = #0) AND (KeyPressed)) THEN
            BEGIN
{To use this program with Turbo Pascal versions prior
    to 4.0, add the 2 lines below:}
            { Read(KBD,Ch);
            Write('<27> '); }
{To use this program with Turbo Pascal versions prior
    to 4.0, remove the 2 lines below:}
            Ch: = ReadKey;
            Write('<0> ');

        END;
        IF NOT Special THEN Write('<',Ch,'> ');
        WriteLn('<',ORD(Ch),'>');
    END;
END. {program showcode}
```

the CheckBreak variable to False. This allows Ctrl-C to be one of the key combinations that is checked. It then determines the number of keystrokes that you want to check and sets up the appropriate loop.

Next the program reads the keystroke and determines whether the character is printable or special. If the character is part of an extended scan code returned by version 4.0 or 5.0 (Ch=#0 and KeyPressed indicate another character is waiting), or an escape sequence returned by earlier versions (Ch=#27 and KeyPressed), the program reads the second character code. Finally, it constructs an appropriate output to report the keystroke and writes it to the screen.

Once your program can identify nonprintable characters, it can handle them in either of two ways. One choice is to ignore them completely and accept only printable characters. Alternatively, some nonprintable characters can take on special meanings in a program, signaling an immediate need for special actions.

The nonprintable character that is most commonly used for a special function in a program is the Escape (Esc) key. It generally allows users to get out of whatever they are doing whenever they want to. Of course, sometimes an escape is not offered immediately because a special sequence of events that cannot be interrupted has been initiated in the program. However, for the most part, an escape should be available whenever a program requests user input. The program also must take care of any file- and record-handling tasks that may be necessary after a user requests an escape.

Two other nonprintable characters frequently encountered in programs are the backspace (which returns a code of 8) and the Enter, or Return, keystrokes. A backspace can allow the user to return to another data-entry field, and a Return or Enter can mean that the user has no entry for that particular field.

IDENTIFYING KEYBOARD RETURN CODES

Turbo Pascal 4.0 and 5.0 provide the new ReadKey function to return scan codes. This function serves the same purpose as the Read (KBD, Ch) statement in earlier versions.

The ReadKeyCode procedure, shown as Tool 3.2, illustrates a simple method of identifying the type of keystroke that has been made. This is the first step in any program that will treat nonprintable characters in a special way. ReadKeyCode returns parameters to the program that indicate the type of keystroke (standard or nonprintable) and the key return code.

Here's how the ReadKeyCode procedure works:

• Wait for a keystroke.

- After reading a keystroke, determine if it was a standard, printable character.

- If it was not a standard character and the return code is either a 0 (versions 4.0 and 5.0) or a 27 (earlier versions), check through the Turbo Pascal function KeyPressed to see whether another character is waiting to be read. If nothing is waiting, the Esc key was pressed (#27); if a character is waiting, a cursor, function, Ctrl, or Alt key combination was entered.

- Place the value of the key return code in the parameter Code and return it to the program.

Test Program 3.2 shows how the ReadKeyCode procedure could be used in a program. The program accepts any keystroke and interprets it through the ReadKeyCode procedure. If it is a printable character, that

```
PROCEDURE ReadKeyCode(VAR Code:Byte; VAR Std:Boolean);

    (For use with versions of Turbo Pascal prior to 4.0)

    VAR
        Ch  :Char;

    BEGIN (read keyboard return code)
        Read(KBD,Ch);
        Std:=(Ch IN[#32..#126]);
        IF NOT Std THEN
            IF ((Ch=#27) AND (KeyPressed)) THEN
                    Read(KBD,Ch);
        Code:=ORD(Ch);
    END;  (read keyboard return code)


PROCEDURE ReadKeyCode(VAR Code:Byte; VAR Std:Boolean);

    (For use with Turbo Pascal versions 4.0 and 5.0)

    VAR
        Ch  :Char;

    BEGIN (read keyboard return code)
        Ch:=ReadKey;
        Std:=(Ch IN[#32..#126]);
        IF NOT Std THEN
            IF ((Ch=#0) AND (KeyPressed)) THEN
                    Ch:=ReadKey;
        Code:=ORD(Ch);
    END;  (read keyboard return code)
```

Tool 3.2: Procedure ReadKeyCode to identify nonprintable characters.

character is displayed on the screen. Otherwise, the program informs you that a nonprintable character was entered and displays its keyboard return code.

```
PROGRAM TestReadKey;

     {To use this program with Turbo Pascal versions prior to
        4.0, remove the Uses statement below.}

Uses DOS,CRT;

VAR
     ReturnCode   :Byte;
     Printable    :Boolean;

{$I ReadKeyC.Inc}

Begin {program test readkey}
     ClrScr;
     WriteLn('Testing ReadKeyCode procedure.');
     WriteLn('  Enter a keystroke.');
     ReadKeyCode(ReturnCode,Printable);
     IF Printable THEN WriteLn(CHR(ReturnCode))
          ELSE WriteLn('Nonprintable character - code: ',
                          ReturnCode);
END.   {program test readkey}
```

Test Program 3.2: Using procedure ReadKeyCode in a program.

SIMPLE KEYBOARD DATA ENTRY

The simplest keyboard data entry is, of course, a single character. Even in this case, your program can prevent improper data entry by screening the input.

To guard single-character entries against mistakes, a series of program statements similar to those shown below can ensure proper data entry and even allow for appropriate nonprintable characters. These lines look for a simple yes (Y) or no (N) answer, but also provide for a backspace (e.g., to a previous data-entry field), a Return (no answer), or an Esc keypress.

```
{locate cursor at proper position}
REPEAT
     Character: = ReadKey {for versions 4.0 and 5.0}
     Read(KBD,Character); {for versions prior to 4.0}
```

```
      {often appropriate to force uppercase}
      Character: = UpCase(Character);
      {see if character is in allowable entry set}
      OK: = (Character IN['Y','N',#8,#13,#27]);
      IF NOT OK THEN Write(#7);  {beep if bad data}
   UNTIL OK;
   {now that character is accepted, write it}
   Write(Character);
```

HANDLING COMPLEX
DATA ENTRY

The Turbo Pascal Read and ReadLn procedures in versions earlier than 4.0 accept keyboard data input, but the user must get it right, or there will be problems immediately. Even with version 4.0 or 5.0, which includes provisions for checking data read from the keyboard, there are plenty of opportunities for run-time and data errors to result from inaccurate keyboard input. For complex data entry that involves more than a single character, you can use a full-scale input routine to protect your program from some of the inevitable data-entry errors.

A Data-Entry Routine

For an effective data-entry routine, you could use a single keyboard entry procedure or multiple procedures, one for each specific data type; each method has its advantages and disadvantages. The InKey procedure, shown as Tool 3.3, is a single procedure for all basic data types (byte, integer, real, and string). This method will conserve program space and avoid the repetition of the same programming for each of the basic data types, and it is still fast enough to accommodate most users' rates of data entry. Although the procedure requires more parameters than one for just a single data type, it minimizes the parameter requirements by returning only the real type when dealing with numbers. You simply use the Turbo Pascal Trunc procedure to convert this value to byte or integer data types when the program variable being input is one of these types. The keyboard-input procedure keeps the data within the proper ranges so that the Trunc procedure will function properly.

```
PROCEDURE InKey(Col, Row, NumChars:Integer;
                TypeInput, Format:Char;
                VAR InString:Str255;
                VAR InReal:Real;
                VAR Result:Integer);

  {If this procedure is used with Turbo Pascal versions prior
     to 4.0, the TypeInput values of (W)ord and (L)ongInt are
     not valid and cannot be used}

VAR
  Count, X, Reslt, Places  : Integer;
  Key                      : Char;
  InRange, Valid, Decimal  : Boolean;


BEGIN {InKey}
  REPEAT {until in range}
    GotoXY(Col,Row);
    {Initialize}
    Count:=0; InString:=''; InReal:=0.0; InRange:=False;
    Decimal:=False; Result:=0; TypeInput:=UpCase(TypeInput);
    Format:=UpCase(Format);
    IF (Format IN['0'..'9']) THEN
      Val(Format,Places,Reslt) ELSE Places:=0;
    Decimal:=(Places=0);
    IF Places>0 THEN Places:=(NumChars-Places-1);
    {Loop until desired number characters read}
    WHILE (Count<NumChars) DO
      BEGIN {while count<numchars}
        {Read the character entered}

        {To use this program with Turbo Pascal versions prior
           to 4.0, add the line below:}
        { Read(KBD,Key); }

        {To use this program with Turbo Pascal versions prior
           to 4.0, remove the line below:}
        Key:=ReadKey;

        {If Esc is hit...}

        {To use this program with Turbo Pascal versions prior
           to 4.0, add the 14 lines below:}
        (* IF (Key=#27) THEN
          BEGIN {Esc key hit}
            IF NOT KeyPressed THEN Result:=3;
            IF KeyPressed THEN
              BEGIN
                Read(KBD,Key);
                IF Key=#35 THEN Result:=4;
              END;
            IF (Result>2) THEN
              BEGIN
                InString:=''; InReal:=0.0; Exit;
              END
                ELSE Key:=#0;
          END;  {Esc key hit} *)

        {To use this program with Turbo Pascal versions prior
           to 4.0, remove the 14 lines below:}
           IF ((Key=#27) OR (Key=#0)) THEN
```

Tool 3.3: Procedure InKey to manage keyboard data entry.

```
                          BEGIN
                            IF (Key=#27) THEN Result:=3;
                            IF (Key=#0) THEN
                              BEGIN
                                Key:=ReadKey;
                                IF (Key=#35) THEN Result:=4;
                              END;
                            IF (Result>2) THEN
                              BEGIN
                                InString:=''; InReal:=0.0; Exit;
                              END
                                ELSE Key:=#0;
                          END;
      {accept any valid character;}
      {backspace if necessary; <CR> ends}
      CASE TypeInput OF
        'B','W': Valid:=(Key IN[#8,#13,#48..#57]);
        'I','L': IF Count=0 THEN
                   Valid:=(Key IN[#8,#13,#45,#48..#57])
                   ELSE Valid:=(Key IN[#8,#13,#48..#57]);
        'R': BEGIN
               IF Count=0 THEN
                 Valid:=(Key IN[#8,#13,#45,#46,#48..#57])
                 ELSE Valid:=(Key IN[#8,#13,#46,#48..#57]);
               IF ((Decimal) AND (Key=#46)) THEN
                 Valid:=False;
             END;
        'S': CASE Format OF
               'A': Valid:=(Key IN[#8,#13,#32..#126]);
               'U': Begin
                      Key:=UpCase(Key);
                      Valid:=(Key IN[#8,#13,#32..#126]);
                    END;
               'L': BEGIN
                      IF (Key IN[#65..#90]) THEN
                        Key:=CHR(ORD(KEY)+32);
                      Valid:=(Key IN[#8,#13,#32..#126]);
                    END;
               'N': Valid:=(Key IN[#8,#13,#48..#57]);
             END;  {case format}
      END;  {case type input}
      {If the first entry is valid then make an underline}
      {for the number of keystrokes}
      IF ((Count=0) AND (Valid)) THEN
        BEGIN {if}
          FOR X:=1 TO NumChars DO Write(#177);
          GotoXY(Col,Row);
        END;  {if}
      IF NOT Valid THEN Key:=#0;
      CASE Key OF
        #32..#126: BEGIN
          Count:=Count+1;  Write(Key);
          IF ((Key=#46) AND (TypeInput='R')) THEN
            BEGIN
              Decimal:=True; Count:=Places+1;
            END;
          InString:=InString+Key;
          IF (TypeInput='R') THEN
            IF ((Places=Count) AND (Decimal=False)) THEN
              BEGIN
                Count:=Count+1; Decimal:=True;
                InString:=InString+'.'; Write('.');
              END;                          END;
```

Tool 3.3: Procedure InKey to manage keyboard data entry. (continued)

```
    #8      : IF (Count>0) THEN
       BEGIN
         IF InString[Count]=#46 THEN Decimal:=False;
         Write(#8#177#8); Count:=Count-1;
         Delete(InString,Length(InString),1);
       END
         ELSE IF (COUNT=0) THEN
           BEGIN
             Result:=2; Exit;
           END;
    #10,#13  : IF (Count>0) THEN Count:=NumChars
       ELSE
         BEGIN
           Result:=1; Exit;
         END;
    ELSE    Write(^G);
   END; {case key statement}
  END;  {while count<numchars}
  Val(InString,InReal,Reslt);
  CASE TypeInput OF
   'B': InRange:=((InReal>=0) AND (InReal<256));
   'W': InRange:=((InReal>=0) AND (InReal<=65535.0));
   'I': InRange:=((InReal>=-32767) AND (InReal<=32767));
   'L': InRange:=((InReal>=-2147483648.0) AND
                  (InReal<=2147483647.0));
   'R': InRange:=(Reslt=0);
   'S': InRange:=True;
  END;  {case type input}
  IF NOT InRange THEN Write(^G);
 UNTIL InRange;
 Result:=0;
END; {InKey}
```

Tool 3.3: Procedure InKey to manage keyboard data entry. (continued)

Note that although Turbo Pascal 4.0 and 5.0 support single, double, extended, and Comp real types, your computer must be equipped with an 8087 coprocessor to compile and run programs that use these types. Version 5.0 can also emulate an 8087 chip. The InKey procedure only supports the default real type so that it will work with any computer system.

The InKey procedure efficiently manages much of the data-entry process. As mentioned previously, allowing a user to begin data entry in a given data input field and then have a change of heart and back out of the field, leaving previous data intact, is a valuable service we can perform to make our software easier to use. The InKey procedure will, used properly in a program, forgive the user for such a mistake.

The procedure first places the cursor at the point where data entry is to begin and then checks the first keystroke. Depending on the keystroke, the procedure will take one of the following actions:

- If it is a Return, we assume that the user does not want to enter data, and the procedure ends, returning a code indicating that no data were entered.
- If a backspace is the first entry, we know that the user does not want to enter data, and the procedure ends, returning a code indicating that the user backspaced out of the data-entry area.
- If the Esc key was pressed, the procedure ends and returns a code indicating that the user escaped the entry procedure.
- If Alt-H is pressed, the procedure ends and returns a code indicating that the user requested help.
- If a valid key was pressed, the procedure accepts normal data entry.

For normal data-entry situations (in which the first key pressed is a valid key for the type of data being entered), the InKey procedure highlights (by block characters) the data-entry area, showing the user the exact number of spaces allotted for the data. It continues accepting data until the allotted number of spaces is filled or until the user otherwise terminates data entry. The character used to highlight the data-entry area is ASCII #177. You may want to change this to another character, such as a #95 for an underline, in your specific application.

The InKey procedure checks the type and format of the data entered using the parameters you defined. If you specify string type data, any printable key is accepted (except when you select a numeric format, which only allows number keys for string data). If the format calls for it, the procedure will convert the character entered to uppercase or lowercase.

When you specify numeric input (type real, integer, or byte), only numeric entries are accepted; the user can enter a minus sign for a negative real or integer (but not bytes or words) and a period for a real number's decimal point. For real numbers, you also specify the number of decimal places allowed. If you have to classify an integer as a real because of its size, specify zero decimal places, and only an integer will be accepted. When you specify byte or integer numbers, the InKey procedure checks that the entry is within the allowable range for a number of that type, and will not accept it if it is out of range.

When the user terminates data entry by pressing Return, InKey accepts the data already entered and returns them to the program. If the user terminates entry by pressing the Esc key, the procedure returns to the program with a code indicating that no data were entered and the user escaped. If the user enters Alt-H, the procedure understands that a help screen is desired and returns to the program with a code indicating a request for help. Backspacing out of the field after beginning data entry returns a code indicating that no data were entered and that the user backspaced out of the data-entry area. Generally, when this happens, the program should return to the previous data-entry field to give the user a chance to reenter that data item.

Parameters for Using the InKey Procedure

The InKey procedure requires the following parameters to be passed to it:

- The Col (for column) and Row parameters are integers telling the procedure where the input is to begin.

- NumChars is an integer parameter that indicates the maximum number of valid keystrokes to allow the user to enter.

- TypeInput is a character parameter that specifies the type of input the user is to enter (B for byte, I for integer, W for word, L for long integer, R for real, or S for string).

- Format is a character parameter indicating either the number of decimal places to allow for a real (0 through 9) or the format of string input (A for accept as entered, U for force to uppercase, L for force to lowercase, and N for numeric input only).

Although it must always be passed, the Format parameter is valid only when the type of input is either real or string. The Format parameter is passed *only* as a character, even if it is a number conforming to the conventions required for an InputType real; that is, you must enclose it in single quotation marks (e.g., 'A', '0', '4', 'L').

The InKey procedure will force all real-number entry fields to have the number of decimal places indicated by the Format parameter. After the user enters data to fill the allowed number of places to the left of the decimal point, the procedure inserts the decimal point automatically at the proper position to ensure that the specified number of positions to the right are entered. For example, if you set Format to 4, and NumChars is 7, the procedure will allow the user to enter two numbers, force a decimal point, and then allow four more numbers to be entered to the right of the decimal point. An entry of 0 for Format indicates that no decimal places are allowed, thus forcing an integer (though of type real) to be returned. A − (for negative) entry is allowed and is counted as one keystroke of the NumChars parameter.

Parameters Returned to the Program

The InKey procedure will return three parameters to the program: Result, InString, and InReal. The Result parameter tells the program how the user ended input at this screen location. The following codes may be returned by Result:

0 = Normal data input

1 = No input, the user bypassed the field by pressing Return

2 = The user backspaced out of the data-input area and, therefore, out of the InKey procedure

3 = The user pressed the Esc key to exit the InKey procedure

4 = The user pressed Alt-H to exit the InKey procedure and is, therefore, requesting a help screen for this input area

You can design your program to respond appropriately to user input by basing its next action on the Result code returned by the InKey procedure. For example, the program might take the following actions:

- If Result is 0, assign one of the returned data parameters (StringVariable or RealVariable) to the variable applicable to the data-entry field.

- If Result is 1, assume that the user does not wish to enter or change data in this field and proceed to the next data-entry field.
- When 2 is returned, go back to the previous data-entry field.
- When 3 is returned, allowed the user to exit this portion of the program.
- If Result is 4, display an appropriate help screen and return to the input field when the user finishes with it.

The InString and InReal parameters are used to return the actual input (if there is any). As noted above, if the InKey procedure returns with a zero Result parameter (for normal entry), the program should assign the input data to the appropriate program variable. Both InString and InReal are returned by the InKey procedure; it is up to the programmer to properly assign the returned input to the program variable. In the case of a string variable, you can make a simple assignment, as in

ProgramVariable: = InString

If the program variable is of type real, a simple assignment will also suffice. However, if the program variable is of type byte or integer, the assignment must be made using the Turbo Pascal Trunc procedure, for example:

ProgByteVariable: = Trunc (InReal)

When you define the TypeInput parameter as an integer, the InKey procedure will not allow input of a number that is out of the range of integers (−32768 to +32767). In the same manner, the procedure controls the range for the input type byte (0 through 255), type word (0 through 65535), and long integer (−2147483648 through 2147483647).

InKey at Work

Here's how the InKey procedure works:

- Locate the cursor at the coordinates passed to the procedure.
- Initialize variables to zero.

INKEY PARAMETERS IN BRIEF

Col and **Row**:	Integers to position the cursor
NumChars:	The number of keystrokes to accept
TypeInput:	B = Byte, I = Integer, W = Word, L = LongInt, R = Real, S = String
Format:	A = Accept string as entered, U = Uppercase string, L = Lowercase string, N = Numeric string, 0–9 = Number of decimal places allowed if input is a real number
InString:	The string passed back to the calling program if the input was type S
InReal:	The real number passed back to the calling program if the input was any numeric type
Result:	Either the result of the input or the ORD (order number) of the last input character

0 = Normal data input
1 = No input (Return pressed)
2 = User backspaced out of input area
3 = User escaped input
4 = User pressed Alt-H for help

- Convert the Format parameter to uppercase, in case it was not passed in this form.

- If the Format character is a number, determine the number of decimal places and assign the value to an integer.

- Loop until the allowed number of characters have been entered (or until the procedure is otherwise terminated).

- Wait for and read a keystroke.

- Determine whether the keystroke is the Esc key or another non-printable character.

- If the Esc key was pressed, assign the Result code a value of 3 to be returned to the program; if an escape sequence is indicated and if the sequence indicates Alt-H as the keystroke, assign Result a value of 4 to return to the program (asking for help).

- If, at this point, the Result code is nonzero, reinitialize the variable parameters pertaining to keyboard input (nullifying any other keystrokes already entered for this data item) and exit the procedure.
- Having gotten this far, the key read is probably a valid character, so handle it as the specified data type.
- Based on the specified input type, decide on the validity of the keystroke.
- If this is the first keystroke and it is valid, display the allotted data-entry area as a line of blocks indicating the size of the input field. (The character used is ASCII #177.) After writing the characters indicating the data-entry area, move the cursor to the beginning of the area.
- Handle the valid keystroke on the screen. Depending on the keystroke, write it as a character, a backspace, or a carriage return.
- Increment or decrement the count for the loop according to whether a printable character, backspace, or Return was entered.
- If the data-entry type is a real number, constantly track the decimal place so that it can only be positioned as specified by the Format parameter.
- If data entry for this item is terminated by backspacing out of the field or by a carriage return, assign the appropriate Result code for return to the program.
- If an invalid character was entered, sound a beep.
- After the allotted number of characters have been entered, make appropriate assignments for the values and check the ranges to be certain that invalid values are not returned to the program.

Using InKey in a Program

The InKey procedure is designed to work best in a program that uses *generic variables* (that is, variables other than the ones actually requested by the program) for data items that will be returned by the procedure with the user input. The program should first display the present data item in the data-entry area, and then call the InKey procedure. When the procedure returns, the program should check the Result parameter and respond appropriately (the actions suggested for each code are listed earlier, in the discussion of parameters returned to the program).

When the InKey procedure finishes, any unused keystrokes that were allowed are still marked with ASCII #177, and the data entered remain left-aligned. Your program should redisplay the current data for the field. This provides for a more attractive screen display and ensures that the data were properly assigned to the program variable. The test program shown later demonstrates how to do this.

Our next procedure can be used in conjunction with InKey to perform most of the tasks mentioned above. It is especially useful when your program presents a data-entry form on the screen or requires a lengthy series of data-entry items.

A SHELL FOR DATA ENTRY

The DataEntry procedure, shown as Tool 3.4, is an example of a shell procedure for all data entry on a given screen. The shell controls the movement from one item to another and allows the user to return to previous

```
Procedure DataEntry(VAR Recrd:DataRec);

    VAR
            Item, Result      :Integer;
            Escape            :Boolean;
            InpType, Fmt      :Char;
            GenericStr        :Str255;
            GenericRl         :Real;

    BEGIN {data entry/display loop}
        Item:=1; Escape:=False;
        REPEAT
        CASE Item OF
            1..4: BEGIN {data items 1-4}
                IF Item=1 THEN Fmt:='U' ELSE
                    IF Item=2 THEN Fmt:='L' ELSE
                        IF Item=3 THEN Fmt:='N' ELSE
                            Fmt:='A';
                GotoXY(1,2+(3*Item)); ClrEol;
                Write(Recrd.Strng[Item]);
                InKey(1,2+(3*Item),60,'S',Fmt,GenericStr,
                    GenericRl,Result);
```

Tool 3.4: Procedure DataEntry to act as a shell for data entry.

```
                                IF (Result=0) THEN
                                     Recrd.Strng[Item]:=GenericStr;
                                GotoXY(1,2+(3*Item)); ClrEol;
                                Write(Recrd.Strng[Item]);
                        END;   {data item 1}
                        5: BEGIN
                                GotoXY(20,16); ClrEol;
                                Write(Recrd.Bite);
                                InKey(20,16,3,'B',Fmt,GenericStr,
                                     GenericRl,Result);
                                IF (Result=0) THEN
                                     Recrd.Bite:=Trunc(GenericRl);
                                GotoXY(20,16); ClrEol;
                                Write(Recrd.Bite);
                        END;
                        6: BEGIN
                                GotoXY(23,18); ClrEol;
                                Write(Recrd.Intgr);
                                InKey(23,18,6,'I',Fmt,GenericStr,
                                     GenericRl,Result);
                                IF (Result=0) THEN
                                     Recrd.Intgr:=Trunc(GenericRl);
                                GotoXY(23,18); ClrEol;
                                Write(Recrd.Intgr);
                        END;
                    7..9: BEGIN
                            IF Item=7 THEN Fmt:='0' ELSE
                                IF Item=8 THEN Fmt:='2' ELSE
                                     IF Item=9 THEN Fmt:='5';
                            GotoXY(39,20+(2*(Item-7))); ClrEol;
                            Write(Recrd.Reel[Item-6]:11:6);
                            InKey(39,(20+(2*(Item-7))),11,'R',Fmt,GenericStr,
                                 GenericRl,Result);
                            IF (Result=0) THEN
                                 Recrd.Reel[Item-6]:=GenericRl;
                            GotoXY(39,20+(2*(Item-7))); ClrEol;
                            Write(Recrd.Reel[Item-6]:11:6);
                        END;
                    END;  {case item of}
                    CASE Result OF
                        0: Item:=Item+1; {normal entry}
                        1: Item:=Item+1; {carriage return}
                        2: IF Item>1 THEN Item:=Item-1;
                        3: Escape:=True;
                        4: BEGIN
                             {provide help if available}
                           END;
                    END; {case result of}
                    UNTIL ((Item>9) OR (Escape));
            END;  {data entry/display loop}
```

Tool 3.4: Procedure DataEntry to act as a shell for data entry. (continued)

data fields and skip ahead to others. It also allows the user to quit data entry at any time by pressing the Esc key. You can construct a similar procedure to act as a shell for keyboard data entry. If your program will display help screens, you can easily add provisions to move to such a screen temporarily when the InKey result indicates that this is a proper response (we'll discuss help screens a little more after reviewing the DataEntry procedure).

Here's how the DataEntry procedure works with the InKey procedure:

- Initialize the procedure by setting the data item to 1 and Escape to False.

- Go into a repeat loop that continues until the final data item on the screen has been addressed or until the Esc key has been pressed.

- Depending on the value of Item, move the loop to the appropriate data-entry area on the screen and display the current data for that item.

- Call the InKey procedure to allow data entry.

- If the result returned by InKey indicates valid input, assign that input to the appropriate program variable.

- Redisplay the current data for an item.

- After addressing each data item, evaluate the result returned by InKey and either increment the item number, decrement the number, provide help, or set Escape to True to exit the DataEntry procedure.

Using Help Screens

To include help screens for the user when you are handling data input with the InKey procedure, your program must first have these screens available. This can be accomplished through either a procedure that reads a text file containing the helpful information or a file of screens created with a screen generator, which can be called upon to flash the appropriate screen when help is called for (see Chapter 8 for more information about making screens with a screen generator).

When the InKey procedure returns to the program with a Result of 4, simply call the appropriate procedure to produce the help screen and then return to the data-input item from which help was requested.

Backspacing Out of a Data-Input Field

Because this capability especially enhances the user-friendliness of a program, let's look a little further into how InKey handles backspacing out of a data-entry area.

As mentioned earlier, the InKey procedure is designed to operate with generic variables. Upon returning from the InKey procedure, if the result indicates normal data input, the program variable being sought is assigned the value of the appropriate generic variable passed back by InKey. Because the real program variable is not being changed within the data-input process, it is possible for a user to begin entering a data item, have a change of mind, and backspace out of the data-entry field. The code returned to the host program will indicate that the field did not receive normal data input and, therefore, the program variable should not be changed. This leaves the original entry for a field intact when the user presses backspace to exit that field after beginning to make a change.

TESTING THE INKEY AND DATAENTRY PROCEDURES

Tool 3.5 shows the TestDataEntryScreen procedure. This procedure in itself is not significant. Its purpose is to construct the data-entry screen for Test Program 3.3, which demonstrates the use of the InKey and Data-Entry procedures.

The test program presents a data-entry screen and allows you to enter various data types under the control of the InKey and DataEntry procedures. It displays the value for each field prior to calling the InKey procedure; this makes the procedure valuable for data revision as well as for initial entry. Also, after returning from the InKey procedure, the program redisplays the present value for the given field; this removes any of the full-field length block characters that the InKey procedure displayed to indicate maximum data-input length and ensures that the user sees the current value of the program variable.

HANDLING CONTROL CHARACTERS AND FUNCTION KEYS

Our current version of the InKey procedure only handles the control characters returned by the Esc key and the Alt-H key combination (for help). If your program uses any other special keys, you can modify the

```
PROCEDURE TestDataEntryScreen;
    BEGIN {produce screen for test data entry}
        ClrScr;
        GotoXY(28,2);
        WriteLn('SAMPLE DATA ENTRY SCREEN');
        GotoXY(1,4);
        Write('Enter string data below -',
                ' it will be forced to uppercase.');
        GotoXY(1,7);
        Write('Enter string data below -',
                ' it will be forced to lowercase.');
        GotoXY(1,10);
        Write('Enter string data below -',
                ' only numeric characters allowed.');
        GotoXY(1,13);
        Write('Enter string data below as you wish.');
        GotoXY(1,16);
        Write('Enter BYTE number:');
        GotoXY(1,18);
        Write('Enter INTEGER number:');
        GotoXY(1,20);
        Write('Enter REAL number - 0 decimal places:');
        GotoXY(1,22);
        Write('Enter REAL number - 2 decimal places:');
        GotoXY(1,24);
        Write('Enter REAL number - 5 decimal places:');
    END;  {produce screen for test data entry}
```

Tool 3.5: Procedure TestDataEntryScreen for testing procedures InKey and DataEntry.

InKey procedure to return their codes to your program or data-entry shell procedure. Your program could then take appropriate action based on the code returned.

Here's how to modify InKey so that it can handle extended ASCII codes:

1. Find the following statement in the InKey procedure:

CASE TypeInput OF
'B','W': Valid: = (Key IN[#8,#13,#48..#57]);

2. Immediately *before* this CASE statement, insert:

IF NOT (Key IN[#8,#10,#13,#32..#126]) THEN
BEGIN
    InString: = ''; InReal: = 0.0;
    Result: = ORD(Key) + 100;
    Exit;
END;

3. Find the following statement in the InKey procedure:

IF Key = #35 THEN Result: = 4;

4. Modify the above statement to read as follows:

Result: = ORD(Key) + 100;

Now, instead of ignoring any extended scan or escape sequence codes other than 35 (the result of striking Alt-H), the procedure will assign the code plus 100 to Result and pass it back to the program.

We added 100 to the return code so that, after the procedure returns, the program can differentiate between an extended scan or escape sequence code of 1 (Ctrl-A) and a Result of 1 (input terminated by a Return). If the

```
PROGRAM TestDataEntry;

     {To use this program with Turbo Pascal versions prior to
        4.0, remove the Uses statement below.}

     Uses DOS,CRT;

     TYPE
          Str255 = STRING[255];
          DataRec = RECORD
               Strng :ARRAY[1..4] OF STRING[60];
               Bite  :Byte;
               Intgr :Integer;
               Reel  :ARRAY[1..3] OF Real;
          END;  {datarec}

     VAR
          InPutRec :DataRec;

     {$I TDES.Inc}  { TestDataEntryScreen procedure}
     {$I InKey.Inc}
     {$I DataNtry.Inc}

     BEGIN {program}
          TestDataEntryScreen;
          {initialize data record}
          WITH InPutRec DO
               BEGIN {with}
                    Strng[1]:=''; Strng[2]:=''; Strng[3]:='';
                    Strng[4]:=''; Bite:=0; Intgr:=0;
                    Reel[1]:=0.0; Reel[2]:=0.0; Reel[3]:=0.0;
               END;  {with}
          DataEntry(InPutRec);
     END.  {program}
```

Test Program 3.3: Using procedures InKey and DataEntry in a program.

Result is greater than 100, you should have your program decrement the value by 100 and respond appropriately to the resulting return code.

You can also use InKey in creating other specialized input routines. Depending on the record structures you normally use, you may find it handy to construct a specialized library of input procedures for telephone numbers, zip codes, dates, and other data in a special format and use the InKey procedure as an integral part of the specialized procedure. Chapter 4, which deals with date handling, also presents a date-input procedure that uses InKey to obtain a valid date in the mm/dd/yy format (Tool 4.6).

DATA-INPUT TEMPLATES

Another technique you can incorporate with the InKey procedure (or other input-handling procedures) to make programming data input and display much faster and simpler is the use of templates. First you construct a generalized data-input and/or data-display procedure, similar to the DataEntry procedure (Tool 3.4). This specialized data-entry procedure, however, calls a file of template records for all information concerning the data input about to take place.

The template record file should contain a template of each data-entry item, with various characteristics of that item represented in a coded format. The specialized procedure then can go on to handle all data entry or display without further programming. No matter how many data-entry/data-display screens a program has, each can be handled by a fast, simple template file. This method can save a great deal of programming time; it handles the display of present data, data entry, and data revisions.

In this section, you'll see how to design and use templates with the InKey procedure (of course, you can use the technique with any keyboard data-entry routine). It presents a program that you can use to create template files and a procedure to read the files.

THE BASIC TEMPLATE

Each set of template records should represent all the data entry or display that will take place on a given screen. Each data entry item must contain the information necessary to obtain the data input and display it properly.

To use templates with the InKey procedure, each data item will need the following information about it placed into the template record file:

- Screen number: If the template file is to hold records for more than one screen, each record must contain the number of its associated screen

- Data item number: A number signifying the order of entry or display for this item

- Beginning position on the screen: The column and row

- Number of positions to be displayed: The maximum number of characters allowed for this data item

- Justification: Display the data for this item as right- or left-aligned

- Data type: Byte, word, integer, long integer, real, or string

- Data format: Number of decimal places, uppercase, lowercase, as entered, or numeric string

CREATING A TEMPLATE FILE

You can easily create a template file by using a brief program that takes the information for each data item on a screen and writes a record to file for that item. It is possible, by adding a number for each screen, to build a single template file with the data for all the data entry or display screens in a program.

The MakeTemp program, shown as Tool 3.6, can be used to create a template file for all the screens in a program.

> **NOTE:** the MakeTemp program is simply structured for purposes of illustration; it does not provide checks on the data entered. Therefore, if you use the program as is, you must be careful to ensure accurate and appropriate data entry.

The MakeTemp program begins by asking you to enter a file name for the template records. This may be an existing template file that will have

```
Program MakeTemp;

        {To use this program with Turbo Pascal versions prior to
            4.0, remove the Uses statement below.}

        Uses DOS,CRT;

        LABEL
            ReDo;

        TYPE
            TemplRec = RECORD
                ScreenNo, ItemNo           :Integer;
                Col, Row, NumChars         :Integer;
                Justify, DataType, Format  :Char;
            END; {templ rec}

        VAR
            TemplateRec           :TemplRec;
            TemplateFile          :FILE OF TemplRec;
            Ans                   :Char;
            Finished, Correct     :Boolean;
            FName                 :STRING[65];

        BEGIN {program to make a template file}
            ClrScr;
            WriteLn('Simple program to create a file of',
                    ' template records');
            Window(1,3,80,25);
            Write('Enter FILE NAME for Template File: ');
            ReadLn(FName);
            Write('Enter SCREEN NUMBER for Template Records: ');
            ReadLn(TemplateRec.ScreenNo);
            Window(1,6,80,25);
            REPEAT   {until finished}
                ReDo:
                WITH TemplateRec DO
                    BEGIN {with templaterec}
                        Write('Enter item number: ');
                        ReadLn(ItemNo);
                        Write('Data entry position COLUMN: ');
                        ReadLn(Col);
                        Write('Data entry position ROW: ');
                        ReadLn(Row);
                        Write('Maximum number keystrokes: ');
                        ReadLn(NumChars);
                        Write('When displaying data - ',
                              'JUSTIFY (R)ight or (L)eft: ');

            {To use this program with Turbo Pascal versions prior
                to 4.0, add the line below:}
                        { Read(KBD,Justify); }
            {To use this program with Turbo Pascal versions prior
                to 4.0, remove the line below:}
                        Justify:=ReadKey;

                        Justify:=UpCase(Justify);
                        WriteLn(Justify);
```

Tool 3.6: Program MakeTemp to create a template file for all the data-entry or display screens in a program.

```
                {To use this program with Turbo Pascal versions prior
                   to 4.0, add the 2 lines below:}
                            { Write('Data type (B)yte, (I)nteger,',
                                  ' (R)eal, (S)tring ');
                            Read(KBD,DataType); }

                {To use this program with Turbo Pascal versions prior
                   to 4.0, remove the 2 lines below:}
                            Write('Data type (B)yte, (W)ord, (I)nteger,'
                                  ' (L)ongInt, (R)eal, (S)tring ');
                            DataType:=ReadKey;

                            DataType:=UpCase(DataType);
                            WriteLn(DataType);

                            IF (DataType='S') THEN
                                 Write('Data format (U)ppercase,',
                                     ' (L)owercase, (N)umeric,',
                                     ' (A)s entered   ');
                            IF (DataType='R') THEN
                                 Write('Number of DECIMAL PLACES',
                                     ' allowed:  (0-9) ');
                            IF (DataType IN['R','S']) THEN
                                 BEGIN

                {To use this program with Turbo Pascal versions prior
                   to 4.0, add the line below:}
                                   { Read(KBD,Format); }

                {To use this program with Turbo Pascal versions prior
                   to 4.0, remove the line below:}
                                 Format:=ReadKey;

                                 Format:=UpCase(Format);
                                 WriteLn(Format);
                            END
                                 ELSE Format:='0';
                            WriteLn;
                            Write('Everything correct? (Y/N) ');

                {To use this program with Turbo Pascal versions prior
                   to 4.0, add the line below:}
                            { Read(KBD,Ans); }

                {To use this program with Turbo Pascal versions prior
                   to 4.0, remove the line below:}
                            Ans:=ReadKey;
                            WriteLn(Ans);
                            Correct:=(UpCase(Ans)='Y');
                            IF NOT Correct THEN GOTO ReDo;
                        END;   {with templaterec}
                Assign(TemplateFile,FName);
                {$I-} Reset(TemplateFile); {$I+}
                IF NOT (IOResult=0) THEN Rewrite(TemplateFile);
                Seek(TemplateFile,FileSize(TemplateFile));
                Write(TemplateFile,TemplateRec);
                Close(TemplateFile);
                WriteLn;
                Write(#7,'>> Enter more records ?  (Y/N) ');
```

Tool 3.6: Program MakeTemp to create a template file for all the data-entry or display
screens in a program. (continued)

```
               {To use this program with Turbo Pascal versions prior
                   to 4.0, add the line below:}
                   { Read(KBD,Ans); }

               {To use this program with Turbo Pascal versions prior
                   to 4.0, remove the line below:}
                   Ans:=ReadKey;

                   WriteLn(Ans);
                   Finished:=(Ans IN['N','n']);
               UNTIL Finished;
               Window(1,1,80,25);
          END.  {program to make a template file}
```

Tool 3.6: Program MakeTemp to create a template file for all the data-entry or display
screens in a program. (continued)

the new template records added to it, or it may be a new file (a new file is
created if the file name given does not exist). You will also be asked to supply a screen number for the data-entry screen. Generally, screens should be
sequentially numbered in order of their appearance within the program.

The program next takes the information for each data item on the screen, in
turn. After making the appropriate entries for a given item, the program asks if
you want to enter another template record for another item.

For each data-entry item on the screen, a separate template record is created. The following information is to be entered for each data-entry area:

- Item number: This represents the sequential order in which a
  given item will be entered or displayed. Normally, the top-
  leftmost data item will be the first, and the bottom-rightmost data
  item will be the last. However, you can arrange the items in any
  order—item numbering permits any data field on the screen to be
  in the entry order you choose.

- Data-entry position: The next two entries are the column and
  row at which data entry or display begins.

- Display area: The next item requested is the maximum number
  of keystrokes allowed for data entry. This also tells the program
  the width of the field for display purposes.

- Justification: The templates will allow a data-display procedure
  to automate the display process. For this reason, it is necessary to

enter a parameter to the template declaring whether the displayed data are to be right- or left-aligned within their area.

- Data type: Because the template records will be used to call the keyboard input routine, InKey, as well as a procedure to display the data, the templates must also contain information about the data type of each given field. Data types are B for byte, W for word, I for integer, L for long integer, R for real, and S for string.

- Format: For those data types requiring formatting (strings and reals), you will be asked to enter either the string format (U for uppercase, L for lowercase, N for numeric only, or A for as entered) or the number of decimal places (0 through 9) to display with real numbers.

- Verification: The final step in entering the template for a given data item is the verification that the previously entered information is correct. If verified, the record is written to file; if not, it must be reentered.

Here's how the MakeTemp program works:

- Clear the screen and write a heading.
- Obtain the template file name and screen number and make them part of the heading.
- Create a window to preserve the heading.
- Establish a repeat loop to allow continued entries of template records until the required number for the given screen have been entered.
- Request the various data items for a given data item one by one.
- After entering all the information for a single template record, verify the accuracy of the data.
- Write the template record just constructed to the end of the template file.
- Decide whether there are more records to be entered.

The simple MakeTemp program requires precise data entry. You may find it useful to enhance this example program by adding procedures to review and revise the template records and, perhaps, even sort them by screen and item number after the file is completed.

READING THE TEMPLATES

After the templates are in a file, your program must read them for three basic functions: to allow entry of new data, to display the present data, and to allow revision of existing data. The ReadTemp procedure, shown as Tool 3.7, will read the template file and place all the template records for a

```
PROCEDURE ReadTemp(FName:Str255; ScreenNum:Integer;
                   VAR TopHeap:Pointr;
                   VAR NumberItems:Integer);

   TYPE
         TemplRec = RECORD
                ScreenNo, ItemNo          :Integer;
                Col, Row, NumChars        :Integer;
                Justify, DataType, Format :Char;
         END; {templ rec}
         MTRPtr = ^MemTemplRec;
         MemTemplRec = RECORD
                ScreenNo, ItemNo          :Integer;
                Col, Row, NumChars        :Integer;
                Justify, DataType, Format :Char;
                Last, Next                :MTRPtr;
         END; {templ rec}

   VAR
         TempRec                   :TemplRec;
         TempFile                  :FILE OF TemplRec;
         First,Last,Current        :MTRPtr;

   BEGIN {read template file}
         NumberItems:=0; First:=NIL;
         Last:=NIL; Current:=NIL;
         Mark(TopHeap);
         Assign(TempFile,FName);
         {$I-} Reset(TempFile); {$I+}
         IF NOT (IOResult=0) THEN
                BEGIN {template file not found}
                       WriteLn(#7,'TEMPLATE FILE NOT FOUND.');
                       Halt;
                END;   {template file not found}
         WHILE NOT EOF(TempFile) DO
                BEGIN {while not eof}
                       Read(TempFile,TempRec);
                       IF (TempRec.ScreenNo=ScreenNum) THEN
```

Tool 3.7: Procedure ReadTemp to read the template file.

```
                          BEGIN {item template for this screen}
                               New(Current);
                               IF (First=NIL) THEN First:=Current;
                               Current^.ScreenNo:=TempRec.ScreenNo;
                               Current^.ItemNo:=TempRec.ItemNo;
                               Current^.Col:=TempRec.Col;
                               Current^.Row:=TempRec.Row;
                               Current^.NumChars:=TempRec.NumChars;
                               Current^.Justify:=TempRec.Justify;
                               Current^.DataType:=TempRec.DataType;
                               Current^.Format:=TempRec.Format;
                               Current^.Last:=Last;
                               Current^.Next:=First;
                               First^.Last:=Current;
                               IF (Last<>NIL) THEN Last^.Next:=Current;
                               Last:=Current;
                               NumberItems:=NumberItems+1;
                          END;   {item template for this screen}
              END;   {while not eof}
        Close(TempFile);
     END;   {read template file}
```

Tool 3.7: Procedure ReadTemp to read the template file. (continued)

given screen in dynamic memory. From there, these templates can be used by data-display and data-entry procedures (presented a little later).

If your computer system has a limited amount of available memory, you should have your program check that there is enough room to store the number of template records required for a screen before calling Read-Temp. Note that the procedure will return variable parameters to the host program denoting the beginning memory location of the templates and the number of templates present.

The ReadTemp procedure must be passed a string parameter containing the name of the template file to be used and the screen number to be chosen. It returns to the program with values set to the variable parameters TopHeap and NumberItems. The NumberItems parameter is used by the program to determine the number of data-entry item templates available for a given screen. The TopHeap parameter is passed to the data-display or data-entry procedure to tell it where, in dynamic RAM, to find the beginning of the template data records.

After your program is finished with the data-display or data-entry procedure, the dynamic memory allocated to the templates should be reclaimed using Turbo Pascal's Release procedure:

Release(TopHeap)

Here's how the ReadTemp procedure works:

- Initialize the NumberItems parameter, which will be returned to the program, and the pointers to the template records about to be created in dynamic RAM.

- Set the TopHeap pointer to the beginning of currently available dynamic RAM. This address will eventually be passed by the program to the data-display and data-entry procedures to enable them to find the appropriate template records in dynamic RAM. Later, the same address will be used with Turbo Pascal's Release procedure to deallocate the memory area occupied by the template records.

- Attempt to open the file containing records. If the attempt fails, halt the program after displaying a message.

- Search the template file for template records with the same screen number passed by the ScreenNum parameter.

- When an appropriate template record is found, allocate dynamic RAM and assign the information from the record in the template file to the appropriate variables in the memory record for templates. Increment the number of items (templates) each time a new template record is found.

- The memory records for templates also contain pointers to other template records in memory. Set appropriate values for these pointers, indicating the next and previous records read.

- Read the memory-resident records for the templates. They form a "circular" list; the Next record after the final one is the First one; the record previous to the First one read is the final one read.

- After reading all appropriate template records from the template file and placing them into dynamic memory, end the procedure.

You'll see how the ReadTemp procedure can be used in a program after we discuss data-display and data-entry procedures that work with it.

USING TEMPLATES TO DISPLAY DATA

Tool 3.8 shows the procedure DataDisp, which you can use in conjunction with ReadTemp to display data items on the screen.

```
PROCEDURE DataDisp(TopHeap:Pointr; ItemNum:Integer;
                   StrItem:Str255; IntItem:LongInt;
                   RealItem:Real);

    {When using this procedure with versions of Turbo Pascal
         prior to 4.0, change the type of the IntItem parameter
         from LongInt to Integer.}

    TYPE
        MTRPtr = ^MemTemplRec;
        MemTemplRec = RECORD
             ScreenNo, ItemNo            :Integer;
             Col, Row, NumChars          :Integer;
             Justify, DataType, Format   :Char;
             Last, Next                  :MTRPtr;
        END; {templ rec}

    VAR
        First,Current :MTRPtr;
        Found         :Boolean;
        X, DecPl      :Integer;
        TempStr       :STRING[18];

    BEGIN {display data on screen using template}
         {using TopHeap, set pointer to first template}
         Current:=Ptr(Seg(TopHeap^),Ofs(TopHeap^));
         First:=Current;
         {search for template for proper item number}
         REPEAT   {until found or current=first}
              Found:=(Current^.ItemNo=ItemNum);
              IF NOT Found THEN Current:=Current^.Next;
         UNTIL ((Found) OR (Current=First));
         IF Found THEN
              BEGIN {display data using template}
                  IF (Current^.Justify<>'L') THEN
                       Current^.Justify:='R';
                  GotoXY(Current^.Col,Current^.Row);
                  FOR X:=1 TO Current^.NumChars DO Write(' ');
                  GotoXY(Current^.Col,Current^.Row);
                  X:=0;
                  IF (Current^.DataType='R') THEN
                       DecPl:=(ORD(Current^.Format)-48);
                  IF (DecPl<0) THEN DecPl:=0;
                  IF (DecPl>9) THEN DecPl:=9;
                  CASE Current^.Justify OF
                    'L': IF (Current^.DataType='S') THEN
                             Write(StrItem) ELSE
                         IF (Current^.DataType
                            IN['B','I','W','L'])
                             THEN Write(IntItem) ELSE
                         IF (Current^.DataType='R') THEN
```

Tool 3.8: Procedure DataDisp to use templates to display data on the screen.

```
                       BEGIN
                          Str(RealItem:18:DecPl,TempStr);
                          WHILE ((Length(TempStr)>0) AND
                               (ORD(TempStr[1])<45)) DO
                               Delete(TempStr,1,1);
                          Write(RealItem:Length(TempStr)
                               :DecPl);
                       END;
                  'R': BEGIN
                         X:=Current^.NumChars;
                         IF (Current^.DataType='S') THEN
                             Write(StrItem:X) ELSE
                         IF (Current^.DataType
                             IN['B','I','W','L'])
                             THEN Write(IntItem:X) ELSE
                         IF (Current^.DataType='R') THEN
                             Write(RealItem:X:DecPl);
                       END;
                 END; {case statement}
            END;  {display data using template}
    END;  {display data on screen using template}
```

Tool 3.8: Procedure DataDisp to use templates to display data on the screen.
(continued)

The DataDisp procedure is called a number of times within a loop to display the various items of data on the screen by using the template records for that screen. The TopHeap parameter passed by the ReadTemp procedure tells DataDisp where to find the appropriate template record.

The following parameters should be passed to the DataDisp procedure:

- The dynamic RAM address of the template records for the data items being displayed on screen. This address was returned by the ReadTemp procedure when it got the template records from the file and placed them into dynamic memory.

- The item number to be displayed. ItemNum is the present loop count when the items are being displayed through a loop (as illustrated in Test Program 3.4).

- Three generic variables: StrItem, IntItem, and RealItem. The genuine program variable values are assigned to the appropriate one of these generic variables through each pass of the loop, and the procedure uses the appropriate one according to the template records.

Here's how the DataDisp procedure works:

- Using the parameter TopHeap, which was set by ReadTemp when it placed the template records into memory, determine the memory location of the first template record. Based on this address, the addresses of all other template records can be determined because each contains the address of the previous and next record.

- Begin a repeat loop to inspect each template record until the one with an ItemNo matching the item specified in the parameter ItemNum is found.

- If no matching template record is found after searching through all template records once, end the search without taking action.

- If a matching template record is found, the data from the appropriate template govern which generic variable parameter will be written to the screen, where it will be displayed, and in what format.

USING TEMPLATES FOR DATA ENTRY AND REVISION

Tool 3.9 shows the procedure EntrRev, which you can use in conjunction with the ReadTemp procedure to allow users to make entries (or revisions) to the various data items displayed on the screen.

Similar to the DataDisp procedure, the EntrRev procedure is called a number of times within a loop to provide keyboard entry or revision of the various items of data on the screen by using the template records for that screen. The TopHeap parameter passed by the ReadTemp procedure provides the address of the appropriate record.

The following parameters should be passed to the EntrRev procedure:

- The dynamic RAM address of the template records for the data items being displayed on the screen. This address was returned by the ReadTemp procedure when it got the template records from the file and placed them into dynamic memory.

- The item number to be displayed. ItemNum is the present loop count when the items are being displayed through a loop, as illustrated in Test Program 3.4.

```
PROCEDURE EntrRev(TopHeap:Pointr; ItemNum:Integer;
                 VAR StrItem:Str255; VAR IntItem:LongInt;
                 VAR RealItem:REAL; VAR Result:Integer);

    {When using this procedure with versions of Turbo Pascal
         prior to 4.0, change the type of the IntItem parameter
         from LongInt to Integer.}


    TYPE
         MTRPtr = ^MemTemplRec;
         MemTemplRec = RECORD
              ScreenNo, ItemNo          :Integer;
              Col, Row, NumChars         :Integer;
              Justify, DataType, Format :Char;
              Last, Next                 :MTRPtr;
         END; {templ rec}

    VAR
         First,Current :MTRPtr;
         Found         :Boolean;
         X, DecPl      :Integer;
         TempStr       :STRING[18];
         InS           :Str255;
         InR           :Real;

    BEGIN {enter/revise data on screen using template}
         {using TopHeap, set pointer to first template}
         Current:=Ptr(Seg(TopHeap^),Ofs(TopHeap^));
         First:=Current;
         {search for template for proper item number}
         REPEAT  {until found or current=first}
              Found:=(Current^.ItemNo=ItemNum);
              IF NOT Found THEN Current:=Current^.Next;
         UNTIL ((Found) OR (Current=First));
         IF Found THEN
              BEGIN {get input then re-display}
                   InKey(Current^.Col,Current^.Row,
                        Current^.NumChars,Current^.DataType,
                        Current^.Format,InS,InR,Result);
                   IF (Result=0) THEN
                        BEGIN {data entered--assign input}
                             StrItem:=InS; RealItem:=InR;
                             IF (Current^.DataType
                                 IN['I','B','W','L'])
                                  THEN IntItem:=Trunc(InR);
                        END;  {data entered--assign input}
                   IF (Current^.Justify<>'L') THEN
                        Current^.Justify:='R';
                   GotoXY(Current^.Col,Current^.Row);
                   FOR X:=1 TO Current^.NumChars DO Write(' ');
                   GotoXY(Current^.Col,Current^.Row);
                   X:=0;
                   IF (Current^.DataType='R') THEN
                        DecPl:=(ORD(Current^.Format)-48);
                   IF (DecPl<0) THEN DecPl:=0;
                   IF (DecPl>9) THEN DecPl:=9;
                   CASE Current^.Justify OF
                     'L': IF (Current^.DataType='S') THEN
                             Write(StrItem) ELSE
```

Tool 3.9: Procedure EntrRev to use templates for data entry and revision.

```
                              IF (Current^.DataType
                                 IN['B','I','W','L'])
                                 THEN Write(IntItem) ELSE
                              IF (Current^.DataType='R') THEN
                                 BEGIN
                                     Str(RealItem:18:DecPl,TempStr);
                                     WHILE ((Length(TempStr)>0) AND
                                          (ORD(TempStr[1])<45)) DO
                                          Delete(TempStr,1,1);
                                     Write(RealItem:Length(TempStr)
                                          :DecPl);
                                 END;
                        'R': BEGIN
                             X:=Current^.NumChars;
                             IF (Current^.DataType='S') THEN
                                 Write(StrItem:X) ELSE
                             IF (Current^.DataType
                                 IN['B','I','W','L'])
                                 THEN Write(IntItem:X) ELSE
                             IF (Current^.DataType='R') THEN
                                 Write(RealItem:X:DecPl);
                             END;
                    END;   {case statement}
                 END;   {get input then redisplay}
      END;   {enter/revise data on screen using template}
```

Tool 3.9: Procedure EntrRev to use templates for data entry and revision. (continued)

- Three generic variables: StrItem, IntItem, and RealItem. The genuine program variable values are assigned to the appropriate one of these generic variables through each pass of the loop, and the procedure uses the appropriate one according to the template records. If new data are input by the user, the generic variables are changed and passed back to the program, which should then alter the genuine program variable values accordingly.

- A Result parameter is passed back to the program describing the type of input that took place (or whether any data were entered). This Result parameter is originally returned by the InKey procedure, and its codes have the same meanings as if it were returned directly by InKey.

Here's how the EntrRev procedure works:

- Using the parameter TopHeap, which was set by ReadTemp when it placed the template records into memory, determine the memory location of the first template record.

- Begin a repeat loop to inspect each template record until the one with an ItemNo matching the item specified in the parameter ItemNum is found.

- If no matching template record is found after searching through all template records once, end the search without taking action.

- If a matching template record is found, call the InKey procedure to allow data input from the keyboard.

- After returning from InKey, if the Result indicates that data were entered, assign the appropriate generic variable so that the new data can be passed back to the program. Adjust the value of the applicable genuine program variable.

- Redisplay the current data for the field, according to the formatting established within the template record for the given data item.

USING TEMPLATES FOR DISPLAY AND REVISION IN A PROGRAM

Test Program 3.4 illustrates the use of procedures ReadTemp, Data-Disp, and EntrRev to read a template file, display present data, and allow data to be entered or revised. The UseTemplate program employs the same data screen as Test Program 3.3 (the simple screen-construction procedure in Tool 3.5).

```
PROGRAM UseTemplate;

     {To use this program with Turbo Pascal versions prior to
       4.0, remove the Uses statement below.}

     Uses DOS,CRT;

     TYPE
          Str255 = STRING[255];
          Pointr = ^Integer;
          DataRec = RECORD
               Strng :ARRAY[1..4] OF STRING[60];
               Bite  :Byte;
               Intgr :Integer;
               Reel  :ARRAY[1..3] OF Real;
          END;  {datarec}
```

Test Program 3.4: Using procedures ReadTemp, DataDisp, and EntrRev in a program.

```
VAR
      TopHeap                                     :Pointr;
      FileName, StrItem                           :Str255;
      ScreenNo, NumItems, Item, Result            :Integer;

      {When using this program with Turbo Pascal versions
          prior to 4.0, change the type of IntItem from
          LongInt to Integer.}
      IntItem                                     :LongInt;

      RealItem                                    :Real;
      InPutRec                                    :DataRec;
      Quit                                        :Boolean;
      Ans                                         :Char;

{$I TDES.Inc}   { TestDataEntryScreen procedure}
{$I InKey.Inc   }
{$I ReadTemp.Inc}
{$I DataDisp.Inc}
{$I EntrRev.Inc }

BEGIN {using templates in a program for data entry/display}
      {get template file name}
      ClrScr;
      Write('Enter FILE NAME used on Template File: ');
      ReadLn(FileName);
      TestDataEntryScreen;
      {initialize data record}
      WITH InPutRec DO
          BEGIN {with}
              Strng[1]:=''; Strng[2]:=''; Strng[3]:='';
              Strng[4]:=''; Bite:=0; Intgr:=0;
              Reel[1]:=0.0; Reel[2]:=0.0; Reel[3]:=0.0;
          END;  {with}
      ReadTemp(FileName,1,TopHeap,NumItems);
      REPEAT  {until quit}
      FOR Item:=1 TO NumItems DO
          BEGIN {display item}
              CASE Item OF
                1..4: StrItem:=InPutRec.Strng[Item];
                5: IntItem:=InPutRec.Bite;
                6: IntItem:=InPutRec.Intgr;
                7..9: RealItem:=InPutRec.Reel[Item-6];
              END; {case statement}
              DataDisp(TopHeap,Item,StrItem,
                      IntItem,RealItem);
          END; {display item}
      Item:=1;
      WHILE (Item<=NumItems) DO
          BEGIN {data entry for item}
              CASE Item OF
                1..4: StrItem:=InPutRec.Strng[Item];
                5: IntItem:=InPutRec.Bite;
                6: IntItem:=InPutRec.Intgr;
                7..9: RealItem:=InPutRec.Reel[Item-6];
              END; {case statement}
              EntrRev(TopHeap,Item,StrItem,IntItem,
                      RealItem,Result);
              CASE Result OF
```

Test Program 3.4: Using procedures ReadTemp, DataDisp, and EntrRev in a program.
(continued)

```
                               0: BEGIN
                                  CASE Item OF
                                   1..4:InPutRec.Strng[Item]:=StrItem;
                                   5: InPutRec.Bite:=IntItem;
                                   6: InPutRec.Intgr:=IntItem;
                                   7..9:InPutRec.Reel[Item-6]:=RealItem;
                                  END; {case item}
                                  Item:=Item+1;
                                  END;
                               1: Item:=Item+1;
                               2: IF (Item>1) THEN Item:=Item-1;
                               3: Item:=NumItems+1; {user escaped}
                               4: BEGIN {help requested}
                                     GotoXY(1,25);
                                     Write(#7,'>> NO HELP AVAILABLE');
                                     Delay(1000);
                                     GotoXY(1,25); ClrEol;
                                  END;
                           END;   {case result}
                        END; {data entry for item}
                GotoXY(1,25);
                Write('Again?  (Y/N)  ');

           {To use this program with Turbo Pascal versions prior
              to 4.0, add the line below:}
              { Read(KBD,Ans); }

           {To use this program with Turbo Pascal versions prior
              to 4.0, remove the line below:}
              Ans:=ReadKey;

              GotoXY(1,25); ClrEol;
              Quit:=(UpCase(Ans)='N');
        UNTIL Quit;
        Release(TopHeap);
    END.   {using templates in a program for data entry/display}
```

Test Program 3.4: Using procedures ReadTemp, DataDisp, and EntrRev in a program. (continued)

Before running the test program, you must construct a template record file for it to read. Table 3.4 lists the information to include in this file. Use the MakeTemp program (Tool 3.6) to create the template file.

The UseTemplate program begins by determining the name of the template file that has been created for it. Your program, when using these procedures, should have this file name as a constant already declared within it. (See Appendix A for details.) Next it creates a data-entry screen using procedure TestDataEntryScreen (Tool 3.5). The demonstration data record for the program is initialized, and the template file is read.

Table 3.4:
Template File Entries for the UseTemplate Program (Test Program 3.4)

FileName: User's choice
Screen Number: 1

Item No.	Column	Row	Max. Chars	Justify	Data Type	Format
1	1	5	60	L	S	U
2	1	8	60	L	S	L
3	1	11	60	L	S	N
4	1	14	60	L	S	A
5	20	16	3	R	B	X
6	23	18	6	R	I	X
7	39	20	11	R	R	0
8	39	22	11	R	R	2
9	39	24	11	R	R	5

Note: Create the template record file with the MakeTemp program (Tool 3.6).

From the parameter NumItems returned by the ReadTemp procedure, the program knows how many data items are to be handled on screen, and loops are set up accordingly. A loop is set up to display the current data for each data item presented on the screen using the DispData procedure. After the current data are presented on screen (for data revision), Item is set to a value of 1 and a WHILE statement is entered to allow entry to and movement among all the data-entry items on the screen.

Following the user's action on the final data item on the screen, the user is offered the choice to repeat the operation. If the operation is repeated, it will be treated as record revision rather than initial data entry. After all the operations using the template records for this screen are completed, the dynamic memory area allocated for these records is freed using Turbo Pascal's Release procedure.

PUTTING IT ALL TOGETHER

The procedures InKey, ReadTemp, DispData, and EntrRev, together with program MakeTemp (or an enhanced program for creating template files), can be used to make powerful and complete data-entry and data-display routines for your programs. In a simple program with just a few items on one data-entry screen, these procedures can save a bit of programming time; in a larger program with a number of screens and more complex data entry and display, this group of procedures can be extremely valuable. Not only can they save a great deal of programming time and effort, but they also provide more reliable results.

Furthermore, as noted previously, the data-entry and data-display procedures presented here can be enhanced to provide for special handling of telephone numbers, dates, social security numbers, and similar items.

CHAPTER 4
HANDLING AND
STORING DATES AND TIMES

....
....
....
....
....
....
....
....
....
....
....
....
....
....
....
....
....
....
....
....
....
....
....

Among the many ways of handling and storing dates and times, there are some that are quite complex and others that are extremely simple; some store a great deal of date or time information in only 2 bytes (as DOS does), while less sophisticated methods require substantially greater storage space for these data. This chapter deals with various methods for determining and entering dates and times, as well as for storing them. For all practical purposes, dates and times are stored and handled in the same manner. Thus, any tool in this chapter that deals with dates is also applicable to times, even if this is not explicitly stated in the text.

DATE AND
TIME STORAGE

As you saw in Chapter 2, in the procedures for decoding the directory-search data stored in the DTA, the method DOS uses for date storage is very efficient; it stores the month, day, year, hour, minute, and second of a file's creation in only 4 bytes. It is also complex. The routine for storing date information in this format requires the use of the formula

$$(\text{Year-1980}) \star 512 + \text{Month} \star 32 + \text{Day}$$

The DOS time storage formula is

$$\text{Hour} \star 2048 + \text{Minute} \star 32 + \text{Second} / 2$$

Turbo Pascal 4.0 and 5.0 handle date and time storage and decoding through the DateTime record and the procedures PackTime and Unpack-Time. For users of earlier versions, another method for decoding the information stored by DOS was presented in Chapter 2 as Tools 2.6 and 2.7. Unfortunately, there is no simple and straightforward technique for interpreting this information in versions of Turbo Pascal prior to 4.0.

The simplest date storage method is the 8-character string, which stores a date in its conventional notation as mm/dd/yy. Along with the obvious disadvantage of requiring a large amount of space, it is also difficult to sort and compare dates stored in this manner.

Another method of date handling, which is only slightly less efficient than the 2-byte technique used by DOS, is to store the date in an array of 3 bytes. In the array, the first byte represents the year, the second byte represents the month, and the final byte represents the day. The same format can be used to store the time, with the bytes representing the hour, minute, and second. You could store the date or time in a string, but that would require one more byte at the beginning of the string to represent its length.

This type of date storage has the advantages of allowing quick sorting and comparisons and being easily decoded. Its disadvantage is that it limits the dates stored to a span of 100 years, but most programs deal with substantially less than that range of dates. When the dates do overlap a century (for example, 1990–2010), the actual span of years will probably be significantly less than 100 years. Then you can fairly assume that dates 50 and higher go with one century and dates 49 and less go with the other. If you must include the century, you could add one more byte to the date field to handle it.

For those applications that use transaction records and sort them chronologically, the date and time the record is created can be critical. For these types of programs, you can increase the date field to 6 bytes to include the hour, minute, and second (in that order). And for the rare occasions when hundredths of a second are also necessary, you could add an extra byte for that information.

ENCODING AND DECODING 3-BYTE DATES

Tool 4.1 consists of four short procedures for encoding and decoding dates stored in 3 bytes, in both string and array formats. Note that to facilitate date comparisons and sorting, the string or array should be arranged in the order of year, month, day. And if you are using the procedures with times, they should be in the order of hour, minute, second.

The EncodeDateString procedure begins by checking that the year is less than 100; then it initializes the date string to three positions. Finally, it assigns a character with an ASCII value equal to the Year, Month, and Day to string positions 1, 2, and 3, respectively.

The DecodeDateString procedure first assigns a value to the integers of Year, Month, and Day, equal to the ASCII value of string characters 1, 2, and 3, respectively. Then it writes the date to the screen in the format mm/dd/yy, using the character values from DateString.

Similarly, the EncodeDateArray procedure checks the year and then assigns the values of Year, Month, and Day to elements 1, 2, and 3 of a byte array. The DecodeDateArray procedure writes the date to the screen in the format mm/dd/yy, using the values from the appropriate elements of the date array.

JULIAN DATES

In a broad sense, any day-numbering system can be referred to as a Julian date. Definitively, a *Julian date* is the number of days that have elapsed since noon on January 1, 4713 B.C., a date chosen to facilitate conversion

```
PROCEDURE EncodeDateString(Month,Day,Year:Integer;
                           VAR DateString:Str255);

    BEGIN {encode date to string}
        WHILE (Year>100) DO Year:=Year-100;
        DateString:='   ';
        DateString[1]:=CHR(Year); {0-99}
        DateString[2]:=CHR(Month);
        DateString[3]:=CHR(Day);
    END;  {encode date to string}

PROCEDURE DecodeDateString(DateString:Str255;
                           VAR Month,Day,Year:Integer);

    BEGIN {decode date string}
        Year:=ORD(DateString[1]);
        Month:=ORD(DateString[2]);
        Day:=ORD(DateString[3]);
        Write('Date is: ',ORD(DateString[2]),'/',
            ORD(DateString[3]),'/',ORD(DateString[1]));
    END;  {decode date string}

    {The following two procedures assume the declaration}
    {in the host program:                               }
    {TYPE                                                }
    {    Arr3 = ARRAY[1..3] OF Byte;                     }

PROCEDURE EncodeDateArray(Month,Day,Year:Integer;
                          VAR DateArray:Arr3);

    BEGIN {encode date array}
        WHILE (Year>100) DO Year:=Year-100;
        DateArray[1]:=Year; {0-99}
        DateArray[2]:=Month;
        DateArray[3]:=Day;
    END;  {encode date array}

PROCEDURE DecodeDateArray(DateArray :Arr3);

    BEGIN {decode date array}
        Write('Date is: ',DateArray[2],'/',DateArray[3],
            '/',DateArray[1]);
    END;  {decode date array}
```

Tool 4.1: Procedures EncodeDateString, DecodeDateString, EncodeDateArray, and DecodeDateArray to encode and decode 3-byte dates.

between various ancient calendar systems. The Julian date, developed by Joseph Julius Scaliger, should not be confused with the Julian calendar, which was established by Julius Caesar.

DOS uses a day-numbering system that begins at midnight, December 31, 1979. In this system, day 1 is January 1, 1980. This system prevents DOS from accepting any date prior to January 1, 1980, as a system date (it will not use negative dates). The Julian date system discussed here is the one used by DOS.

ADDING AND SUBTRACTING DATES

If you need to add or subtract dates, you will find that Julian dates are the easiest to handle. The Julian function, shown as Tool 4.2, will convert a calendar date (month, day, year) to a Julian date. After you've obtained Julian dates for the days involved, you can add or subtract them to calculate new dates, compare dates, or subtract one from another to determine days elapsed. If you are going to perform numerous date calculations, you may even want to store dates in their Julian form (a real number occupying 6 bytes) and only convert them to calendar dates when you need to display them on the screen or print them (Tool 4.4, presented a little later, can be used for this conversion).

```
FUNCTION Julian(Year,Month,Day:Integer):Real;

    VAR
        Yr, Mth                        :Integer;
        NoLeap, Leap, Days, Yrs        :Real;

    BEGIN {function julian}
        IF Year<0 THEN Yr:=Year+1
            ELSE Yr:=Year;
        Mth:=Month;
        IF (Month<3) THEN
            BEGIN
                Mth:=Mth+12;
                Yr:=Yr-1;
            END;
        Yrs:=365.25*Yr;
        IF ((Yrs<0) AND (Frac(Yrs)<>0)) THEN
            Yrs:=Int(Yrs)-1
            ELSE Yrs:=Int(Yrs);
        Days:=Int(Yrs) + Int(30.6001*(Mth+1)) +Day-723244.0;
        IF Days<-145068.0 THEN Julian:=Days
            ELSE
                BEGIN
                    Yrs:=Yr/100.0;
                    IF ((Yrs<0) AND (Frac(Yrs)<>0)) THEN
                        Yrs:=Int(Yrs)-1;
                    NoLeap:=Int(Yrs);
                    Yrs:=NoLeap/4.0;
                    IF ((Yrs<0) AND (Frac(Yrs)<>0)) THEN
                        Yrs:=Int(Yrs)-1;
                    Leap:=2 - NoLeap + Int(Yrs);
                    Julian:=Days+Leap;
                END;
    END;   {function julian}
```

Tool 4.2: Function Julian to convert a calendar date to a Julian date.

The Julian function returns a real number as the Julian date for the integer parameters Year, Month, and Day, which are passed to it by the program. The Julian date returned is the number of days passed since December 31, 1979. The Year parameter must be the entire year, not just the last two digits. If you use 88 instead of 1988, the Julian function will return the number for the year 88 A.D. The function returns negative Julian dates for days prior to December 31, 1979. Year, Month, and Day are all integers.

Here's how the Julian function works:

- If the year is negative (B.C.), reduce the absolute value of the year by 1 to allow for the absence of a year zero (that is, the year before 1 A.D. was −1, or 1 B.C., not 0; for the procedure, though, it must be year 0).

- Change month numbering so that January and February are months 13 and 14 and there are no months 1 and 2 (March is month 3). This makes February, with its varying number of days, easier to work with.

- Get the number of days elapsed in the completed years.

- Get the total number of days elapsed (days from completed years + days elapsed year-to-date to the beginning of the month + days elapsed month-to-date − days elapsed 1/1/1 to 1/1/1980.

- The Julian calendar (Julius Caesar) date is now ready. If the number of days indicates it (more than or equal to −145068), use the Gregorian calendar method for computing the date.

- If the Gregorian method is used, determine the number of leap year days that should have been left out and make the necessary adjustments.

You'll see how to use function Julian within another procedure in Tool 4.5 and in a program in Test Program 4.1.

DETERMINING THE DAY OF THE WEEK

Often, it is convenient to know what weekday a given date falls on. For dates that fall within the valid date range for DOS (January 1, 1980, to December 31, 2099), the weekday can be determined automatically by

DOS. You could also use a procedure that calculates the weekday from the Julian date. First let's see how to get this information from DOS.

Getting the Weekday from DOS

DOS automatically calculates and keeps the weekday for the current system date. A call to DOS function 42 (as illustrated in Chapter 1, Tool 1.3) will return an integer code for the weekday of the system date. The Get-Date procedure in Turbo Pascal 4.0 and 5.0 also returns the weekday by using this method. To get the weekday for any date within DOS's valid range, you must take the following four steps:

1. Read and store the present system date.
2. Set the system date to the date for which the weekday is desired.
3. Read the new system date (set in step 2) and receive the weekday code along with that date.
4. Reset the system date to the correct system date from step 1.

DOS returns the weekday in the form of an integer representing the day of the week. To convert this code into the name of the day, make the following type of declaration in your program.

```
CONST
WeekDay:ARRAY[0..6] OF STRING[9] = ('Sunday', 'Monday',
'Tuesday', 'Wednesday', 'Thursday', Friday', 'Saturday');
```

Then you can display the date on the screen by using the statement

```
Write(WeekDay[WeekDayNumber]);
```

where WeekDayNumber is the variable containing the integer code returned by DOS.

Calculating the Weekday from the Julian Date

The function WeekDayNo, shown as Tool 4.3, returns the weekday by taking the Julian number for a given date and finding the corresponding day. To use this function, you must first calculate the calendar date using the Julian function (Tool 4.2) and pass the resulting real number Julian date to WeekDayNo as the parameter. The weekday is represented by an integer number returned in the range of zero through six, where 0 is Sunday, 1 is Monday, and so on.

```
FUNCTION WeekDayNo(Date:Real):Integer;

    VAR
        JDays:Real;

    BEGIN {function weekdayno}
        JDays:=Date;
        WHILE (JDays>28000.0) DO JDays:=JDays-28000.0;
        WHILE (JDays<0) DO JDays:=JDays+28000.0;
        WeekDayNo:=((Trunc(JDays)+1) MOD 7);
    END;  {function weekdayno}
```

Tool 4.3: Function WeekDayNo to calculate the weekday from the Julian date.

Here's how the WeekDayNo function works:

- Rapidly reduce the Julian date to integer range by deducting 28000 (a large multiple of 7) from it until it is less than 28000.
- Convert the reduced Julian date to an integer.
- Use the MOD operator to find the weekday number.

Refer to Tool 4.5 and Test Program 4.1 to see how the WeekDayNo function can be used within another procedure and within a program.

CONVERTING A JULIAN DATE TO A CALENDAR DATE

After you've converted a calendar date to a Julian date and performed operations to calculate a new Julian date, you will usually want to convert the result back into a calendar date. To accomplish this, you can use procedure CalendarDate, shown as Tool 4.4. It is also useful for checking that a date entered in Julian format is the correct calendar date.

When the CalendarDate procedure is called, the parameter JulianDate, a real number, is passed to it. The procedure then returns the variable integer parameters Month, Day, and Year as a valid date.

```
PROCEDURE CalendarDate (JulianDate:Real;
                        VAR Year, Month, Day:Integer);

    VAR
        JulCalDay, TempDay, Correction, Century,
            Days, Mo, JulDate                    :Real;
        Yr                                       :Integer;

    BEGIN {procedure calendar date}
        JulDate:=Int(JulianDate + 2444239.0);
        IF (JulianDate<-145078.0) THEN JulCalDay:=JulDate
            ELSE
            BEGIN
                TempDay:=Int((JulDate-1867216.25)/36524.25);
                JulCalDay:=JulDate+1+TempDay;
                TempDay:=TempDay/4.0;
                IF ((TempDay<0) AND (Frac(TempDay)<>0)) THEN
                    TempDay:=INT(TempDay)-1;
                JulCalDay:=JulCalDay-Int(TempDay);
            END;
        Correction:=JulCalDay+1524.0;
        Century:=Int((Correction-122.1)/365.25);
        Days:=Int(365.25 * Century);
        Mo:=Int((Correction-Days)/30.6001);
        DAY:=Trunc(Correction-Days-Int(30.6001*Mo));
        IF (Mo>13.5) THEN Month:=Trunc(Mo-13.0)
            ELSE Month:=Trunc(Mo-1.0);
        IF (Month>2) THEN Yr:=Trunc(Century-4716.0)
            ELSE Yr:=Trunc(Century-4715.0);
        Year:=Yr;
    END;   {procedure calendar date}
```

Tool 4.4: Procedure CalendarDate to convert a Julian date to a calendar date.

Here's how the CalendarDate procedure works:

- Assuming that the Julian date provided is figured from 1/1/80, add the days elapsed from 1/1/1 to 1/1/1980 to adjust the number to a true Julian date.

- Having the Julian date, correct the number for the Julian calendar, if appropriate.

- Calculate the calendar Year, Month, and Day.

CalendarDate is used in Tool 4.5 and Test Program 4.1.

CHECKING AND CORRECTING DATES

An invalid date can be a mistake (for example, a user enters 2/29/87) or a programming convenience (say, to compute the date from March 15 to 45 days later by simply adding the 45 to 15 to get March 60). Procedure

ValidDate, shown as Tool 4.5, is useful for correcting such dates. The procedure calls function Julian (Tool 4.2), function WeekDayNo (Tool 4.3), and procedure CalendarDate (Tool 4.4) to accomplish this task.

```
PROCEDURE ValidDate (VAR Month, Day,
                         Year, WeekDay:Integer);

     VAR
          DayNo          :Real;
          AdditionMade   :Boolean;                  {XXXXX}

     BEGIN {procedure valid date}
          AdditionMade:=False;                       {XXXXX}
          IF Year<100 THEN                           {XXXXX}
               BEGIN
                    Year:=1900+Year;
                    AdditionMade:=True;
               END;
          DayNo:=Julian(Year,Month,Day);
          CalendarDate(DayNo,Year,Month,Day);
          IF AdditionMade THEN Year:=Year-1900;      {XXXXX}
          WeekDay:=WeekDayNo(DayNo);
     END;  {procedure valid date}
```

Tool 4.5: Procedure ValidDate to check and correct dates.

The ValidDate procedure, when passed integer numbers for the Month, Day, Year, and WeekDayNumber, checks the date for validity and corrects it to a valid date if necessary. For example, if it found the date to be 2/31/85, it would correct it to 3/2/85. It also returns a parameter indicating the ordinal day of the week (that is, 0 for Sunday, 1 for Monday, 2 for Tuesday, and so on). The parameters Month, Day, and Year must be passed. WeekDayNo may be zero or any other integer number. The ValidDate procedure uses the Julian and WeekDayNo functions and CalendarDate procedure to check and correct the date and return the correct weekday number.

The ValidDate procedure can even handle negative dates, resulting from date subtraction, and convert them to correct dates. For example, 3/−1/86 would be corrected to 2/27/86.

The procedure uses the following date equivalents: 1/0/86 = 12/31/85; 3/0/86 = 2/28/86. It assumes that any Year less than 100 is short notation for the current century, and adds the number 1900 to the value. If you want to defeat this precaution and make the procedure suitable for years long passed (for example, 1776), remove the statements commented with {XXXXX}.

Here's how the ValidDate procedure works:

- If the year passed to ValidDate is less than 100, add 1900 to the year. Note is made of the fact that 1900 is added through the Boolean variable AdditionMade.

- Use the Julian function to get a Julian date for the calendar date passed.

- Submit the Julian date to the CalendarDate procedure to get an absolutely valid calendar date.

- If 1900 was added to the year, deduct it now to return the date in the same format in which it was passed.

- Submit the Julian date to the WeekDayNo function to obtain a correct weekday number.

- Pass the values obtained back to the program.

The use of procedure ValidDate within other procedures is shown in Tools 4.6 and 4.7. It is also demonstrated in Test Program 4.1.

SYSTEM DATES AND TIMES

Date-sensitive programs that work with files and records often use the system date as the default entry in the date field presented to the user. Inventory programs sometimes even stamp transaction records with the current system time. Because the accuracy of the date is so important in these operations, the user must be given an opportunity to correct the system date and time. Although you may use an autoexec batch (AUTOEXEC.BAT) file to set the system time and date, time- and date-sensitive programs should offer a more direct route. Any application program that depends on date and time information should check the system date and time, and reset it if necessary, from within itself.

CHECKING AND SETTING THE SYSTEM DATE AND TIME

The ChekDate procedure, shown as Tool 4.6, can be used at the beginning of a program to allow the user to verify the system date and time and, if they are not correct, alter either or both of them.

The ChekDate procedure begins with system calls to obtain the date and time from the computer, using the Turbo Pascal 4.0 or 5.0 procedures Get-Date and GetTime or, for versions prior to 4.0, the procedures presented earlier in this book, GetDate (Tool 1.9) and GetTime (Tool 1.11) from Chapter 1. It then constructs a screen that displays the current system date and time. If the user accepts them as correct, these values are returned to the program. If N is selected to reject them, the procedure requests a correct date and time, and then it uses the ValidDate procedure (Tool 4.5) to check the new date's validity. It handles all keyboard entries through the InKey procedure (Tool 3.3) from Chapter 3.

If necessary, the procedure sets a new system date and time using Turbo Pascal 4.0 or 5.0 procedures SetDate and SetTime or, for prior versions, procedures SetDate (Tool 1.10) and SetTime (Tool 1.12) from Chapter 1. It gets the current date and time from the system again and displays them on the screen for the user's verification. The procedure does not end until the user accepts the displayed date and time as correct.

ChekDate returns the variable integer parameters Hours, Mins, Secs, Month, Day, and Year. These supply the system date and current time to the program.

Here's how the ChekDate procedure works:

- Clear the screen.
- Check the operating system for its date and time.
- Establish reverse video.
- Set up a screen to display the system date and time.
- Enter a repeat loop to continue until the user accepts the date and time as correct.
- Display the system date and time and ask the user if it is correct.
- If the user accepts the displayed date, end the loop.

```
PROCEDURE ChekDate(VAR Hours,Mins,Secs,
                       Month,Day,Year:Word);

    {When using this procedure with Turbo Pascal versions
        prior to 4.0, change all variable declarations of
        type Word to type Integer.}

    VAR
        Correct                    :Boolean;
        CH                         :Char;
        Dummy                      :Str255;
        Value                      :Real;
        Result, X, M, D, Y         :Integer;
        WD, Secs100                :Word;

    BEGIN {check system date & time}
        ClrScr;

        {To use this program with Turbo Pascal versions prior
            to 4.0, add the 2 lines below:}
        { GetDate(Month,Day,Year,WD);
        GetTime(Hours,Mins,Secs); }

        {To use this program with Turbo Pascal versions prior
            to 4.0, remove the 2 lines below:}
        GetDate(Year,Month,Day,WD);
        GetTime(Hours,Mins,Secs,Secs100);

        TextColor(0); TextBackground(7); {reverse video}
        GotoXY(22,2); Write(#201);
        FOR X:=1 TO 33 DO Write(#205);
        Write(#187);
        GotoXY(22,3);
        Write(#186,' VERIFY  SYSTEM  DATE  AND  TIME ',#186);
        GotoXY(22,4); Write(#200);
        FOR X:=1 TO 33 DO Write(#205);
        Write(#188);
        NormVideo;
        REPEAT {until correct}
            GotoXY(25,6);
            Write('System Date: ',Month:2,'/',
                    Day:2,'/',Year:2);
            GotoXY(25,7);
            Write('System Time: ',Hours:2,':',
                    Mins:2,':',Secs:2);
            GotoXY(25,10);
            Write('Date and Time correct?  (Y/N) ');
            REPEAT

        {To use this program with Turbo Pascal versions prior
            to 4.0, add the line below:}
                { Read(KBD,Ch); }
        {To use this program with Turbo Pascal versions prior
            to 4.0, remove the line below:}
                Ch:=ReadKey;


                Ch:=UpCase(Ch);
            UNTIL Ch IN['Y','N'];
            Write(Ch);
            Correct:=(Ch='Y');
            IF NOT Correct THEN
```

Tool 4.6: Procedure ChekDate to check and set the system date and time.

```
       BEGIN {set correct system date & time}
            GotoXY(25,15);
            Write('Enter correct DATE:  mm/dd/yy');
            GotoXY(25,16);
            Write('Enter correct TIME:  hh:mm');
            REPEAT
                 InKey(46,15,2,'B','X',Dummy,
                       Value,Result);
                 IF Result=0 THEN
                      Month:=Trunc(Value);
            UNTIL (Month<13);
            REPEAT
                 InKey(49,15,2,'B','X',Dummy,
                       Value,Result);
                 IF Result=0 THEN
                      Day:=Trunc(Value);
            UNTIL (Day<32);
            REPEAT
                 InKey(52,15,2,'B','X',Dummy,
                       Value,Result);
                 IF Result=0 THEN
                      Year:=Trunc(Value);
            UNTIL ((Year+1900)>=1980);
            Year:=Year+1900;
            REPEAT
                 InKey(46,16,2,'B','X',Dummy,
                       Value,Result);
                 IF Result=0 THEN
                      Hours:=Trunc(Value);
            UNTIL (Hours<24);
            REPEAT
                 InKey(49,16,2,'B','X',Dummy,
                       Value,Result);
                 IF Result=0 THEN
                      Mins:=Trunc(Value);
            UNTIL (Mins<60);
            Secs:=0;  Secs100:=0;
            M:=Month; D:=Day; Y:=Year;
            ValidDate(M,D,Y,Result);
            Month:=M; Day:=D; Year:=Y;
        {"result" ^^above^^ is a dummy variable }
        {it will contain the week day number which}
        {is not used in this procedure}

{To use this program with Turbo Pascal versions prior
     to 4.0, add the 2 lines below:}
                 { SetDate(Month,Day,Year);
            SetTime(Hours,Mins,Secs); }

{To use this program with Turbo Pascal versions prior
     to 4.0, remove the 2 lines below:}
            SetDate(Year,Month,Day);
            SetTime(Hours,Mins,Secs,Secs100);

            GotoXY(25,10); ClrEOL;
            GotoXY(25,15); ClrEOL;
            GotoXY(25,16); ClrEOL;
            Delay(200);
```

Tool 4.6: Procedure ChekDate to check and set the system date and time. (continued)

```
        {To use this program with Turbo Pascal versions prior
            to 4.0, add the 2 lines below:}
                        { GetDate(Month,Day,Year,WD);
                        GetTime(Hours,Mins,Secs); }

        {To use this program with Turbo Pascal versions prior
            to 4.0, remove the 2 lines below:}
                        GetDate(Year,Month,Day,WD);
                        GetTime(Hours,Mins,Secs,Secs100);

                    END;    {set correct system date & time}
            UNTIL Correct;
    END;    {check system date & time}
```

Tool 4.6: Procedure ChekDate to check and set the system date and time. (continued)

- If the user responds negatively, request the correct date and time, then call the ValidDate procedure to ensure a correct date has been entered.

- Send the date and time the user entered to the system.

- Check the system for its date and time; this will be the date and time just entered unless the user made an invalid entry. If the new date was invalid, the system date will not have changed.

- Go back to the top of the loop—display, ask, and change until the date is accepted.

A KEYBOARD INPUT ROUTINE FOR DATES

Even though a date is only a single information item, handling its input from the keyboard in a way that protects the program's integrity and ensures a valid date can be tedious. The InpDate procedure, shown as Tool 4.7, incorporates several of our earlier procedures into a single keyboard input routine. It obtains a valid date in the format mm/dd/yy.

Similar to the ChekDate procedure, InpDate calls on procedure InKey (Tool 3.3) for the actual numeric input. It allows entry of month values in the range of 1 through 12, day values in the range of 1 through 31, and year values from 0 through 99. It also uses the ValidDate procedure (Tool 4.5) to check and correct the date if necessary.

The parameters to be passed to InpDate are two integers representing the column and row where input is to begin and three byte variables to receive the mm(Month), dd(Day), and yy(Year) inputs.

```
PROCEDURE InpDate(Column,Row:Integer;
                    VAR mm,dd,yy,DayNo,Result:Integer);

    VAR
        Count           :Integer;
        SVal            :Str255;
        RVal            :Real;

    BEGIN {procedure get date}
        Count:=1;
        {count tracks the fields in the date format}
        {3 fields = mm, dd, yy}
        WHILE ((Count<4) AND (Count>0)) DO
            BEGIN {while count < 4}
                CASE Count OF
                1: REPEAT
                    InKey(Column, Row, 2, 'B','X',
                            SVal,RVal,Result);
                    IF Result=0 THEN MM:=Trunc(RVal);
                    GotoXY(Column,Row); Write(MM:2);
                    UNTIL ((MM>=1) AND (MM<=12));
                2: REPEAT
                    InKey(Column+3, Row, 2, 'B','X',
                            SVal,RVal,Result);
                    IF Result=0 THEN DD:=Trunc(RVal);
                    GotoXY(Column+3,Row); Write(DD:2);
                    UNTIL ((DD>=1) AND (DD<=31));
                3: REPEAT
                    InKey(Column+6, Row, 2, 'B','X',
                            SVal,RVal,Result);
                    IF Result=0 THEN YY:=Trunc(RVal);
                    GotoXY(Column+6,Row); Write(YY:2);
                    UNTIL (YY>=0);
                END;  {case statement}
                {a backspace out of a field = result 2}
                IF Result=2 THEN Count:=Count-1
                    ELSE Count:=Count+1;
                IF Result=3 THEN Exit;
            END;  {while count < 4 and > 0}
        ValidDate(MM,DD,YY,DayNo);
        GotoXY(Column,Row);
        Write(mm:2,'/',dd:2,'/',yy:2);
    END;  {procedure get date}
```

Tool 4.7: Procedure InpDate to handle keyboard input of dates.

The procedure returns the integer parameter Result to convey the manner in which input was handled: 0 for normal input, 1 for Return pressed (no input), 2 for backspaced out of field, and 3 for Esc pressed. You can design your program to respond appropriately, as described in the discussion of the InKey procedure in Chapter 3. The InpDate procedure allows the user to backspace to previous fields in the date format (backspacing from yy takes the user to the dd field) without leaving the procedure or requiring further handling by the host program.

The procedure also returns the proper weekday number code for the date (0 for Sunday, 1 for Monday, and so on) to the program through the integer parameter DayNo.

Here's how the InpDate procedure works:

- Set up a loop to handle the three fields associated with the date: mm, dd, and yy.
- Depending on the loop count (1, 2, or 3), call the InKey procedure to handle the keyboard input of a byte number at either the mm (count 1), dd (count 2), or yy (count 3) date field.
- Accept entries only within the generally valid range for months (1–12), days (1–31), and years (0–99).
- If a backspace is entered, place the user at the previous date field; if this occurs at the first date field, exit the procedure.
- If Escape is entered, exit the procedure.
- After a date has been entered, pass it to the ValidDate procedure to be certain that it is a correct (valid) calendar date.
- Write the valid date to the screen.

A DEMONSTRATION PROGRAM

Test Program 4.1 illustrates the use of the InpDate procedure, along with functions Julian and WeekDayNo and procedures CalendarDate, ValidDate, and ChekDate (Tools 4.2 through 4.6). It also employs the procedures from Chapter 1 to get and set the system time and date (Tools 1.9 through 1.12), or the Turbo Pascal 4.0 or 5.0 procedures that get and set the time and date.

The TestDate program begins by calling the ChekDate procedure to display and validate the system date. Next it displays instructions on the screen. The InpDate procedure is called to allow keyboard entry of a date in the format mm/dd/yy. Finally, the program displays the date just entered and the weekday name on the screen.

```
PROGRAM TestDate;

     {To use this program with Turbo Pascal versions prior to
        4.0, remove the Uses statement below.}

  Uses DOS,CRT;

  TYPE
       Str255 = STRING[255];

  VAR

       {To use this program with Turbo Pascal versions prior
          to 4.0, change the variable declaration of type
          Word to type Integer.}
       H,M,S,Mo,D,Y,WD         :Word;
       Ho,Mi,Se,Mon,Da,Ye,WkD :Integer;
       Result                  :Integer;

  CONST
       WeekDay:ARRAY[0..6] OF STRING[9] = ('Sunday','Monday',
          'Tuesday','Wednesday','Thursday','Friday',
          'Saturday');


       {To use this program with Turbo Pascal versions prior
          to 4.0, add the 4 lines below:}
  (*
  {$I GetDate.Inc}
  {$I SetDate.Inc}
  {$I GetTime.Inc}
  {$I SetTime.Inc}
  *)

       {All versions need the following files}

  {$I InKey.Inc}
  {$I Julian.Inc}
  {$I WeekDay.Inc}
  {$I CalDate.Inc}
  {$I ValiDate.Inc}
  {$I ChekDate.Inc}
  {$I InpDate.Inc}

  BEGIN {program}
       ChekDate(H,M,S,Mo,D,Y);
       ClrScr;
       WriteLn('Enter any date below.');
       WriteLn('The date will be checked for validity.');
       WriteLn('The valid date will be printed on screen.');
       WriteLn;
       Write('mm/dd/yy');
       Mon:=Mo; Da:=D; Ye:=Y; WkD:=WD;
       InpDate(1,5,Mon,Da,Ye,WkD,Result);
       Mo:=Mon; D:=Da; Y:=Ye; WD:=WkD;
       WriteLn; WriteLn;
       WriteLn('Valid date is: ',WeekDay[WD],
          Mo:4,'/',D,'/',Y);
  END.   {program}
```

Test Program 4.1: Using functions Julian and WeekDayNo and procedures
CalendarDate, ValidDate, ChekDate, and InpDate in a program.

FISCAL DATES

Business programs, particularly those for accounting, often use fiscal months and years that differ from the calendar date. If your programs must calculate fiscal dates, you will find the next tool very handy.

OBTAINING A FISCAL DATE

Procedure Fiscal, shown as Tool 4.8, will return the fiscal month and year, as integers, to the program. To use the procedure, integer parameters must be passed indicating the month the fiscal year begins (StartFisYr) and the calendar month and year to calculate from (CalMo, CalYr).

```
PROCEDURE Fiscal(VAR StartFisYr,CalMo,CalYr,FisMo,FisYr:Integer);

    BEGIN {get fiscal month, year}
        IF (StartFisYr=1) THEN
            BEGIN
                FisMo:=CalMo; FisYr:=CalYr;
            END;
        IF (CalMo>=StartFisYr) THEN
            BEGIN
                FisMo:=CalMo+1-StartFisYr;
                FisYr:=CalYr+1;
            END;
        IF (CalMo<StartFisYr) THEN
            BEGIN
                FisMo:=CalMo+13-StartFisYr;
                FisYr:=CalYr;
            END;
        IF FisYr>99 THEN FisYr:=0;
    END;  {get fiscal month, year}
```

Tool 4.8: Procedure Fiscal to obtain the fiscal month and year.

Here's how the Fiscal procedure works:

- If the fiscal year begins in January (StartFisYr = 1), the fiscal and calendar years are the same.
- If the fiscal year begins in a month less than the calendar month, compute the elapsed months and increment the year.
- If the fiscal year begins in a month later than the calendar month, compute the months elapsed.

• If, by incrementing it, the fiscal year has hit 100, let it equal zero (for a new century).

Test Program 4.2 illustrates the use of the Fiscal procedure. It first requests the month that the fiscal year begins and the calendar month and year. Then it calls the Fiscal procedure to make the calculations. Finally, the program displays the fiscal month and year on the screen.

```
PROGRAM TestFiscal;

     {To use this program with Turbo Pascal versions prior to
        4.0, remove the Uses statement below.}

     Uses DOS,CRT;

     VAR
          SFY, Mo, Yr, FMo, FYr        :Integer;

     {$I Fiscal.Inc}

     BEGIN {program}
          WriteLn('>>>>> TEST CALCULATE FISCAL YEAR <<<<<');
          WriteLn;
          Write('Enter MONTH fiscal year begins (1-12) : ');
          ReadLn(SFY);
          Write('Enter calendar MONTH (1-12) : ');
          ReadLn(Mo);
          Write('Enter calendar year (00-99) : ');
          ReadLn(Yr);
          Fiscal(SFY,Mo,Yr,FMo,FYr);
          WriteLn;
          WriteLn('This is month ',FMo,' of fiscal year 19',FYr);
          WriteLn;
     END. {program}
```

Test Program 4.2: Using procedure Fiscal in a program.

ELAPSED TIME

Occasionally, it is handy to have a procedure to compute elapsed time. Such a procedure could be used in accumulating time or to obtain an hour factor to multiply against an hourly rate (as for computing wages for a payroll).

CALCULATING THE ELAPSED TIME

Procedure ElapsedTime, shown as Tool 4.9, will return integers for the elapsed number of hours, minutes, and seconds. It also returns a real number for the elapsed hours and decimal portion of an hour, which can be used as a multiplier for an hourly rate.

```
PROCEDURE ElapsedTime(VAR StHour,StMin,StSec,
                          EndHour,EndMin,EndSec,
                          ElHour,ElMin,ElSec:Integer;
                          VAR Time:Real);

    VAR
        Temp, Elapsed, Start, Stop :Real;

    BEGIN {figure elapsed time}
        Start:=StHour*60;                  {minutes}
        Start:=Start+StMin;                {minutes}
        Start:=Start*60;                   {seconds}
        Start:=Start+StSec;                {seconds}
        Stop:=EndHour*60;                  {minutes}
        Stop:=Stop+EndMin;                 {minutes}
        Stop:=Stop*60;                     {seconds}
        Stop:=Stop+EndSec;                 {seconds}
        Elapsed:=Stop-Start;               {seconds}
        Time:=Int(Elapsed/60);             {minutes}
        Time:=Time/60;                     {hours}
        ElHour:=Trunc(Time);               {hours}
        Temp:=ElHour*60;                   {minutes}
        Temp:=Temp*60;                     {seconds}
        Elapsed:=Elapsed-Temp;             {seconds}
        ElMin:=Trunc(Elapsed/60);          {minutes}
        Elapsed:=Elapsed-(ElMin*60);       {seconds}
        ElSec:=Trunc(Elapsed);             {seconds}
    END;   {figure elapsed time}
```

Tool 4.9: Procedure ElapsedTime to calculate the elapsed time.

The ElapsedTime procedure requires six integer parameters to be passed to it from the host program. These parameters are the starting time as hours, minutes, and seconds (StHour, StMin, StSec) and the ending time in the same form (EndHour, EndMin, EndSec). When the procedure returns to the program, it will have the elapsed time in integers representing hours, minutes, and seconds (ElHour, ElMin, ElSec) and a real number (Time), which will be the elapsed hours and decimal fraction.

Here's how the ElapsedTime procedure works:

- Convert the starting times to seconds.
- Convert the ending times to seconds.

- Determine the elapsed number of seconds.
- Load the elapsed hours and decimal fraction of an hour to the real variable parameter Time.
- Load the elapsed hours to the integer variable parameter ElHour, the elapsed minutes to ElMin, and the elapsed seconds to ElSec.

Test Program 4.3 shows how the ElapsedTime procedure could be used in a program. It simply takes a starting and ending time from the user, calls

```
PROGRAM TestElapsed;

      {To use this program with Turbo Pascal versions prior to
         4.0, remove the Uses statement below.}

      Uses DOS,CRT;

      VAR
            SHour, SMin, SSec, EHr, EMin, ESec,
              THr, TMin, TSec                      :Integer;
            ElHrs                                  :Real;

      {$I Elapsed.Inc}

      BEGIN {program}
            WriteLn;
            WriteLn('>>>>> TEST ELAPSED TIME PROCEDURE <<<<<');
            WriteLn;
            WriteLn('Enter start time below.');
            Write('Hour: ');
            ReadLn(SHour);
            Write('Minutes: ');
            ReadLn(SMin);
            Write('Seconds: ');
            ReadLn(SSec);
            WriteLn('Enter stop time below.');
            Write('Hour: ');
            ReadLn(EHr);
            Write('Minutes: ');
            ReadLn(EMin);
            Write('Seconds: ');
            ReadLn(ESec);
            ElapsedTime(SHour,SMin,SSec,EHr,EMin,ESec,
                        THr,TMin,TSec,ElHrs);
            WriteLn;
            WriteLn('Elapsed time is:  ',THr,':',TMin,':',TSec);
            WriteLn('Hour multiplier is: ',ElHrs:7:4);
      END.  {program}
```

Test Program 4.3: Using procedure ElapsedTime in a program.

the ElapsedTime procedure, and displays the calculated elapsed time on the screen. The elapsed time is displayed in actual hours, minutes, and seconds, as well as a decimal number representing the elapsed hours and fraction of an hour.

CHAPTER 5
PROGRAMMING MENUS

Virtually all programs that interact with people have some form of a menu. Some programmers use icons to present menu selections because they feel that the pictures speed up the process while giving users the image of utterly simple and easy-to-use computer systems and software. The drawbacks to icon types of menus are the difficulty of producing a satisfactory picture graphically on a computer screen and the fact that people may interpret a given picture, however simple, in different ways. A verbal menu has the distinct advantages of communicating more precisely what a given selection really means and being quicker and easier to program.

MENU CRITERIA

Any menu should be as logical, from the ordinary user's viewpoint, as possible and, equally important, as easy as possible to make selections from. In complex programs, a multilevel set of menus, in which the user begins selecting from broad categories of operations and gradually works toward specific tasks, may provide the clearest choices to the user.

All menus within a program should follow the same basic format, with the same selection process. In most older programs, users select from menus by entering a letter or number. New programs usually have the user highlight the desired option (using the cursor-movement keys) and then pressing Enter (or Return) to make the selection. From the user's viewpoint, the best type of menu is the one that is the most familiar and the simplest to operate.

GENERAL OPERATION OF THE MENU PROCEDURES

This chapter presents two menu procedures which differ only in the placement of the menu on the screen; one centers the menu on the screen, and the other displays the menu wherever the programmer specifies.

In accordance with the criteria outlined above, both procedures produce attractive, easy-to-use menus, with minimal programming effort. They allow for a reasonable number of header lines and a lengthy list of selections on each menu. If the number of selections is greater than the number of lines available on the screen, the selections will scroll.

The menu procedures read a menu file (created by the programmer, as described in the next section), select the lines for the appropriate menu in that file by the menu number passed as a parameter, and display them on the screen.

When the menu is called, it will move the existing screen to memory and then restore that screen when the procedure is complete, just prior to returning to the host program. Saving and restoring the previous screen is handled through the WindowIn and WindowOut procedures, presented in Chapter 7 as Tools 7.3 and 7.5.

NOTE: If you want your menu to be more attention-catching, substitute the ExWindow procedure (Tool 7.4) for the WindowIn procedure in the menu procedures presented in this chapter.

The user makes selections from the menu using only the up and down cursor-movement keys. Pressing the up arrow from the first menu selection places the user at the final selection; pressing the down arrow from the final selection places the user at the first selection. The current selection is always highlighted, and pressing the Enter key will end the procedure and return the number of the current selection to the host program. Line numbers are not necessary; the number returned is the ordinal number of the selected menu line in the menu file.

Because each menu procedure requires use of only the arrow keys, it first deactivates the Num Lock status of the number pad keys and activates them as cursor-movement keys. This is accomplished through the KbdCtrol procedure, presented as Tool 3.1 in Chapter 3.

MENU PROGRAMMING REQUIREMENTS

To include either menu procedure in a program, you must first create an ASCII menu text file with a word processor or with the Turbo Pascal screen editor, and then call the menu procedure from your program, passing to it the number of the desired menu and the name of the file containing the menu. Numerous menus for the same program may be included in one menu file. We'll get to the details of this file shortly.

You must also determine the size (columns by rows) that the menu should be and pass those dimensions to the procedure. Each time the procedure is called (with different menu selections), it can present a menu of a different size.

Another programming consideration is the availability of computer memory. The menu procedures use dynamic RAM to store the menu choices and the screen being temporarily replaced. The procedures assume that you have allowed sufficient RAM for this task. They cannot check to see if sufficient memory is present because there is no way to determine ahead of time how many selections and headers will be found in the text file for any given menu. Generally, 5 kilobytes of RAM will be sufficient for the menu operations; 4 kilobytes will be necessary for the storage of the previous screen; and 1 kilobyte will be used for the menu selections.

MENU TEXT FILE CONVENTIONS

The ASCII text file lines that are read by the menu procedures must begin with three characters indicating the menu number (for example, 001). The rest of the line is either a heading or menu selection. In a menu heading line, the three characters immediately following the menu number are ⋆H⋆, and the following text is a menu header line, which will be centered. In menu selection lines, the text to identify the selection follows the menu number. The lines for each particular menu must be grouped together, one following the other.

You can use as many heading lines as you like; the rest of the space allocated to the menu will be used for the selections. If there are too many selections to fit the remaining space, they will scroll as the user cursors up or down.

NOTE: Your menu headings and selection lines can include blank lines or lines of any ASCII character, including spaces. Regardless of content, each heading line must begin with the menu number and heading indicator (for example, 001⋆H⋆), each selection must begin with the menu number, and all lines are limited to no more than 79 characters following the prefix.

SAMPLE MENU TEXT FILE LINES

001⋆H⋆Program Name
001⋆H⋆

001⋆H⋆Master Program Menu

001Exit this program

001A Menu Selection

001Another Menu Selection

001Final Menu Selection

Generally, you will use a CASE statement to have your program respond to the menu selection chosen by the user; a CASE statement following the menu procedure will call the appropriate program procedures to handle the selected program function. The selections for each menu are entirely up to you. However, I suggest that you always include a choice that allows the user to exit the program or a particular function of the program and return to a previous menu. (See Test Program 5.1 for an example.)

MENU PROCEDURES

The two menu procedures presented are CMenu and Menu. The CMenu procedure centers the menu within the screen, based on the overall size of the menu in relation to the screen. The Menu procedure will place the menu exactly where the programmer specifies. The only differences between the procedures are the calculation of the menu window size and the additional parameters passed for this calculation.

DISPLAYING A MENU IN THE CENTER OF THE SCREEN

The CMenu procedure, shown as Tool 5.1, requires that the following parameters be passed to it:

- The parameter MenuNumber, which is a string of three numeric characters (such as '001', '002', '003'), tells the menu procedure which of the headings and selections in the menu text file are to be used.

- The parameter MenuFileName, which is a string containing the name of the text file that holds the menu data, tells the menu procedure the menu text file to be read.

- The parameters ScreenWidth and ScreenLength, which are the dimensions of the menu, tell the menu procedure where to center the menu in the screen area.

The minimum menu width is 40 characters (because the prompt line requires it); even if the menu is called with a ScreenWidth of less than 40

```
PROCEDURE CMenu(MenuNumber,MenuName:Str255;
               ScreenWidth, ScreenLength:Integer;
               VAR Choice:Integer);


TYPE
  LnPtr = ^MnuLn;
  MnuLn = RECORD
    MLine               :STRING[85];
    Next, Last          :LnPtr;
  END;

VAR
  MenuFile                              :Text;
  TopL, BotR, TopRow, BotRow, Col, Row,
      CharacterOffset, AttributeOffset,
      HdgLines, MenuLines,
      Len, Start, Line, MenuSize, NumLines,
      CurrentLine, CurrentChoice, Count, CCol,
      CRow, Result                      :Integer;

          {To use this program with Turbo Pascal versions prior
              to 4.0, add the line below:}
          { ScreenAddress              :Integer; }


          {To use this program with Turbo Pascal versions prior
              to 4.0, remove the line below:}
          ScreenAddress                 :Word;

  TextLine                              :STRING[85];
  FirstHdg, LastHdg, NewHdg, FirstLine,
      LastLine, NewLine, TopLine, BotLine   :LnPtr;
  TopHeap, WindowInMemory               :Pointr;
  MenuFound, EndOfMenu                  :Boolean;
  ThisLine                              :MnuLn;
  Operation,Setting                     :STRING[3];


  PROCEDURE CalculateWindow;

    {This procedure takes the desired screen length and width}
    {parameters and calculates the placement of the menu on the}
    {screen, based on an 80 column by 25 row screen.          }

    BEGIN {calculate window}
      TopRow:=((25-ScreenLength) DIV 2);
      BotRow:=TopRow+ScreenLength;
      TopL:=((80-ScreenWidth) DIV 2);
      BotR:=TopL+ScreenWidth;
    END;  {calculate window}


  PROCEDURE MenuBackGround;

    {This procedure sets the screen background in the menu   }
    {window to reverse video, centers the instruction line;  }
    {writes the menu heading lines (from the menu text        }
    {file); and places two lines (MMMMM), one below the      }
    {heading and one above the instruction line.             }

    VAR
      Spaces, Line  :Integer;
```

Tool 5.1: Procedure CMenu to display a menu in the center of the screen.

```
      BEGIN {set menu background}
        TextColor(0); TextBackground(7); {reverse video}
        ClrScr;
        GotoXY(1,ScreenLength+1);
        Spaces:=ScreenWidth-40;
        Spaces:=Spaces DIV 2;
        IF Spaces<1 THEN Spaces:=1;
        Write(#32:Spaces,'CURSOR = Move Up/Dn      Enter = Select ');
        NewHdg:=FirstHdg;
        FOR Line:=1 TO (HdgLines) DO
          BEGIN {write heading lines}
            ThisLine.MLine:=NewHdg^.MLine;
            Len:=Length(ThisLine.MLine);
            Start:=((ScreenWidth-Len) DIV 2);
            GotoXY(Start+1,Line);
            Write(ThisLine.MLine);
            NewHdg:=NewHdg^.Next;
          END;   {write heading lines}
        GotoXY(1,HdgLines+1);
        FOR Line:=1 TO ScreenWidth+1 DO Write(#205);
        GotoXY(1,ScreenLength);
        FOR Line:=1 TO ScreenWidth+1 DO Write(#205);
      END;  {set menu background}


PROCEDURE GetFile;

    VAR
        Count  :Integer;

    {This procedure reads the menu text file, decides if a given}
    {line is a header or selection line, and then strips the    }
    {line of the menu number and puts the remaining part of the }
    {line into RAM.                                             }

    BEGIN {get menu file}
      {initialize}
      HdgLines:=0; MenuLines:=0; MenuFound:=FALSE;
      EndOfMenu:=FALSE; FirstHdg:=NIL; LastHdg:=NIL;
      FirstLine:=NIL; LastLine:=NIL;
      Assign(MenuFile,MenuName);
      {$I-} Reset(MenuFile); {$I+}
      IF IOResult<>0 THEN
        BEGIN {file not found}
          Write('Menu file not found.  Abort.');
          Halt;
        END;  {file not found}
      {mark top of heap so it can be released later}
      Mark(TopHeap);
      REPEAT
        BEGIN {search for desired menu}
          ReadLn(MenuFile,TextLine);
          IF ((MenuNumber[1]=TextLine[1]) AND
              (MenuNumber[2]=TextLine[2]) AND
              (MenuNumber[3]=TextLine[3])) THEN
            BEGIN {found a desired menu line}
              MenuFound:=TRUE;
              IF ((TextLine[4]='*') AND (TextLine[5]='H')
                  AND (TextLine[6]='*')) THEN
                BEGIN {heading line}
                  FOR Count:=1 TO 6 DO DELETE(TextLine,1,1);
                  WHILE (LENGTH(TextLine)>(ScreenWidth-2)) DO
                    Delete(TextLine,LENGTH(TextLine),1);
```

Tool 5.1: Procedure CMenu to display a menu in the center of the screen. (continued)

```
                    New(NewHdg);
                    HdgLines:=HdgLines+1;
                    NewHdg^.Last:=NIL;
                    NewHdg^.MLine:=TextLine;
                    NewHdg^.Last:=NIL;
                    IF FirstHdg=NIL THEN FirstHdg:=NewHdg
                      ELSE
                          LastHdg^.NEXT:=NewHdg;
                    LastHdg:=NewHdg;
                    LastHdg^.NEXT:=NIL;
                  END    {heading line}
                    ELSE
                      BEGIN {menu line}
                        FOR Count:=1 TO 3 DO Delete(TextLine,1,1);
                        WHILE (Length(TextLine)>(ScreenWidth-2)) DO
                          Delete(TextLine,LENGTH(TextLine),1);
                        New(NewLine);
                        MenuLines:=MenuLines+1;
                        NewLine^.MLine:=TextLine;
                        NewLine^.Last:=LastLine;
                        IF FirstLine=NIL THEN FirstLine:=NewLine
                          ELSE
                            LastLine^.NEXT:=NewLine;
                            LastLine:=NewLine;
                            LastLine^.NEXT:=FirstLine;
                            FirstLine^.Last:=LastLine;
                        END;    {menu line}
                    END    {found a desired menu line}
                      ELSE
                        IF MenuFound THEN EndOfMenu:=True;
                END;   {search for desired menu}
              UNTIL EndOfMenu OR EOF(MenuFile);
              IF NOT MenuFound THEN
                BEGIN {menu not found}
                  Write('Menu number not found.  Abort.');
                  Halt;
                END;   {menu not found}
              Close(MenuFile);
            END;   {get menu file}


PROCEDURE MenuWindow;

  {This procedure uses Turbo's Window command to establish a}
  {window for the selections on the menu and calculates how }
  {many selection lines remain after the heading lines.     }

  BEGIN {make menu window}
    Window(TopL+1,TopRow+HdgLines+2,BotR+1,BotRow-1);
    MenuSize:=((BotRow-1)-(TopRow+HdgLines+1));
  END;   {make menu window}


PROCEDURE WriteMenuSelections;

  VAR
    Line,Col  :Integer;

  {This procedure initializes the menu with the first (top) }
  {selection being highlighted and lists as many selections }
  {on the menu as space allows.  The cursor is moved to the }
  {bottom-right corner of the CRT screen.                   }
```

Tool 5.1: Procedure CMenu to display a menu in the center of the screen. (continued)

```
        BEGIN {write first set of menu selections}
          NewLine:=FirstLine; TopLine:=FirstLine;
          IF MenuSize>MenuLines THEN NumLines:=MenuLines
            ELSE NumLines:=MenuSize;
          FOR Line:=1 TO (NumLines) DO
            BEGIN {write menu lines}
              ThisLine.MLine:=NewLine^.MLine;
              BotLine:=NewLine;
              GotoXY(1,Line);
              Write(' ',ThisLine.MLine);
              NewLine:=NewLine^.Next;
            END;  {write menu lines}
          Window(1,1,80,25);
          GotoXY(80,25);
          MenuWindow;
          CurrentLine:=1; CurrentChoice:=1;
          Row:=(TopRow+HdgLines+CurrentLine);
          FOR Col:=TopL TO BotR DO
            BEGIN {normal video}
              CharacterOffset:=(Row*160)+(Col*2);
              AttributeOffset:=CharacterOffset+1;
              Mem[ScreenAddress:AttributeOffset]:=$07;
            END;  {normal video}
        END; {write first set of menu selections}


PROCEDURE ReadKeyBoard;

  {This procedure reads keystrokes entered by the user and   }
  {then reacts accordingly on the menu screen.  When a key is}
  {pressed, the selection is returned to reverse video       }
  {(nonhighlighted).  The procedure interprets the keypress  }
  {and, if it was a cursor-movement key, moves the selection }
  {indicator (the highlighted area) up or down on the menu   }
  {and scrolls the screen, if necessary.                     }

  LABEL NoKey;

  VAR
      Ch   :Char;
      Col  :Integer;

  BEGIN {read key board}
    {decide size of usable screen - number of selection lines}
    IF MenuSize>MenuLines THEN NumLines:=MenuLines
      ELSE NumLines:=MenuSize;
    REPEAT

        {To use this program with Turbo Pascal versions prior
            to 4.0, add the line below:}
      { Read(KBD,Ch); }


        {To use this program with Turbo Pascal versions prior
            to 4.0, remove the line below:}
      Ch:=ReadKey;


      Row:=(TopRow+HdgLines+CurrentLine);
      FOR Col:=TopL TO BotR DO
        BEGIN {reverse video}
```

Tool 5.1: Procedure CMenu to display a menu in the center of the screen. (continued)

```
            CharacterOffset:=(Row*160)+(Col*2);
            AttributeOffset:=CharacterOffset+1;
            Mem[ScreenAddress:AttributeOffset]:=$70;
        END;  {reverse video}

     {To use this program with Turbo Pascal versions prior
         to 4.0, add the line below:}
{ IF ((Ch=#27) AND (KeyPressed)) THEN Read(KBD,Ch)
  ELSE IF (Ch<>#13) THEN GOTO NoKey; }


     {To use this program with Turbo Pascal versions prior
         to 4.0, remove the line below:}
 IF ((Ch=#0) AND (KeyPressed)) THEN Ch:=ReadKey
  ELSE IF (Ch<>#13) THEN GOTO NoKey;


IF ORD(CH)=80 THEN
  BEGIN {move cursor down}
  CurrentLine:=CurrentLine+1;
  CurrentChoice:=CurrentChoice+1;
  IF CurrentChoice>MenuLines THEN
    BEGIN
        CurrentChoice:=1;
        IF NumLines=MenuLines THEN CurrentLine:=1;
    END;
  IF CurrentChoice<=MenuLines THEN
    BEGIN {move to next line & choice}
      IF CurrentLine>MenuSize THEN
        BEGIN {scroll menu}
            CurrentLine:=MenuSize;
            GotoXY(1,1);
            DelLine;
            GotoXY(1,MenuSize);
            InsLine;
            NewLine:=BotLine^.Next;
            TopLine:=TopLine^.Next;
            BotLine:=NewLine;
            ThisLine.MLine:=NewLine^.MLine;
            GotoXY(1,CurrentLine);
            Write(' ',ThisLine.MLine);
            Window(1,1,80,25); GotoXY(80,25); MenuWindow;
        END; {scroll menu}
    END;  {move to next line & choice}
  END;  {move cursor down}
IF ORD(CH)=72 THEN (*IF CurrentChoice>1 THEN*)
  BEGIN {move cursor up}
  CurrentLine:=CurrentLine-1;
  CurrentChoice:=CurrentChoice-1;
  IF CurrentChoice<=0 THEN    (*new line*)
    BEGIN
    CurrentChoice:=MenuLines;
    IF NumLines=MenuLines THEN CurrentLine:=NumLines;
  END;
IF CurrentChoice>0 THEN
  BEGIN {move to previous line & choice}
    IF CurrentLine<1 THEN
```

Tool 5.1: Procedure CMenu to display a menu in the center of the screen. (continued)

```
                        BEGIN {scroll menu}
                          CurrentLine:=1;
                          GotoXY(1,MenuSize);
                          DelLine;
                          GotoXY(1,1);
                          InsLine;
                          NewLine:=TopLine^.Last;
                          BotLine:=BotLine^.Last;
                          TopLine:=NewLine;
                          ThisLine.MLine:=NewLine^.MLine;
                          GotoXY(1,CurrentLine);
                          Write(' ',ThisLine.MLine);
                          Window(1,1,80,25);
                          GotoXY(80,25);
                          MenuWindow;
                        END;  {scroll menu}
                    END;  {move to previous line & choice}
                END;  {move cursor up}
            NoKey:
            Row:=(TopRow+HdgLines+CurrentLine);
            FOR Col:=TopL TO BotR DO
              BEGIN  {normal video}
                CharacterOffset:=(Row*160)+(Col*2);
                AttributeOffset:=CharacterOffset+1;
                Mem[ScreenAddress:AttributeOffset]:=$07;
              END;  {normal video}
          UNTIL CH IN[#10,#13];
      END;  {read keyboard}


BEGIN {procedure centered menu}
  {make certain that NumLock is off and cursor pad on}
  Operation:='NUM';
  Setting:='OFF';
  KbdCtrl('S',Operation,Setting,Result);
  {determine if color card or monochrome card}
  IF (Mem[0000:1040] AND 48) <> 48 THEN ScreenAddress:=$B800
    ELSE ScreenAddress:=$B000;
  {make sure menu is at least 40 characters wide}
  IF ScreenWidth<40 THEN ScreenWidth:=40;
  GetFile;
  {make sure screen is long enough for at least 5 selections}
  IF ScreenLength<(HdgLines+5) THEN ScreenLength:=HdgLines+5;
  CalculateWindow;
  WindowIn(TopL+1,TopRow+1,BotR+1,BotRow+1,CCol,
           CRow,WindowInMemory);
  MenuBackGround;
  MenuWindow;
  WriteMenuSelections;
  ReadKeyBoard;
  Choice:=CurrentChoice;
  {Release the RAM used to store the previous screen}
  Release(TopHeap);
  WindowOut(CCol,CRow,WindowInMemory);
  Window(1,1,80,25); NormVideo;
END;  {procedure centered menu}
```

Tool 5.1: Procedure CMenu to display a menu in the center of the screen. (continued)

characters, the menu window will automatically be presented as 40 characters in width.

The CMenu procedure has several subprocedures. Each of these will be explained separately.

Procedure CalculateWindow calculates the position of the window for the menu. The window calculation is based on a screen width of 80 columns and a screen height of 25 rows. The desired width and length of the menu screen is centered within the full screen when the four window positions are calculated.

Procedure MenuBackground clears the menu window and gets it ready for selections to be listed. In this procedure, reverse video is established; the menu window is cleared; the instruction line to inform the user how the menu is operated is written; the heading lines are recalled from dynamic RAM, centered, and written on the menu; and a border line is written below the heading lines and above the instruction line.

Procedure GetFile finds the text file containing menu selections and reads the appropriate selections to memory.

Here's how this subprocedure works:

- Perform necessary initialization.
- Search for the specified menu file. If the file is not found, halt the program and display a message.
- Record the first open dynamic memory address.
- Search the menu text file for lines that belong to the menu about to be displayed. If the first three characters of the text file match the menu number passed, the line belongs to the desired menu.
- If a heading line has been found (with the characters following the number), strip the line of the first six characters, allocate dynamic RAM for storing the new heading line and references to other heading lines, increment the heading line count, and transfer information concerning this heading line to the memory record space just allocated.
- If a selection line has been found, strip the line of the first three characters, allocate dynamic RAM for the new selection line,

increment the selection line count, and transfer information concerning this selection line to the memory space just allocated.

- When a menu line which does not belong to the specified menu is encountered, halt the search. (This is why the lines for a given menu must be together, one after the other, in the menu text file.)

Procedure MenuWindow creates a final window in which only the selections will appear. It establishes a new window within the menu window, below the heading lines and above the instruction line. (This is where the actual selections will go.) Then the procedure calculates the actual number of selections which may appear in the available space at a given time.

Procedure WriteMenuSelections initializes the menu with the first selections to be displayed. Here's how this subprocedure works:

- Perform necessary initialization.
- Calculate the number of lines to be written. If the available lines are greater than the number of selections, the number of lines to be written is the number of selections; if the number of selections is greater than the available lines, the number of lines to be written is the available number of lines.
- Establish a loop to write the selections. A selection is written on each pass through the loop.
- Set the window to the full screen and place the cursor at the bottom corner.
- Set the window back to the actual area allowed for selections when the MenuWindow procedure is called.
- Initialize the current line and selection number at 1.
- Determine the actual row number on the screen of the first selection.
- Directly manipulate the screen attributes in video RAM to change this row from reverse to normal video and thus highlight the selection appearing on this line. (The direct video RAM manipulations used in this procedure are detailed in Chapter 7.)

Procedure ReadKeyBoard reads the keystrokes entered and takes the appropriate action. Here's how this subprocedure works:

- Determine the number of lines being worked with. If the number of selections is greater than the number of lines available for display, the number being worked with is the number available for display; if the number of selections is less than or equal to the number of available lines, the number of lines being worked with equals the number of selections.

- Wait to read a keystroke.

- After a keystroke is read, change the attributes of the current line to reverse video through direct video RAM manipulation (so it is no longer highlighted).

- Check if an extended scan code (4.0 and 5.0) or an escape sequence (earlier versions) has been read; if so, this may be a cursor-movement key. If no escape sequence has been read and the key pressed was not Enter (Return), ignore the keystroke.

- If the character read in the scan code or escape sequence is 80, the down arrow key was pressed, which means that the user wishes to move to the selection below the current selection. In this case, increment the current line count and selection count. If the current selection is greater than the total number of selections, go back to the top of the menu and make it selection number one. If the number of selections fits in the menu window, go to line one; no need to scroll. If the current selection is less than or equal to the total number of selections and the current line is greater than the available number of lines, scroll by deleting a line and inserting a line. Keep track of the present top, bottom, and current lines. Write the new selection in the space created by scrolling. Move the cursor back to the bottom of the whole screen.

- If the character read in the escape sequence is 72, the up arrow key was pressed, which means the user wishes to move to the selection above the current selection. Follow the same procedures as with the down arrow key, but move the selection in the other direction.

- The screen has now been set up correctly. Go to the appropriate row and highlight that selection by changing the video RAM attributes to those of normal video.

- End the procedure when the Enter key is pressed, indicating that the user has made a selection.

The CMenu procedure first calls the KbdCtrl procedure to make certain that the cursor-movement keys are operative, not the number keys. (See Chapter 3 for a complete explanation of this procedure.) Then it determines whether a color video display card is active and sets the video RAM address accordingly. If the ScreenWidth parameter indicates less than 40 columns, it is reset to 40 columns so that the window will be wide enough for the instruction line. Next the GetFile subprocedure is called to read the menu text file. The ScreenLength parameter is checked to be certain that it will display at least one selection line after showing the heading lines, instruction line, and border lines below the headings and above the instructions. If there have not been enough lines provided, the length is arbitrarily increased. If too many heading lines are used, it is possible to force the screen length to be longer than the 25 lines available on PCs; this will be immediately obvious when the menu is displayed.

The CMenu procedure continues by calling the CalculateWindow subprocedure to determine the window placement on screen. The WindowIn procedure is called to save the present screen and create a window for the menu. (This procedure is presented and explained in Chapter 7.) Next the MenuBackground subprocedure is called to begin setting up the menu on screen, the MenuWindow subprocedure is called to set the active window to the area which will actually be used for displaying menu selections, and the WriteMenuSelections subprocedure is called to place the initial selections on the menu screen. Finally, the ReadKeyBoard subprocedure is called to await and read the user's keystrokes and act accordingly.

After returning from ReadKeyBoard, some choice has been made; the value of the choice is set to the parameter Choice to be returned to the host program as an indication of the selection made by the user. All dynamic RAM allocated for storage of the previous screen and the menu headings and selections is released. The WindowOut procedure (see Chapter 7) is called to restore the screen to the way it was immediately prior to calling the CMenu procedure. The active window is set to the full screen, and normal video mode is set as the procedure ends.

DISPLAYING A MENU ANYWHERE ON THE SCREEN

The only difference between the Menu procedure, shown as Tool 5.2, and the CMenu procedure is that Menu allows you to determine where the menu will appear on the screen. (Only the portion of the procedure that is different from Tool 5.1 is listed in Tool 5.2.) Procedure Menu requires the same parameters to be passed to it as the CMenu procedure, plus two parameters to identify the menu location. These additional parameters are TLCol and TLRow, which tell the procedure the top left column and top left row of the menu position, respectively.

```
PROCEDURE Menu(MenuNumber,MenuName:Str255;
              TLCol, TLRow, ScreenWidth, ScreenLength:Integer;
              VAR Choice:Integer);


TYPE
    {same as CMenu}

VAR
    {same as CMenu}

  PROCEDURE CalculateWindow;

    {This procedure takes the desired screen length and width}
    {parameters and calculates the placement of the menu on the}
    {screen                                                    }

    BEGIN {calculate window}
      TopL:=TLCol;
      TopRow:=TLRow;
      BotRow:=TopRow+ScreenLength;
      BotR:=TopL+ScreenWidth;
    END;   {calculate window}


BEGIN   {procedure menu}

    {same as CMenu}

END;   {procedure menu}
```

Tool 5.2: Procedure Menu to display a menu anywhere on the screen.

In order to position the menu, the CalculateWindow subprocedure begins the window calculation from the top left menu corner, as specified in the TLCol and TLRow parameters. The desired width and length of the menu screen is added to the top left corner positions to calculate the four window corner positions.

USING THE MENU PROCEDURES IN A PROGRAM

Test Program 5.1 illustrates the use of the menu procedures within a program. In order for this demonstration program to operate, you must create a text file for the menu procedures to read. Here is the text of a sample menu selection file to be used with the test program. Name this file MENUDEMO.MNU.

```
001*H*****************************************
001*H*
001*H*Sample Menu Number 1
001*H*
001*H*****************************************
001Selection 1
001 Selection 2
001   Selection 3
001     Selection 4
001        Selection 5
001          Selection 6
001Quit
002*H*Sample Menu Number 2
002Subselection 1
002Subselection 2
002Subselection 3
002Subselection 4
002Subselection 5
002Subselection 6
002Subselection 7
002Subselection 8
002Subselection 9
002Subselection 10
002Subselection 11
002Subselection 12
002Subselection 13
```

```
Program TestMenus;

    {To use this program with Turbo Pascal versions prior to
        4.0, remove the Uses statement below.}

    Uses DOS,CRT;

    {$V-}  {relaxed parameter type checking}

    TYPE
        Str255 = STRING[255];
        Pointr = ^Integer;

    VAR
        Selection1, Selection2    :Integer;
        MenuNum                   :STRING[3];

    CONST
        MenuFile = 'MENUDEMO.MNU';

    {$I WindowIn.Inc}
    {$I WindoOut.Inc}
    {$I SetBits.Inc}
    {$I BitSet.Inc}
    {$I KbdCtrl.Inc}
    {$I Menu.Inc}
    {$I CMenu.Inc}

BEGIN {program}
    WriteLn;
    WriteLn('>>> Test Centered Menu <<<');
    Delay(1500);
    REPEAT   {until Selection2<>25}
        MenuNum:='001';
        CMenu(MenuNum,MenuFile,40,15,Selection1);
        WriteLn;
        WriteLn('Main-Menu selection was number ',Selection1);
        WriteLn;
        Delay(1500);
        MenuNum:='002';
        CASE Selection1 OF
          1..6: CMenu(MenuNum,MenuFile,40,15,Selection2);
          7: Selection2:=0;
        END;   {case selection1 statement}
        WriteLn;
        WriteLn('Sub-Menu selection was number ',Selection2);
        WriteLn;
        Delay(1500);
    UNTIL (Selection2<>25);
    REPEAT   {until selection 2 <> 25}
        WriteLn;
        WriteLn('>>> Test Menu Procedure <<<');
        Delay(1500);
        MenuNum:='001';
        Menu(MenuNum,MenuFile,1,1,40,15,Selection1);
        WriteLn;
        WriteLn('Main-Menu selection was number ',Selection1);
        WriteLn;
        Delay(1500);
        MenuNum:='002';
        CASE Selection1 OF
```

Test Program 5.1: Using the menu procedures in a program.

```
          1..6: Menu(MenuNum,MenuFile,Selection1+1,Selection1+1,
                      40,15,Selection2);
           7: Selection2:=0;
          END;   {case selection1 statement}
          WriteLn;
          WriteLn('Sub-Menu selection was number ',Selection2);
          WriteLn;
          Delay(1500);
      UNTIL (Selection2<>25);
  END.   {program}
```

Test Program 5.1: Using the menu procedures in a program. (continued)

```
002Subselection 14
002Subselection 15
002Subselection 16
002Subselection 17
002Subselection 18
002Subselection 19
002Subselection 20
002Subselection 21
002Subselection 22
002Subselection 23
002Subselection 24
002Return to Previous Menu
```

Note that this text file is set up for two separate menus, Menu 1 and Menu 2. Theoretically, Menu 2 is a submenu which is called for more specific choices after the broader choices have been made from Menu 1. Note also that Menu 1 is a short menu that will fit on the screen; Menu 2 is a longer menu that will demonstrate the scrolling function of the menu procedures.

Here's how the TestMenus program works:

- Mark the necessary files for operation for inclusion.
- Test the centered menu first.
- Present a primary menu with a few selections.
- If any selection is chosen other than Quit, present a secondary menu. In this demonstration program, the same secondary menu is presented regardless of the primary menu selection; in your

program, the secondary menus would differ based on the primary menu selection.

- If any secondary menu selection other than Return to Previous Menu is made, end this portion of the program. Your program would have a CASE statement to call the appropriate program functions based on the secondary menu selection.

- Test the menu that allows the programmer to determine screen placement. All operations are the same as with the centered menu.

- The screen placement of the secondary menu is based on the primary menu selection; this is only to demonstrate different placements and has no other significance.

- After each menu selection, primary or secondary, display the number of the selection chosen, as reported back to the host program by the menu procedures.

The menu procedures presented in this chapter will allow your programs to have consistent menu formats throughout, with virtually no programming effort. At the same time, placing all menu headers and selections in an ASCII file will help save program code with a minimal sacrifice in execution time.

If it is not important in your program to preserve the current screen when a menu is called, you could design a special background screen for the menu. For example, if your program is called My Program, you might wish to have a screen filled repetitively with *My Program* as a backdrop for the menus. You could write your own procedure to create such a screen before calling the menus themselves, or use the screen generator discussed in Chapter 8.

CHAPTER 6
BIT MAPPING FOR EFFICIENT DATA STORAGE

....
....
....
....
....
....
....
....
....
....
....
....
....
....
....
....
....
....
....
....
....
....
....
....
....

Just as you can think of a string as an array of characters, you can consider a byte or an integer as an array of bits. You can store a great deal of simple data in a compact area by manipulating the individual bits in a byte. One way to do this is to store each data item as true or false. A byte could contain eight items stored this way (one data item for each bit), and an integer could hold sixteen items. Another method is to let the status of certain bits (1 for set, or on; 0 for unset, or off) apply to certain information. This is how DOS stores a complete date in 2 bytes and time in another 2 bytes, as discussed in Chapter 2. In fact, DOS makes extensive use of bytes and integers for storing data about the system configuration because a great deal of information can be contained in an extremely small area.

EXAMPLES OF BIT MAPPING

The DOS flags register is a good example of bit mapping. This integer contains 16 bits that can be turned on or off individually to indicate certain occurrences within the operating system. A flag commonly used when dealing with function calls to the operating system through interrupt 33 is the carry flag, which is often set to indicate that an error occurred. Turbo Pascal 4.0 and 5.0 include, in the Dos unit, a set of flag constants that can be used to test six of the bits of the DOS flags integer: the carry, parity, auxilliary, zero, sign, and overflow flags. Other bit maps used by DOS include the file attribute byte (discussed in Chapter 1) and the keyboard status bytes (discussed in Chapter 3).

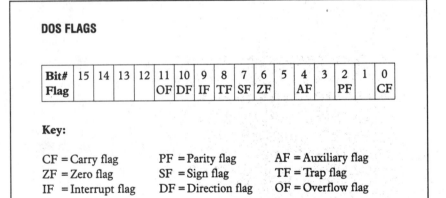

DOS FLAGS

Bit#	15	14	13	12	11	10	9	8	7	6	5	4	3	2	1	0
Flag					OF	DF	IF	TF	SF	ZF		AF		PF		CF

Key:

CF = Carry flag   PF = Parity flag   AF = Auxiliary flag
ZF = Zero flag   SF = Sign flag   TF = Trap flag
IF = Interrupt flag DF = Direction flag   OF = Overflow flag

For data which are slightly more complex, such as the date and time of a file's creation as stored by DOS, sets of bits can be used. Two bits can handle four possibilities (on/on, on/off, off/on, or off/off), three bits can handle eight possibilities, and so on. You can think of these more complex bit sets as various on/off combinations or, more simply, as smaller binary numbers, where 2 bits can contain any number from 0 to 3, 3 bits can contain any number from 0 to 7, and so on. Table 6.1 shows the decimal values of each bit of a byte, along with the settings for several decimal numbers. Note that each is double the previous value, and the values accumulate. The 8 bits of a byte can contain 256 possible combinations, or values in the range of 0 through 255.

Table 6.1:
Bit Values and Settings for Decimal Numbers

BIT VALUES

Bit	Value
7	128
6	64
5	32
4	16
3	8
2	4
1	2
0	1

SETTINGS FOR VARIOUS DECIMAL NUMBERS

Number	Setting							
0	0	0	0	0	0	0	0	0
1	0	0	0	0	0	0	0	1
2	0	0	0	0	0	0	1	0
3	0	0	0	0	0	0	1	1
4	0	0	0	0	0	1	0	0
128	1	0	0	0	0	0	0	0
255	1	1	1	1	1	1	1	1

USES OF BIT MAPPING

Bit maps have many practical applications. For example, say that you are constructing a program with a database for storing a large number of names for a commercial mailing list, and you want to include a great deal of personal and credit data for screening the names for specific product mailings. This information might be the income bracket, marital status, home ownership status, education, and age group for each person in the list. Stored conventionally, with a variable representing each item, these data could occupy 8 or more bytes. Here's how you could use bit mapping to store the information in 2 bytes:

15	14	13	12	11	10	9	8	7	6	5	4	3	2	1	0
AG	AG	RA	CA	CA	CA	CA	MO	ED	ED	OR	CH	MS	IN	IN	IN

IN = Income bracket: Bits 0, 1, and 2

Bits Set		Bracket
none	1	< $10,000
0	2	$10,000–15,000
1	3	$15,000–22,500
0,1	4	$22,500–30,000
2	5	$30,000–40,000
2,0	6	$40,000–55,000
2,1	7	$55,000–75,000
2,1,0	8	> $75,000

MS = Married: Bit 3

    1 = Yes   0 = No

CH = Children: Bit 4

    1 = Yes   0 = No

OR = Own/Rent: Bit 5

1 = Own   0 = Rent

ED = Education: Bits 6 and 7

Bits Set	Education
none	< High school
6	High school
7	Some college
6,7	College +

MO = Former mail order buyer: Bit 8

1 = Yes   0 = No

CA = Credit approved date: Bits 9, 10, 11, and 12

Bits Set	Date
9,10 off	1st quarter
9	2nd quarter
10	3rd quarter
9,10	4th quarter
11,12 off	old or not approved
11	current year
12	previous year
11,12	2 years old

RA = Race: Bit 13

1 = White   0 = Nonwhite

AG = Age group: Bits 14 and 15

Bits Set	Group
none	<25
14	25–30

15   30–45

14,15   45+

For an individual record, 6 bytes one way or another is hardly significant. When multiplied by one million, two million, or more names in a large database, we suddenly begin speaking in terms of 6, 12, or more megabytes of disk space, and the numbers get quite significant in a hurry.

Another use of bit maps is to track certain program operations. If several operations are to be performed on each record in a file, it can be worthwhile to have a status byte with the various flags set as each operation is performed. This information can save you a lot of time and effort if the operations are interrupted for some reason—you will know what has been done and what is left to do. While you could accomplish this tracking easily through Boolean variables, it can usually be done almost as easily, and with a lot less memory space, through a byte or integer used as a flag set, with each bit significant to a specific operation. For those programs that begin to stretch the limits of Turbo Pascal's program capacity, saving this memory space can be very important.

In general, when large amounts of data are to be stored, it is beneficial to use as little space as possible for the data items in order to run faster sorts, speed up access time, and allow more records in a given file. Using an integer to store 16 pieces of information or a byte to store 8 pieces can make data storage and access more efficient for any program.

BIT-MAPPING PROCEDURES

Bit mapping, or setting flags, operates the same in bytes or integers. The only difference is that a byte has only 8 bits to set, and an integer consists of 2 bytes, providing 16 bits that may be manipulated. The procedures presented in this chapter deal with bit mapping in integers. Some could be used as they are with byte values, but others arbitrarily seek 16 bits and would have to be rewritten for bytes so that they would seek only 8 bits.

SETTING BITS

The procedure SetBits, shown as Tool 6.1, allows you to change any of the 16 bits in an integer. You can set the bit to 0, set it to 1, or simply change it to its opposite state (if it is 0, change it to 1; if it is 1, change it to 0). The procedure will return the changed integer to the program.

```
PROCEDURE SetBits(Operation:Char;
                  Position :Integer;
                  VAR Flag :Integer);

     VAR
          Y :Integer;

     BEGIN {set a bit}
          Operation:=UpCase(Operation);
          Y:=1 SHL Position;
IF Operation='S' THEN Flag:=Flag OR Y;
IF Operation='U' THEN Flag:=Flag AND NOT Y;
IF Operation='X' THEN
          IF Odd(Flag SHR Position) THEN Flag:=Flag AND NOT Y
               ELSE Flag:=Flag OR Y;
     END;   {set a bit}
```

Tool 6.1: Procedure SetBits for setting flags.

We used SetBits in the KbdCtrl procedure, presented in Chapter 3 (Tool 3.1) to set the appropriate keyboard control bit. It was also employed in the InterpretTime and InterpretDate procedures (for Turbo Pascal versions earlier than 4.0), presented in Chapter 2 (Tools 2.6 and 2.7) to set the bits of an integer to hours, minutes, or seconds and the month, day, or year, respectively.

The procedure uses the following parameters:

- The parameter FlagInteger is the integer to be changed and returned to the program in its changed format. All 16 bits of FlagInteger are available for change (one at a time).

- The parameter Operation tells the procedure whether a bit is to be set (to 1), unset (to 0), or switched to its opposite state. It is either an S for set, a U for unset, or an X for switch to the opposite state.

- The Position parameter indicates the bit to be changed. It is an integer value of 0 through 15, representing the corresponding bit.

Here's how the SetBits procedure works:

- Convert the Operation parameter to uppercase, in case it was passed as a lowercase character.
- Regardless of the operation to be performed, set the integer Y to the appropriate bit (do not set any other of its bits). This is accomplished through Turbo Pascal's SHL operator. A value of 1 is given to Y, and the SHL operator shifts this value to the appropriate bit position.
- If the operation is to set this particular bit in the FlagInteger, use an arithmetic OR operator.
- If the operation is to unset the bit, use the arithmetic AND NOT operator.
- If the present bit setting is to be reversed, test to determine if it is presently set, and then use the appropriate operator (OR or AND NOT) to perform the operation.

The use of the SetBits procedure, as well as the other bit-mapping tools, is demonstrated in Test Program 6.1, presented at the end of this chapter.

CHECKING THE PRESENT STATUS OF A BIT

If you are setting flags to store data items, you will want your programs to retrieve this information and act accordingly. Function BitSet, shown as Tool 6.2, checks a single data item (bit) within the flag set to determine its present state.

```
FUNCTION BitSet(Position :Integer; Flag :Integer):Boolean;

  BEGIN {bit set ?}
    BitSet:=(Odd(Flag SHR Position));
  END;  {bit set ?}
```

Tool 6.2: Function BitSet to check the status of a bit.

BitSet is a Boolean function that returns a true if the bit in the integer parameter FlagInteger is set (1) or a false if the bit is not set (0). The bit to be checked is indicated by the Position parameter, which is an integer between 0 and 15. We used the BitSet function in the KbdCtrl procedure of Chapter 3 to see if a specified keyboard control bit was set.

Here's how the BitSet function works:

- Move the bit to be checked to position zero. In this position, it will have a value of 1 if it is set and a value of zero if it is not set. The altered FlagInteger will have an odd value if the specified bit is set, or an even value if it is not set.

- Return the Boolean value True if FlagInteger, with the bits shifted to the right, became an odd number.

- Return the Boolean value False if FlagInteger became an even number.

CHECKING ALL THE FLAGS AT ONE TIME

When you are interested in the status of a number of bits, you may find it tedious to check each single bit. You can use procedure ReadBits, shown as Tool 6.3, to obtain the setting of all the flags at one time. This procedure may, for example, be used to determine the setting of each flag in the flags register returned when a DOS service routine is called.

```
PROCEDURE ReadBits(InputNo:Integer; VAR FlagString:Str255);

    VAR
        X          :Integer;

    BEGIN {read bits}
        FlagString:='                ';  {16 spaces}
        FOR X:=15 DOWNTO 0 DO
            IF (Odd(InputNo SHR X)) THEN
                    FlagString[X+1]:='1'
                        ELSE FlagString[X+1]:='0';
    END;   {read bits}
```

Tool 6.3: Procedure ReadBits to check the status of all 16 bits.

We used the ReadBits procedure in the InterpretTime and Interpret-Date procedures of Chapter 2 to read the bits from the directory data on the time and date of file creation.

The procedure reads the parameter FlagInteger and determines which bits are set and which are not. The information about all 16 bits is returned in the parameter FlagString as a string of 16 characters representing the respective bit flags. The FlagString parameter is a string of ones and/or zeroes corresponding to bits 0 through 15 of the integer.

> **NOTE:** Because element[0] of the string contains a byte denoting the length of the string, the flags are represented by elements 1 through 16, with the element number being 1 more than the flag it represents (for example, Flag 0 = FlagString[0 + 1]; Flag 15 = FlagString[15 + 1]).

Here's how the ReadBits procedure works:

- Initialize the FlagString parameter to be returned to the program to 16 spaces.
- Check each bit of the flag integer InputNo to determine if it is set.
- If a specific bit is set, load the corresponding character in the FlagString parameter with 1; if the bit is not set, load the corresponding FlagString character with 0.

This procedure expects an integer of 16 bits. To use it with byte flags, change this line:

```
FOR X: = 15 DOWNTO 0 DO
```

to

```
FOR X: = 7 DOWNTO 0 DO
```

CHECKING ALL THE FLAGS USING AN ARRAY

Procedure ReadBit2, presented as Tool 6.4, is a variation of the ReadBits procedure. In this procedure, the variable parameter is a Boolean array.

This method has the advantage of having the array element correspond exactly to the bit (for example, ArrayElement[0] = Bit 0). Aside from passing the data as a Boolean array, the procedure works the same as the Read-Bits procedure.

```
PROCEDURE ReadBit2(InputNo:Integer;
                   VAR FlagArray:BoolArray);

     VAR
          X :Integer;

     BEGIN {read bits}
          FOR X:=15 DOWNTO 0 DO
               FlagArray[X]:=(Odd(InputNo SHR X));
     END;   {read bits}
```

Tool 6.4: Procedure ReadBit2 to check all flags using an array.

The ReadBit2 procedure requires the following declaration in the program for the array to be passed:

TYPE
BoolArray = ARRAY[0..15] OF Boolean;

To use the ReadBit2 procedure with byte flags rather than integer flags, make the same change as noted for using the ReadBits procedure with a byte.

BIT MAP
TEMPLATES

If you are storing many data items in a bit-mapped array, you may need to access certain records that match a particular set of criteria. You can speed up the comparison process by using a template of the desired bit-map configuration. For example, using the credit-data flag set presented for the commercial mailing list program example earlier in this chapter, you might want to select only those records that were flagged as:

Income > $75,000; Married; No children; Own home; College +; Former mail order buyer; Credit approved 1st quarter of current year; White; Age 45+

The template for this specific combination (with spaces separating the various components for visual clarity) would be:

(Bit 0>   111 1 0 1 11 1 0010 1 11   <Bit 15)

GETTING A TEMPLATE VALUE

Function Template, shown as Tool 6.5, will return a template integer. You can use this value to quickly compare and select bit-mapped integers in your records.

```
FUNCTION Template(Pattern:Str255):Integer;

    VAR
         X, Y, Z  :Integer;

    BEGIN {construct a template bit map}
         X:=1; Z:=0;
         WHILE ((X<=16) AND (X<=LENGTH(Pattern))) DO
              BEGIN {while}
                   IF (Pattern[X]<>'0') THEN
                        BEGIN {if}
                             Y:=1 SHL (16-X);
                             Z:=Z OR Y;
                        END;   {if}
                   X:=X+1;
              END;  {while}
         Template:=Z;
    END;  {construct a template bit map}
```

Tool 6.5: Function Template to get a bit-map template value.

The Template function is to be passed a 16-character string consisting of a series of ones or zeroes that match the bit pattern to be sought. The leftmost character (1 or 0) corresponds to bit 15; the rightmost corresponds to bit 0. The function will return an integer number. Your program can use that value to find matching bit patterns in your records, as illustrated below:

```
VAR
    DesiredPattern :Integer;
    PatternString :STRING[16];
         {Record.BitMapInteger is the bit-mapped integer}
```

```
{that is part of the record being considered }
{for selection.   }
DesiredPattern: = Template(PatternString);
IF (Record.BitMapInteger = DesiredPattern) THEN
   {select the record}
```

Here's how the Template function works:

- Initialize variables.
- Do not read more than 16 positions, nor past the length of the string.
- If the pattern for the position being considered is not zero, consider it to be set.
- If the position being considered is set, set the appropriate bit in procedure variable Z.
- After setting all appropriate bits, set the value of Template to the value of Z and return to the program with the appropriate value.

The Template function expects 16 bits. To use it with byte flags, change both occurrences of the number 16 to 8, and redefine it as a byte function rather than an integer one.

USING BIT MANIPULATION WITHIN A PROGRAM

Test Program 6.1 illustrates the general use of all the bit-manipulation procedures presented in this chapter. The results of all operations are graphically displayed on screen in this demonstration program.

For clarity, the program uses four subprocedures:

- The ClrLines procedure goes to specified screen positions and clears the lines.
- The WriteData procedure goes to specified screen positions and writes current data to the screen display.

```
PROGRAM TestBits;

     {To use this program with Turbo Pascal versions prior to
        4.0, remove the Uses statement below.}

     Uses DOS,CRT;

     TYPE
          BoolArray = ARRAY[0..15] OF Boolean;
          Str255    = STRING[255];

     VAR
          FlagArray    :BoolArray;
          FlagString   :Str255;
          X, Y, Z      :Integer;
          Ch           :Char;
          Quit         :Boolean;

     {$I SetBits.Inc}
     {$I BitSet.Inc}
     {$I ReadBits.Inc}
     {$I ReadBit2.Inc}
     {$I Template.Inc}

     PROCEDURE ClrLines;
        BEGIN
             GotoXY(6,22); ClrEol;
             GotoXY(6,23); ClrEol;
             GotoXY(20,18); ClrEol;
             GotoXY(10,2); ClrEol;
        END;

     PROCEDURE WriteData;
        BEGIN
             GotoXY(20,18); ClrEol;
             Write(Y);
             GotoXY(6,22); ClrEol;
             FOR Z:=16 DOWNTO 1 DO
                  Write(FlagString[Z],'  ');
             GotoXY(6,23); ClrEol;
             FOR Z:=15 DOWNTO 0 DO
                  IF FlagArray[Z] THEN Write('T  ')
                       ELSE Write('F  ');
        END;


     PROCEDURE Again;
        BEGIN
             GotoXY(1,25);
             Write('Try it again? (Y/N) '):
     {To use this program with Turbo Pascal versions prior
        to 4.0, add the line below:}
             { Read(KBD,Ch); }

     {To use this program with Turbo Pascal versions prior
        to 4.0, remove the line below:}
             Ch:=ReadKey;


             Quit:=(UpCase(Ch)<>'Y');
             GotoXY(1,25); ClrEol;
        END;
```

Test Program 6.1: Using the bit-manipulation procedures in a program.

```
PROCEDURE Screen;
    BEGIN
        ClrScr;
        WriteLn('TESTING bit manipulation procedures.');
        WriteLn('TESTING: ');
        GotoXY(1,18);
        Write('Flag integer value:');
        GotoXY(1,20);
        WriteLn('Bit  15 14 13 12 11 10  9  8  7  6  5  4',
                '  3  2  1  0');
        WriteLn('       __ __ __ __ __ __ __ __ __ __ __ __',
                '  __ __ __ __');
        WriteLn('Set');
        WriteLn('T/F');
    END;

BEGIN {program}
    Screen;
    GotoXY(10,2);
    Write(#7,'ReadBits and ReadBit2');
    FOR Y:=1 TO 20 DO
        BEGIN {for y=1 to 20}
            ReadBits(Y,FlagString);
            ReadBit2(Y,FlagArray);
            WriteData;
            Delay(1500);
        END;    {for x=1 to 20}
    ClrLines;
    Write(#7,'SetBits, BitSet, ReadBits, ReadBit2');
    GotoXY(1,4);
    WriteLn('<S>et bits    <U>n-set bits    <X>change bits');
    WriteLn('Which bit ?   (0 - 15)');
    Y:=0;
    REPEAT {until quit}
        GotoXY(46,4);
        REPEAT
{To use this program with Turbo Pascal versions prior
    to 4.0, add the line below:}
            { Read(KBD,Ch); }

{To use this program with Turbo Pascal versions prior
    to 4.0, remove the line below:}
            Ch:=ReadKey;

            Ch:=UpCase(Ch);
        UNTIL (Ch IN['S','U','X']);
        Write(Ch);
        REPEAT
            GotoXY(25,5);
            ReadLn(X);
        UNTIL (X IN[0..15]);
        SetBits(Ch,X,Y);
        GotoXY(1,19);
        Write('Bit ',X,' is ');
        IF (BitSet(X,Y)) THEN Write('SET    ')
            ELSE Write('NOT SET');
        ReadBits(Y,FlagString);
        ReadBit2(Y,FlagArray);
        WriteData;
        Again;
```

Test Program 6.1: Using the bit-manipulation procedures in a program. (continued)

```
            UNTIL Quit;
            GotoXY(1,19); ClrEol;
            ClrLines;
            Write(#7,'Template, ReadBits, ReadBit2');
            GotoXY(1,4); ClrEol;
            Write('Enter template below as a series of 16 0s and 1s');
            GotoXY(1,5); ClrEol;
            REPEAT {until quit}
                 GotoXY(1,5);
                 FOR X:=1 TO 16 DO Write('_');
                 GotoXY(1,5);
                 ReadLn(FlagString);
                 FlagString[0]:=Chr(16);
                 Y:=Template(FlagString);
                 ReadBits(Y,FlagString);
                 ReadBit2(Y,FlagArray);
                 WriteData;
                 Again;
            UNTIL Quit;
   END.   {program}
```

Test Program 6.1: Using the bit-manipulation procedures in a program. (continued)

- The Again procedure asks the user if he or she wishes to continue trying the current operation.

- The Screen procedure builds the original screen display, which remains throughout the program.

The program begins by calling the Screen procedure and listing the current operation on the screen. It establishes a 20-count loop to display the bit mapping for each integer in the range of 1 to 20.

It tests the accuracy of the ReadBits and ReadBit2 procedures by having them read the bit settings on each of the 20 numbers that come up in the loop sequence. The setting for each bit is displayed on the screen for every number in the loop. A delay gives you an opportunity to read the settings.

Next the program tests the SetBits and BitSet procedures. Portions of the screen are refreshed, and the new operation and data-entry instructions are displayed.

You are offered the option to set, unset, or exchange (switch the current bit setting) bits and asked to specify which of the 16 available bits is to be changed. The appropriate bit is manipulated with the SetBits procedure, the BitSet procedure is called to report whether the selected bit is set or not, and the current settings of all bits are read and displayed on the screen. The program asks if you want to repeat this test. You can continue changing the settings of bits or proceed to the next test. During the repeat loop, the flag integer is not reinitialized; thus, your bit manipulations have a cumulative effect.

Finally, the program tests the Template function. It displays the instructions on the screen and asks you to enter a bit-map pattern as a series of ones and zeroes in the set of 16 underlines it has placed on the screen. The program creates a template integer from the bit-map pattern, reads the bit mapping of the template integer, and displays the decimal value of the template, as well as its bit mapping, on the screen. You can continue entering different bit-map patterns or choose to quit the program.

CHAPTER 7
SCREEN HANDLING

··
··
··
··
··
··
··
··
··
··
··
··
··
··
··
··
··
··
··
··
··
··
··
··
··
··
··
··
··
··
··
··

This chapter provides information and tools for handling two important aspects of the screen display: video display attributes and windows. In the first part of the chapter, you'll learn how to work directly with the memory area controlling the video display in order to manipulate various screen attributes. The second part presents procedures for placing one or more windows on the screen while preserving, and later restoring, the original screen display. The windowing procedures include methods for framing windows and creating "exploding" windows.

SCOPE OF THE SCREEN-HANDLING PROCEDURES

The screen-handling procedures described in this chapter apply directly to working in text mode with the standard and extended ASCII character set, as used on IBM-compatible computers. Advances in display adapters since the original monochrome ones have made many options available for screen displays. Some cards offer multiple pages of screen memory, a vast array of color combinations, and graphics capabilities. Even the color/graphics adapter (CGA) card, with 16 kilobytes of memory allocated to it, can hold four text screens at once. The material presented here deals with only those screen applications that can be used with both color and monochrome monitors and display adapters. The procedures will operate on any IBM (PC, XT, and AT) compatible, in either color or monochrome modes. However, many of the principles, and some of the mechanics, can also be applied to working with screen graphics and the more advanced display adapters.

One of the essential mechanics of the screen-handling procedures is writing to screen memory. Some programmers believe that screen handling should be done through the operating system as opposed to through direct manipulation of the video RAM. Despite all of the arguments against direct RAM manipulation, many applications take this approach because it allows faster screen displays than can be obtained by going through the operating system (the BIOS). Some of the tools presented here perform conventional screen-handling functions through the operating system, but most will work directly with video RAM.

For more in-depth information about the various screen modes and controlling the video display, you can refer to *The MS-DOS Handbook,* Second Edition, by Richard Allen King (SYBEX, 1986).

CONTROLLING VIDEO-DISPLAY ATTRIBUTES

Controlling video-display attributes involves determining where video-display memory begins, calculating specific screen locations, and reading and setting screen information bytes. This section explains the methods for manipulating the screen display and presents procedures that perform the necessary functions.

VIDEO-DISPLAY MEMORY

The video-display memory is physically located on the adapter card, but is logically a part of the computer's main memory address space. Memory blocks A and B set aside a full 128 kilobytes of memory for display at hex addresses A0000 through BFFFF, even though the original display adapters use only two small parts of this memory. The monochrome card provides 4 kilobytes of memory beginning at hex address B000, and the original color/graphics card provides 16 kilobytes beginning at B800; the remaining space is set aside for advance display use, such as for the extended graphics adapter (EGA) card.

In order to work with the character and attribute cells, we must know their location in RAM. The monochrome display adapter cards and color/graphics display adapter cards begin their video-display memory at different addresses; therefore, we must first determine the type of monitor or display adapter in use (color or monochrome). The computer must also know this in order to operate the screen, so the information is available from RAM.

 ### Checking for a Color Card

The procedure CheckForColor, presented as Tool 7.1, will check for the presence of a color card and report its findings back to the program. It also returns the address of video memory in the host computer, which will be $B800 for a color card or $B000 for a monochrome card.

The procedure uses two variables; Color is a Boolean value of True or False and ScreenAddress is a word (for Turbo Pascal 4.0 and 5.0) or an integer (for earlier versions) of $B800 or $B000.

> **NOTE:** The video-memory address used in this procedure for color monitors or display adapters is based on the IBM CGA card. Although other cards may have a great deal more memory and other features, the address returned by the CheckForColor procedure will still work with most of them (without taking into consideration their extended memory or capabilities).

```
PROCEDURE CheckForColor(VAR Color:Boolean;
                        VAR ScreenAddress:Word);
      {To use this procedure with versions of Turbo Pascal prior
   to 4.0, change the type declaration of ScreenAddress from Word to
   Integer.}

      BEGIN {procedure check for color card}
            IF ((Mem[0000:1040] AND 48)<>48) THEN
               BEGIN {color = true}
                     ScreenAddress:=$B800;
                     Color:=True;
               END
               ELSE
                     BEGIN {color = false}
                           ScreenAddress:=$B000;
                           Color:=False;
                     END;
      END;  {procedure check for color card}
```

Tool 7.1: Procedure CheckForColor to check for a color card.

Here's how the CheckForColor procedure works:

- Check a low-memory location bit map to get the initial video mode (80-column color or 80-column monochrome).
- Based on the indication of the display card present, set the base address for video RAM and the Boolean variable Color.

THE VIDEO MODE

Video modes of monitors and adapters include 40- and 80-column text and graphics. The video mode is controllable through DOS commands, to a degree, and through software. For the procedures presented in this book, it is assumed that the video mode will be 2 (80-column black and white text), 3 (80-column color text), or 7 (80-column monochrome text). See Table 7.1 for a list and description of the various video modes available.

The CheckForColor procedure will obtain the information about the display adapter and the address of video memory necessary for all the procedures presented in this chapter. Because the user cannot invoke a graphics video mode through DOS commands, the procedures assume that the host computer will be in 80-column text mode whenever a program is initially invoked. However, if you are writing a program that needs to know

Table 7.1:
Video Modes

Mode	Address	Columns	Rows	Description
0	$B800	40	25	Black & white text
1	$B800	40	25	Color text
2	$B800	80	25	Black & white text
3	$B800	80	25	Color text
4	$B800	320	200	Color graphics
5	$B800	320	200	Black & white graphics
6	$B800	640	200	Black & white graphics
7	$B000	80	25	Monochrome text
8	$B800	160	200	PC Jr
9	$B800	320	200	PC Jr
10	$B800	640	200	PC Jr
11				EGA
12				EGA
13	$A800	320	200	Color graphics
14	$A800	640	200	Color graphics
15	$A000	640	350	Monochrome graphics
16	$A800	640	350	Color graphics

the video-mode setting, you could use an interrupt to access the BIOS video service 15, or, more easily, you could check the video-memory location. This can be accomplished by using the following statement within a program:

    VideoMode: = Mem[0000:1097];

DETERMINING SCREEN LOCATIONS

In text mode, each screen position is a *cell*. The cell contains enough screen space to display each of the various available ASCII characters. The ROM BIOS turns on and off various pixels within the cell to display the character patterns on the screen.

If you know the base screen address of video memory, it is relatively simple to compute the location of any given screen cell. The screen cell locations are the same as those used in Turbo Pascal to position the cursor in the GotoXY(Col,Row) command, with one important exception: Turbo Pascal counts the screen cells beginning from 1,1, and video memory begins with 0,0. For an 80-column by 25-row screen (as used in the procedures presented here), Turbo Pascal recognizes columns 1 through 80 and rows 1 through 25; when working with screen memory, these are referred to as columns 0 through 79 and rows 0 through 24.

Each screen cell has two associated information bytes. The first byte contains the character being displayed, and the second byte contains the screen attribute for displaying that character. You can determine where a specific character resides in video memory by calculating its offset from the base memory address. The following formula calculates the offset of the character byte for a given screen cell:

CharOfs = (Row * 160) + (Col * 2)

and this is the formula for calculating the attribute byte offset:

AttOfs = CharOfs + 1

or

AttOfs = (Row * 160) + (Col * 2) + 1

Table 7.2 shows some examples of the application of these formulas. Note that the addresses are contiguous; that is, they follow the order of cell character attribute, cell screen attribute, next cell character attribute, and so on.

Getting Addresses of Specific Screen Locations

The procedure GetOffset, shown as Tool 7.2, uses the formulas presented above to return the base screen address and the offsets for the character and attribute at a specific location. You specify this location in typical Turbo Pascal format.

The procedure uses the same Col and Row parameters as those in a GotoXY(Col,Row) statement, and decrements each position by one

Table 7.2:

Offsets to Base Address for Various Screen Cells

Turbo Cursor Position	DOS Cursor Position	Offset for Character	Offset for Attribute	Formula for Character Offset
1, 1	0, 0	0	1	$(0\star160)+(0\star2)$
2, 1	1, 0	2	3	$(0\star160)+(1\star2)$
3, 1	2, 0	4	5	$(0\star160)+(2\star2)$
79, 1	78, 0	156	157	$(0\star160)+(78\star2)$
80, 1	79, 0	158	159	$(0\star160)+(79\star2)$
1, 2	0, 1	160	161	$(1\star160)+(0\star2)$
2, 2	1, 1	162	163	$(1\star160)+(1\star2)$
80, 2	79, 1	318	319	$(1\star160)+(79\star2)$
1, 3	0, 2	320	321	$(2\star160)+(0\star2)$
80,24	79,23	3838	3839	$(23\star160)+(79\star2)$
1,25	0,24	3840	3841	$(24\star160)+(0\star2)$
80,25	79,24	3998	3999	$(24\star160)+(79\star2)$

```
PROCEDURE GetOffset(Col,Row :Integer;
                 VAR BaseAddress :Word;                          Var
CharacterOffset,
                    AttributeOffset:Integer);

    {To use this procedure with versions of Turbo Pascal prior
to 4.0, change the type declaration of BaseAddress from Word to
Integer.}

    BEGIN {get offsets}
        IF ((Mem[0000:1040] AND 48)<>48) THEN
            BaseAddress:=$B800
                ELSE BaseAddress:=$B000;
        CharacterOffset:=((Row-1)*160)+((Col-1)*2);
        AttributeOffset:=CharacterOffset+1;
    END;  {get offsets}
```

Tool 7.2: Procedure GetOffset to get the address of specific screen locations.

(Col:=Col−1; Row:=Row−1) so that it will return the proper video-memory offsets. It computes the character offset, then sets the attribute byte offset to the character offset +1 (because the attribute byte immediately follows the corresponding character byte).

Here's how the GetOffset procedure works:

- Check memory to determine the base video RAM address.
- Compute the offset to the base address of the character byte for the screen cell specified by the parameters Col and Row. Because Col and Row are passed as Turbo Pascal screen positions, decrement the value of each by 1 during the computation.
- Compute the offset to the base address of the attribute byte by adding 1 to the character byte offset.

INTERPRETING THE BYTES FOR A SCREEN CELL

After you calculate the offsets for a given screen cell, you can read its character and attribute bytes and reset both if you want to change the character's appearance. The menu procedures in Chapter 5 (Tools 5.1 and 5.2) alter the screen attributes in order to move the highlighting each time the user makes a new menu selection by pressing the down or up arrow; the current selection returns to reverse video and the newly selected item goes to normal video solely by changing the associated attribute bytes.

The character byte is, simply, the character number to be displayed (for example, A = 65 and a = 97). The attribute byte is a bit more complex. It's actually a register of 8 bits, with each bit representing the absence or presence of a specific attribute. Table 7.3 shows the various attribute bits in the attribute byte and what each represents when set to 1 (on).

Setting the Character and Attribute Bytes

You can set the character and attribute bytes by simply making an assignment of the desired value to the appropriate memory location.

To set the character byte to a desired character, such as A, you need the base video RAM address, the offset for the location to be set, and the

Table 7.3:

Bit Flags of the Attribute Byte

Bit								Meaning
7	6	5	4	3	2	1	0	
1	_	_	_	_	_	_	_	Blinking foreground character
_	1	_	_	_	_	_	_	Red component of background
_	_	1	_	_	_	_	_	Green component of background
_	_	_	1	_	_	_	_	Blue component of background
_	_	_	_	1	_	_	_	Intensity of foreground
_	_	_	_	_	1	_	_	Red component of foreground
_	_	_	_	_	_	1	_	Green component of foreground
_	_	_	_	_	_	_	1	Blue component of foreground

value to set there. For example, A = Chr(65), so the character byte value would be 65. The following program statement would set and display the character A:

```
Mem[BaseAddress:CharacterOffset]: = 65;
```

You use the same procedure to set the attribute byte, except the address offset is 1 more byte. Prior to setting the attribute byte, however, you must determine what value you should assign to it to have the character displayed with the desired attributes.

To determine the setting for the attribute byte, you could use either of two methods. You could set the individual flags within the byte by using the procedures presented in Chapter 6 for working with bit maps or, probably a great deal more simply, you could use binary arithmetic to determine the attributes desired and assign the resulting number as the value of the attribute byte. In the binary arithmetic method, you calculate the appropriate decimal number by adding the binary values of the bits to be set. Table 7.4 illustrates some example attributes and their calculation.

In the monochrome mode (including color graphics being displayed on a monochrome screen), the blinking and intensity bits are used. Only five

Table 7.4:
Examples of Using Binary Arithmetic to Determine the Attribute Byte

Attribute	Attribute Byte	Decimal Value of Attribute Byte
Normal video/low intensity	00000111	7
Reverse video	01110000	112
Normal video/high intensity	00001111	15
Normal video/low blinking	10000111	135

**PROGRAM LINES TO GET OR SET THE CHARACTER
OR ATTRIBUTE FOR A SCREEN CELL**

Get the value of the character byte for a cell:

CharacterVal: = Mem[ScreenAddress:CharacterOffset]

Get the value of the attribute byte for a cell:

AttributeVal: = Mem[ScreenAddress:AttributeOffset]

Set the value of the character byte for a cell:

Mem[ScreenAddress:CharacterOffset]: = Value

Set the value of the attribute byte for a cell:

Mem[ScreenAddress:AttributeOffset]: = Value

---

foreground and background "color" combinations produce good results:

- Normal white on black (00000111)
- High-intensity white on black (00001111)
- Underline characters—blue foreground, black background (00000001)

- Reverse video—black foreground, white background (01110000)
- Invisible characters—black on black (00000000).

WINDOWING

Turbo Pascal provides the Window procedure to place windows on screen and manipulate the display in each of them. The procedures presented in this section take the process a step further: they allow you to save and restore the present screen while creating the desired window. They also return the cursor to its original position on the screen when the windowing procedure was first called.

The procedures do not check to be certain that sufficient dynamic RAM remains for screen storage. Each screen requires 4 kilobytes of RAM. If there is any possibility that the program's screen storage requirements would exceed the dynamic RAM, you should have your program check RAM first, and then take appropriate action. As long as sufficient RAM exists, you can nest the windowing procedures and create multiple windows. Each time, the screen as it existed immediately prior to calling the procedure will be saved and later restored.

SAVING THE CURRENT SCREEN AND CREATING A WINDOW

Procedure WindowIn, shown as Tool 7.3, saves the present screen to memory by allocating dynamic RAM and moving the entire present screen image to it, and then creates the desired window and clears it.

When the WindowIn procedure is called, it first marks the top of the memory heap and will pass this pointer back to the host program through the parameter DataPtr, which must be of type Pointr. You must have globally declared this type in the host program as

    TYPE Pointr = ^ Integer;

The procedure next determines the current cursor position and passes this information back to the calling program through the integer parameters CursorCol and CursorRow. It allocates dynamic RAM and stores the current screen in RAM. Finally, it creates and clears a window with the

```
PROCEDURE WindowIn(TopL,TopRow,BotR,BotRow:Integer;
                   VAR CursorCol, CursorRow:Integer;
                   VAR DataPtr:Pointr);

    TYPE
          ScrnArray = ARRAY[0..3999] OF Byte;
          ScreenPtr = ^ScrnArray;

    VAR

    {To use this procedure with versions of Turbo Pascal prior
 to 4.0, change the type declaration of ScreenAddress from Word to
 Integer.}
          ScreenAddress           :Word;
          ScrnPtr                 :ScreenPtr;

    BEGIN {window in}
          IF (Mem[0000:1040] AND 48) <> 48 THEN
               ScreenAddress:=$B800
                    ELSE ScreenAddress:=$B000;
          Mark(DataPtr);
          New(ScrnPtr);
          CursorCol:=WhereX;
          CursorRow:=WhereY;
          Move(Mem[ScreenAddress:0000],ScrnPtr^,4000);
          Window(TopL,TopRow,BotR,BotRow);
          ClrScr;
    END;   {window in}
```

Tool 7.3: Procedure WindowIn to save the current screen and create a window.

following coordinates (all of which are integer parameters):

- TopL, the column of the top-left corner of the window
- TopRow, the top row of the window
- BotR, the column of the bottom-right corner of the window
- BotRow, the bottom row of the window

These are the same coordinates that would be used with the Turbo Pascal Window statement.

> **NOTE:** When using WindowIn (or ExWindow) and Window-Out, these two procedures should form the outer shell of anything which transpires between calling them. The WindowIn procedure allocates dynamic memory to store the present screen; the WindowOut procedure releases this memory after restoring the present screen. If any other portions of the programming between WindowIn and WindowOut have made use of dynamic memory, the data stored there may be lost when

WindowOut releases the dynamic memory allocated for the screen stored by WindowIn (or ExWindow).

Here's how the WindowIn procedure works:

- Determine the base address of video RAM.
- Mark the beginning of RAM available for allocation to be passed to the WindowOut procedure through the host program. (This is the beginning of the area which will be used to store the existing screen.)
- Allocate space for storage of the current screen.
- Note the present cursor position to be passed to the host program and, eventually, to the WindowOut procedure.
- Duplicate the present video RAM in the allocated dynamic RAM area, so that the screen may be restored later.
- Create and clear the desired window.

CREATING EXPLODING WINDOWS

The ExWindow procedure, presented as Tool 7.4, takes the WindowIn procedure a step further by adding a glitzy twist. Instead of simply clearing the

```
PROCEDURE ExWindow(TopL,TopRow,BotR,BotRow :Integer;
                   VAR CursorCol, CursorRow:Integer;
                   VAR DataPtr:Pointr);

    TYPE
        ScrnArray = ARRAY[0..3999] OF Byte;
        ScreenPtr = ^ScrnArray;

    VAR

    {To use this procedure with versions of Turbo Pascal prior
to 4.0, change the type declaration of ScrAddr from Word to
Integer.}
        ScrAddr                                  :Word;
        Row, Col, CharacterOffset, Rings,
            Positions, CRow, CCol, TopRows, Counter,
            BotRows, LftCols, RtCols, Freq, StartPos,
            LoopCount, PresPosition, Count1         :Integer;
        ScrnPtr                                  :ScreenPtr;
```

Tool 7.4: Procedure ExWindow to create "exploding" windows.

```
BEGIN {exploding window}
    IF (Mem[0000:1040] AND 48) <> 48 THEN
        ScrAddr:=$B800
            ELSE ScrAddr:=$B000;
    Mark(DataPtr);
    New(ScrnPtr);
    CursorCol:=WhereX;
    CursorRow:=WhereY;
    Move(Mem[ScrAddr:0000],ScrnPtr^,4000);
    Window(TopL,TopRow,BotR,BotRow);
    {the 'window-in' has been handled above}
    {now, instead of a simple clear, "explode" the window}
    Freq:=500; {initialize sound frequency}
    {get center of active window}
    CRow:=(BotRow-TopRow) DIV 2;
    CCol:=(BotR-TopL) DIV 2;
    TopRows:=CRow;
    BotRows:=BotRow-CRow-TopRow;
    LftCols:=CCol;
    RtCols:=BotR-CCol-TopL;
    Rings:=TopRows;
    IF BotRows>Rings THEN Rings:=BotRows;
    IF LftCols>Rings THEN Rings:=LftCols;
    IF RtCols>Rings THEN Rings:=RtCols;
    CRow:=CRow+TopRow;
    CCol:=CCol+TopL;
    CharacterOffset:=( ((CRow-1)*160) + ((CCol-1)*2) );
    {clear the center position}
    Mem[ScrAddr:CharacterOffset]:=32;
    Mem[ScrAddr:CharacterOffset+1]:=7;
    Positions:=1;
    FOR LoopCount:=1 TO Rings DO
        BEGIN {for loopcount}
            Freq:=Freq+(10*LoopCount);
            Sound(Freq);
            Positions:=Positions+2;
            StartPos:=CharacterOffset; {center}
            IF (LoopCount<=TopRows) THEN
                BEGIN {top row}
                    IF (LftCols+RtCols>=Positions) THEN
                        Counter:=Positions
                        ELSE Counter:=LftCols+RtCols+1;
                    PresPosition:=StartPos-
                            (LoopCount*160);
                    IF LoopCount<=LftCols THEN
                        PresPosition:=PresPosition-
                            (LoopCount*2)
                        ELSE PresPosition:=PresPosition-
                            (LftCols*2);
                    FOR Count1:=1 TO Counter DO
                        BEGIN {count1}
                            Mem[ScrAddr:PresPosition]:=32;
                            Mem[ScrAddr:PresPosition+1]:=7;
                            PresPosition:=PresPosition+2;
                        END;  {count1}
                END;  {top row}
            IF (LoopCount<=LftCols) THEN
                BEGIN {left side}
                    IF (TopRows+BotRows+1>=Positions-2) THEN
                        Counter:=Positions-2
                        ELSE Counter:=TopRows+BotRows+1;
                    PresPosition:=StartPos-(LoopCount*2);
```

Tool 7.4: Procedure ExWindow to create "exploding" windows. (continued)

```
                              IF LoopCount<=TopRows THEN
                                 PresPosition:=PresPosition-
                                           (LoopCount*160)+160
                                 ELSE PresPosition:=PresPosition-
                                              (TopRows*160);
                           FOR Count1:=1 TO Counter DO
                              BEGIN {count1}
                                  Mem[ScrAddr:PresPosition]:=32;
                                  Mem[ScrAddr:PresPosition+1]:=7;
                                  PresPosition:=PresPosition+160;
                              END;  {count1}
                        END;  {left side}
                 IF (LoopCount<=RtCols) THEN
                    BEGIN {right side}
                        IF (TopRows+BotRows+1>=Positions-2) THEN
                           Counter:=Positions-2
                               ELSE Counter:=TopRows+BotRows+1;
                        PresPosition:=StartPos+(LoopCount*2);
                     IF LoopCount<=TopRows THEN
                        PresPosition:=PresPosition-
                                     (LoopCount*160)+160
                        ELSE PresPosition:=PresPosition-
                                      (TopRows*160);
                     FOR Count1:=1 TO Counter DO
                        BEGIN {count1}
                            Mem[ScrAddr:PresPosition]:=32;
                            Mem[ScrAddr:PresPosition+1]:=7;
                            PresPosition:=PresPosition+160;
                        END;  {count1}
                     END;  {right side}
                 IF (LoopCount<=BotRows) THEN
                    BEGIN {bottom row}
                        IF (LftCols+RtCols>=Positions) THEN
                           Counter:=Positions
                           ELSE Counter:=LftCols+RtCols+1;
                        PresPosition:=StartPos+(LoopCount*160);
                        IF LoopCount<=LftCols THEN
                           PresPosition:=PresPosition-
                                       (LoopCount*2)
                           ELSE PresPosition:=PresPosition-
                                       (LftCols*2);
                        FOR Count1:=1 TO Counter DO
                           BEGIN {count1}
                               Mem[ScrAddr:PresPosition]:=32;
                               Mem[ScrAddr:PresPosition+1]:=7;
                               PresPosition:=PresPosition+2;
                           END;  {count1}
                     END;  {bottom row}
                  Delay(7);
                  NoSound;
               END;  {for loopcount}
   END;   {exploding window}
```

Tool 7.4: Procedure ExWindow to create "exploding" windows.

created window, the window is cleared in concentric circles from the center. This windowing display is accompanied by a sound effect. The result gives the impression of the window literally exploding onto the screen.

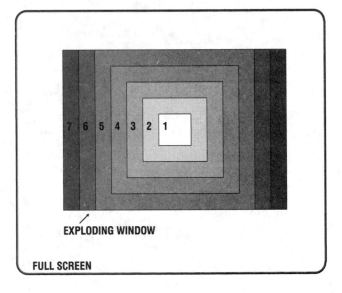

PROGRESSION OF SCREEN CLEARING FOR EXPLODING WINDOW

The exploding window starts with the centermost cell first, progresses to the 8 cells surrounding the centermost cell, the 16 cells surrounding the cells just cleared, and so on until the entire window is cleared. This progression is illustrated below, with the numbers representing the order of cell clearance.

The ExWindow procedure operates in the same manner as WindowIn, with the exception of the method of clearing the window. Where WindowIn uses the Turbo Pascal ClrScr command, ExWindow moves to each screen cell and sets the character to a space and the attribute to normal video. Even with this rather involved process, the screen would still clear too rapidly to be visually appreciated, so a slight time delay is used along with the sound effect; together, they make an impact.

The ExWindow procedure duplicates functions of the WindowIn procedure, except for clearing the screen. At this point, the real ExWindow operations begin:

- Set the initial frequency for the sound accompanying the exploding window. (You may want to change the frequency to produce a different sound.)

- Determine the center cell of the window created, as well as the number of rows and columns above, below, left, and right of center; the number of "rings" to be made around the center cell (the largest of the left, right, top or bottom columns or rows); and the character offset for the center cell; then clear the center cell (normal video attribute, space as character).

- Begin a loop that will continue for as many times as necessary to complete the rings of cells to be cleared around the center cell; gradually increase the frequency at each pass through the loop.

- Give the Sound command to start the sound.

- Set the number of positions to be covered by this pass through the loop. This number gradually increases as the area of the screen being cleared progresses away from the center.

- Set StartPos (the starting position) to the center cell offset.

- If there are still rows above the center cell to be cleared, determine the width of area to be cleared this time, compute PresPosition (the position at which clearing will begin) from StartPos, and initiate a loop to clear the appropriate number of cells during this pass. Clear a cell, and then increment the position to the next position.

- If there are still rows left of, right of, or below the center cell to be cleared, continue the clearing process.

- Issue a slight delay to make certain that the window "explodes" slowly enough to be visual.

- Shut off the sound so that it may be started again at the next repeat loop at a higher frequency or, if the screen clearing is completed, so it will be off as the procedure ends.

- End the loop (and the procedure) when the screen area is cleared.

RESTORING THE ORIGINAL SCREEN

After all operations are completed with the window created by the WindowIn or ExWindow procedure, you can restore the previous screen by calling the WindowOut procedure, shown as Tool 7.5.

When WindowOut is called, it uses the parameter DataPtr (as returned by WindowIn or ExWindow) to find the original screen stored by the windowing procedure. The procedure removes the window that has been in place, and the new window becomes the full screen. The full screen, as it was prior to calling WindowIn or ExWindow, is restored, and the cursor is repositioned to its former position using the parameters CursorCol and CursorRow returned by WindowIn or ExWindow. Finally, the dynamic memory allocated by WindowIn or ExWindow is released.

In order for WindowOut to work correctly, the parameters returned by WindowIn or ExWindow (CursorCol, CursorRow, and DataPtr) must be used as the parameters for calling WindowOut and must have the same values as those returned by either windowing procedure. CursorCol and CursorRow are integers. DataPtr must be of type Pointr, which must have been globally declared in the host program as

TYPE Pointr = ^ Integer

```
PROCEDURE WindowOut(CursorCol,
                    CursorRow:Integer;
                    DataPtr:Pointr);

    VAR

    {To use this procedure with versions of Turbo Pascal prior
to 4.0, change the type declaration of ScreenAddress from Word to
Integer.}
        ScreenAddress      :Word;

    BEGIN {window out}
        IF (Mem[0000:1040] AND 48) <> 48 THEN
            ScreenAddress:=$B800
                ELSE ScreenAddress:=$B000;
        Move(DataPtr^,Mem[ScreenAddress:0000],4000);
        Release(DataPtr);
        Window(1,1,80,25);
        GotoXY(CursorCol,CursorRow);
    END;   {window out}
```

Tool 7.5: Procedure WindowOut to restore the original screen.

Here's how the WindowOut procedure works:

- Determine the base address of video RAM.
- Move the screen to be restored from the memory location where it was stored by WindowIn to video RAM, thus restoring the previous screen.
- Release the memory allocated for storage of the previous screen.
- Make the full screen the active window.
- Position the cursor as it was prior to the invocation of the WindowIn or ExWindow procedure.

When a screen is restored by WindowOut, it will appear exactly as it was prior to calling WindowIn or ExWindow, and the cursor will be restored to its position at that time. However, these procedures have no way of determining what the active window was at the time WindowIn or ExWindow was originally called; it is assumed to be the full screen. If a window was in effect at that time (for example, if nested calls to these procedures are made), it will be necessary to restore that active window after the screen is restored. The window can be reactivated by using the standard Turbo Pascal Window statement.

FRAMING A WINDOW

When creating a window on the screen, a simple frame is an effective method of marking its borders. The procedure Frame, shown as Tool 7.6, is handy for placing a frame at any position on the screen. The frame has as its coordinates TopLeftCol (the column of the top-left corner), TopRow (the top row), BottomRightCol (the column of the bottom-right corner), and BottomRow (the bottom row). The frame will be created in low-intensity video (as opposed to the brighter, high-intensity video) and will be drawn as a simple box with the double-line characters. TopLeftCol, TopRow, BottomRightCol, and BottomRow are all integers.

If you use this procedure immediately after creating a window in order to frame it, recall that the top-left corner of the newly created window is now position 1,1, not the position at which it was created.

```
PROCEDURE Frame(TopLeftCol, TopLeftRow,
                BotRightCol, BotRightRow:Integer);

    CONST
        {Declared constants for frame}
        TL = #201;   TR = #187;     {Top left and right    }
        BL = #200;   BR = #188;     {Bottom left and right }
        H =  #205;   V =  #186;     {horizontal and vertical}

    VAR
        X :Integer;

    BEGIN {frame }
        LowVideo;
        GotoXY(TopLeftCol,TopLeftRow);
        Write(TL);
        GotoXY(BotRightCol,TopLeftRow);
        Write(TR);
        GotoXY(TopLeftCol,BotRightRow);
        Write(BL);
        GotoXY(BotRightCol,BotRightRow);
        Write(BR);
        FOR X:=TopLeftRow+1 TO BotRightRow-1 DO
            BEGIN
                GotoXY(TopLeftCol,X);
                Write(V);
                GotoXY(BotRightCol,X);
                Write(V);
            END;
        FOR X:=TopLeftCol+1 TO BotRightCol-1 DO
            BEGIN
                GotoXY(X,TopLeftRow);
                Write(H);
                GotoXY(X,BotRightRow);
                Write(H);
            END;
        NormVideo;
    END;   {frame }
```

Tool 7.6: Procedure Frame for framing windows.

STEPS FOR CREATING WINDOWS

Windows can often work best if you create them in three basic steps:

1. Create the window two columns wider and two rows longer than is necessary for the display.

2. Frame the window. The frame will occupy the extra two columns and rows, one each top, bottom, left, and right.

3. Display a functional window inside the frame with the Turbo Pascal Window statement.

Here's how the Frame procedure works:

- Declare the ASCII characters for producing the frame as constants.
- Establish low-intensity video.
- Write each of the frame corners to the screen.
- Write the vertical framing characters to the sides of the frame.
- Write the horizontal framing characters to the top and bottom of the frame.
- Reset normal video, assuming this was the setting when the procedure was entered.

TESTING THE WINDOWING PROCEDURES

Test Program 7.1 demonstrates the correct method of using and nesting the WindowIn or ExWindow and WindowOut procedures. This program also demonstrates the use of the Frame procedure with the windows being created.

```
PROGRAM WindowExample;

     {To use this program with Turbo Pascal versions prior to
        4.0, remove the Uses statement below.}

     Uses DOS,CRT;

     TYPE
         Pointr  = ^Integer;
         Str255  = STRING[255];

     VAR
         DtaPtr1, DtaPtr2, DtaPtr3            :Pointr;
         CursCol1, CursCol2, CursCol3,
             CursRow1, CursRow2, CursRow3,
             X, Y                            :Integer;

     {$I WindowIn.Inc}
     {$I WindoOut.Inc}
     {$I ExWindow.Inc}
     {$I Frame.Inc}

     PROCEDURE PressKey;
```

Test Program 7.1: Using Procedures WindowIn, ExWindow, WindowOut, and Frame in a program.

```
          VAR
               Ch  :Char;

          BEGIN
               Write('Press any key to continue...');

          {To use this program with Turbo Pascal versions prior
to 4.0, add the line below:}
                   { Read(KBD,Ch); }
          END;

  BEGIN {window example}
    {program statements}
    ClrScr;
    FOR X:=1 TO 79 DO
      FOR Y:=1 TO 25 DO
        BEGIN
          GotoXY(X,Y); Write('Z');
        END;
    {create 1st window}
    WindowIn(3,3,77,22,CursCol1,CursRow1,DtaPtr1);
        {program statements}
        Frame(1,1,74,20);
        GotoXY(3,4);
        Write('Window 1...');
        GotoXY(1,1);
        PressKey;
        {create 2nd window}
        WindowIn(6,6,71,16,CursCol2,CursRow2,DtaPtr2);
            {program statements}
            Frame(1,1,65,10);
            GotoXY(3,4);
            Write('window 2...');
            GotoXY(1,1);
            PressKey;
            {create 3rd window}
            WindowIn(9,9,68,13,CursCol3,CursRow3,DtaPtr3);
                {program statements}
                Frame(1,1,59,4);
                GotoXY(3,2);
                Write('Window 3...');
                GotoXY(1,1);
                PressKey;
                {finished with 3rd window}
            WindowOut(CursCol3,CursRow3,DtaPtr3);
            {reset active screen window for 2nd WindowIn}
            Window(6,6,71,16);
            {program statements}
            Delay(1500);
            {finished with 2nd window}
        WindowOut(CursCol2,CursRow2,DtaPtr2);
        {reset active screen window for 1st WindowIn}
        Window(3,3,77,22);
        {program statements}
        Delay(1500);
        {finished with 1st window}
    WindowOut(CursCol1,CursRow1,DtaPtr1);
    {program statements}
    Delay(1500);
```

Test Program 7.1: Using Procedures WindowIn, ExWindow, WindowOut, and Frame
in a program. (continued)

```
      ExWindow(3,3,77,22,CursCol1,CursRow1,DtaPtr1);
      Frame(1,1,74,20);
      GotoXY(5,10);
      Write('This is an "exploding window" with a frame.');
      GotoXY(5,12);
      PressKey;
      WindowOut(CursCol1,CursRow1,DtaPtr1);
      Delay(1500);
      ExWindow(5,2,12,24,CursCol1,CursRow1,DtaPtr1);
      Delay(1500);
      WindowOut(CursCol1,CursRow1,DtaPtr1);
      Delay(1500);
      ExWindow(3,8,73,14,CursCol1,CursRow1,DtaPtr1);
      Frame(1,1,70,7);
      Delay(1500);
      WindowOut(CursCol1,CursRow1,DtaPtr1);
      Delay(1500);
      ClrScr;
   END.   {window example}
```

Test Program 7.1: Using Procedures WindowIn, ExWindow, WindowOut, and Frame in a program. (continued)

The program begins by clearing the screen and filling it with the character Z to make the process more visual. Three standard windows are created, one inside another, to illustrate nesting windows.

Each window created has its window number printed within it, along with a message to press any key to continue. Each window created is also framed using the Frame procedure.

After all three windows have been created, the process is reversed; the windows are destroyed and the previous screens restored. A delay is issued between each WindowOut in order to make the process more visible.

Finally, the program creates three exploding windows, two of which are framed. Two remove themselves after a time delay. The program clears the final window and ends.

CHAPTER 8
DESIGNING SCREENS
WITH A SCREEN GENERATOR

A screen generator is a program that gives programmers the capability to quickly and easily build screen designs. A screen generator may be very simple, allowing only text screens to be generated in monochrome; it may use all of the extended ASCII characters for more complex and interesting screen designs; or it may incorporate color and even graphics to produce artistic or very complex screens. This chapter presents procedures for simple to moderately complex designs for screen generators and suggests enhancements for more complex ones.

ADVANTAGES OF USING
A SCREEN GENERATOR

With a screen generator, an existing screen may be quickly and easily modified or a number of similar screens may be produced from a basic design, which is automatically copied and then slightly modified. If a number of people are involved in the design and decision process for a programming effort, many ideas can be portrayed on the screen in a minimal amount of time.

Screen generators also can save a great deal of program code and programming time. You can create a screen with a generator, save the screen information from video RAM into a file, and then have the main program open the file and read the screen information directly to video RAM. It is also possible to have the screen generator build a procedure containing the program code for the screen for inclusion into the program when it is compiled.

In addition to a time and program code savings when creating screens, the actual flow of the program and the file structures may be much more apparent when the screen set is reviewed. Flaws in design may be spotted more quickly, and the coding of other necessary functions of the program may proceed more smoothly.

Another advantage of a screen generator is that after you've constructed a file of screens, they can be used in demonstration programs. The only two things the end user really sees from any program are the screens and printed output; having the ability to show the user what the screens will look like and how the program will work when completed can be a decided edge and can help eliminate troublesome misconceptions, oversights, and misunderstandings. After the program is completed, a series of actual program screens that have been modified to include explanatory material on the processes that involve the user can be a good learning tool for any user.

You could also use a screen generator to create a file of help screens to accompany a program. When help is appropriate, the program could simply store the present screen, read the help screen file, and display the appropriate help screen. When the user signals that he or she is finished with the help screen, your program could redisplay the screen that was saved when help was requested.

THE SCREEN FILE

You can record screens in a file in either of two forms: as captured images or as source code that creates the images. I prefer to record screens by capturing the image from the present screen (that is, from video RAM). When the screen file is read, the screen image is moved directly to video RAM and displayed instantly. If you will be using extended graphics characters or effects such as high- and low-intensity or reverse video, capturing screen images will save you quite a bit of space and time. The alternative is to read the screen, line by line and character by character, and write it to a text file containing the other elements necessary to write a procedure suitable for inclusion in a program.

If you use captured-screen images, you can store several of them in a random-access file. Generally, such files can hold all the screens to be used in a program. However, screens stored as code are much easier to work with when each procedure that reproduces a screen is stored in a separate text file.

GETTING THE NAME OF A SCREEN FILE

The first step in recording screens to a file is obtaining the name of the file that will hold the screen data. The NameFile procedure, shown as Tool 8.1, accomplishes this task.

The NameFile procedure checks the integer parameter IOResult to see if the file name provided by the user already exists. If IOResult has a value other than zero, the file is new; if it is zero, the file exists. The procedure returns the accepted screen file name to the program in the variable string parameter FName.

Here's how the NameFile procedure works:

- Clear the screen and ask the user to supply a file name for the screen about to be generated.

- Attempt to open a file with the name supplied by the user. The IOResult parameter indicates whether such a file already exists. Note that the file type is unimportant at this point; the only relevant issue is whether a file by the name supplied exists.

```
PROCEDURE NameFile(VAR FName:Str255);

    VAR
        OK                      :Boolean;
        ScreenFile              :FILE;
        Result                  :Integer;
        Ch                      :Char;

    BEGIN {name for screen file}
        ClrScr;
        REPEAT {until ok}
            Write('Enter file name for screen to be created: ');
            ReadLn(FName);
            Assign(ScreenFile,FName);
            {$I-} Reset(ScreenFile); {$I+}
            Result:=IOResult;
            IF (Result<>0) THEN
                    BEGIN {new file}
                            Write('This is a new file.  OK? (Y/N) ');
                            REPEAT

        {To use this program with Turbo Pascal versions prior
            to 4.0, add the line below:}
                            { Read(KBD,Ch); }

        {To use this program with Turbo Pascal versions prior
            to 4.0, remove the line below:}
                            Ch:=ReadKey;

                                Ch:=UpCase(Ch);
                            UNTIL (Ch IN['Y','N']);
                            WriteLn(Ch);
                            WriteLn;
                    END;  {new file}
            IF (Result=0) THEN
                    BEGIN {if file already exists}
                            Write(#7,'This file already exists.  ',
                                'Add to this file? (Y/N) ');
                            REPEAT

        {To use this program with Turbo Pascal versions prior
            to 4.0, add the line below:}
                            { Read(KBD,Ch); }



        {To use this program with Turbo Pascal versions prior
            to 4.0, remove the line below:}
                            Ch:=ReadKey;
                            Ch:=UpCase(Ch);
                            UNTIL (Ch IN['Y','N']);
                            WriteLn(Ch);
                            WriteLn;
                    END;  {if file already exists}
            OK:=(Ch='Y');
            {$I-} Close(ScreenFile); {$I+}
            Result:=IOResult;
        UNTIL OK;
    END;  {name for screen file}
```

Tool 8.1: Procedure NameFile to get the name of a screen file.

- If the file name exists, immediately close the file to prevent any possible problems.
- If the file name does not exist, ask the user if he or she wishes to create a new file for this screen.
- If the file name does exist, ask the user if this screen is to be added to the existing file.
- Check IOResult again so it will be clear (in case an attempt was made to open a nonexistent file).
- If the user does not reply positively in either case, ask him or her to supply another file name. End the procedure when a file name has been supplied and accepted.
- Return the accepted file name to the program in the FName parameter.

Recording Screens

As I mentioned at the beginning of this section, screens can be stored in a file of captured images or in a text file of program code. Procedures for both methods are presented here, so you can use whichever one best suits your programming requirements.

Recording Screen Images

Procedure ImageRecord, shown as Tool 8.2, copies the screen image from video RAM to a record and writes the record to a file. The name of the screen file that this screen record is to be written to is passed as a parameter to the procedure. The file name should already be verified through the NameFile (or similar) procedure.

Here's how the ImageRecord procedure works:

- If the data are to be recorded in a new file, begin with a Rewrite statement.
- If the data are going to an existing file, seek the end of file to ensure that the new screen is appended to the file and does not overwrite anything else in the file.

- Determine the base address of video RAM (see Chapter 7 for details).
- Copy the screen image from video RAM to the screen record.
- Write the screen record to file.
- Clear the screen and display the name of the file that the screen was written to and the record number of this particular screen.

Recording Screens as Procedures

Procedure TextRecord, shown as Tool 8.3, records the screen as text and adds the code necessary to form a proper Turbo Pascal procedure. As with the ImageRecord procedure, the name of the screen file that this screen record is to be written to is passed as a parameter to the TextRecord procedure (after the name has been verified by a procedure such as NameFile).

```
PROCEDURE ImageRecord(FName:Str255);

    TYPE
        ScreenRec = RECORD
            ScreenArray :ARRAY[0..3999] OF Byte;
        END;

    VAR
        Screen                :ScreenRec;
        ScreenFile            :FILE OF ScreenRec;

    {To use this procedure with versions of Turbo Pascal
     prior to 4.0, change the type declaration of
     ScrAddr from Word to Integer.}

        ScrAddr               :Word;

    BEGIN {write record of screen image to file}
        Assign(ScreenFile,FName);
        {$I-} Reset(ScreenFile); {$I+}
        IF NOT (IOResult=0) THEN Rewrite( ScreenFile);
        Seek(ScreenFile,FileSize(ScreenFile));
        IF ((Mem[0000:1040] AND 48) <> 48) THEN
            ScrAddr:=$B800
                ELSE ScrAddr:=$B000;
        Move(Mem[ScrAddr:0000],Screen,4000);
        Write(ScreenFile,Screen);
        ClrScr;
        WriteLn('Screen image written to file: ',FName);
        WriteLn;
        WriteLn('This screen is record number ',
                FileSize(ScreenFile)-1);
        Close(ScreenFile);
    END;   {write record of screen image to file}
```

Tool 8.2: Procedure ImageRecord to record a screen image and write it to a file.

```
PROCEDURE TextRecord(FName:Str255);

      VAR
           ScreenFile                      :Text;
           X, Y, Row, Col, Cols            :Integer;

      {To use this procedure with versions of Turbo Pascal
       prior to 4.0, change the type declaration of
       ScrAddr from Word to Integer.}

           ScrAddr                         :Word;

           ProcedureName                   :STRING[65];
           Ch                              :Char;

      BEGIN {write a procedure which will reproduce the screen}
           IF ((Mem[0000:1040] AND 48) <> 48) THEN
                 ScrAddr:=$B800
                       ELSE ScrAddr:=$B000;
           Assign(ScreenFile,FName);
           Rewrite(ScreenFile);
           ProcedureName:=Copy(FName,1,Length(FName)-4);
           WHILE (Length(ProcedureName)>8) DO
                 Delete(ProcedureName,1,1);
           WHILE (Pos('\',ProcedureName)>0) DO
                 Delete(ProcedureName,1,1);
           WHILE (Pos(':',ProcedureName)>0) DO
                 Delete(ProcedureName,1,1);
           WriteLn(ScreenFile,'PROCEDURE ',ProcedureName,';');
           WriteLn(ScreenFile);
           WriteLn(ScreenFile,'     BEGIN {procedure}');
           WriteLn(ScreenFile);
           WriteLn(ScreenFile,' ':10,'ClrScr;');
           FOR Y:=1 TO 25 DO
                 BEGIN {for y}
                       Write(ScreenFile,' ':10,'Write(',#39);
                       Row:=((Y-1) * 160);
                       IF Y<25 THEN Cols:=80 ELSE Cols:=79;
                       FOR X:=1 TO Cols DO
                             BEGIN {for x}
                                   Col:=((X-1) * 2);
                                   Ch:=Chr(Mem[ScrAddr:Row+Col]);
                                   IF (Ch=#39) THEN
                                         Write(ScreenFile,#39,',#39,'#39)
                                               ELSE Write(ScreenFile,Ch);
                             END;   {for x}
                       WriteLn(ScreenFile,#39,');');
                 END;   {for y}
           WriteLn(ScreenFile);
           WriteLn(ScreenFile,'     END; {procedure}');
           Close(ScreenFile);
           ClrScr;
           WriteLn('Procedure written to file: ',FName);
      END;   {write a procedure which will reproduce the screen}
```

Tool 8.3: Procedure TextRecord to record a screen as a procedure and write it to a text file.

Here's how the TextRecord procedure works:

- Determine the base address of video RAM.

- Assign the file name and issue a Rewrite statement to begin the file fresh; overwrite any existing file with this name.

- Give the procedure to be written the same name as the file. Strip the file name of the extension (the last four characters, which are assumed to be .EXT, the file name extension) and any leading characters that are part of a drive name or path (indicated by the presence of a colon or backslash within the file name).

- Write the procedure heading and name, a blank line, and then BEGIN, which initiates the procedure statement.

- Write a ClrScr statement to the procedure.

- Initiate a loop for each of the 25 screen lines.

- Begin each of the next 25 statements in the procedure with the Write statement, followed by the left parenthesis and a single quotation mark. This denotes the beginning of the literal that is to be written to the screen. Indent the Write statement for clarity.

- Initiate a loop to read each of the columns in this particular screen row.

NOTE: For rows 1 through 24, there are 80 columns read; for row 25 only 79 columns are read. If the eightieth column of row 25 was read, writing the 80 columns of row 25 would cause the screen to scroll, and row 1 would be lost. A procedure that allows writing to the eightieth character of line 25 without losing the top screen line is presented later in this chapter.

- Calculate the video RAM offset of each character from the base video RAM address.

- Read a character from the screen (video RAM) and write it to the procedure (text file) for each column position in the row being operated upon. If the screen contains a single quotation mark (ASCII #39), handle it differently (to allow the procedure to operate correctly—a literal single quotation mark cannot be used in a Turbo Pascal line).

- When all columnar positions in a given row have been read and written to the procedure, add the closing single quotation (ASCII #39), the right parenthesis, and a semicolon to complete the Write statement.
- When all 25 lines have been handled, write the END for the procedure to the text file and close the file.
- Clear the screen and notify the user that the procedure has been written to the named file.

BASIC SCREEN GENERATOR DESIGN

The most basic design for a screen generator gives it the ability to request a file name for the screen to be recorded, give the user a blank screen, accept keystrokes and display them on the screen and, finally, at a signal from the user, save the screen created into a file for future use.

A SIMPLE SCREEN GENERATOR

Test Program 8.1 is a simple screen-generator program. The program demonstrates the use of the NameFile, ImageRecord, and TextRecord procedures (Tools 8.1 through 8.3). It is a very basic and rudimentary generator, with the following limitations:

- It accepts standard characters only.
- It ends when the seventy-ninth character on the twenty-fifth line is input or when the Escape key is pressed.
- Backspacing will operate only on the current line (the user cannot backspace to a previous line).

When using this program, pressing Enter (ASCII #13) will take you to the beginning of the current line. Pressing Ctrl-Enter will generate ASCII #10 and move the cursor to the next line.

The program user first determines whether the screen will be captured to an image file or recorded as source code for a procedure in a text file.

```
Program SimpleScreenGen1;

      {To use this program with Turbo Pascal versions prior to
         4.0, remove the Uses statement below.}

      Uses DOS,CRT;

      {$V-}   {relaxed parameter type checking}

      TYPE
          Str255 = STRING[255];

      VAR
          FName                 :STRING[65];
          Ch, Ans               :Char;
          Escape                :Boolean;


      {$I NameFile.Inc}
      {$I ImageRec.Inc}
      {$I TextRec.Inc}

      BEGIN {simple screen generator program 1}
          ClrScr;
          WriteLn('From the screen generated, I wish to produce:');
          WriteLn('A.  A capture of the screen image.');
          WriteLn('B.  A text file with a procedure to ',
                   'produce a screen like mine.');
          WriteLn;
          Write('CHOICE:  (A/B) ');
          REPEAT

          {To use this program with Turbo Pascal versions prior
             to 4.0, add the line below:}
              {Read(KBD,Ans); }
          {To use this program with Turbo Pascal versions prior
             to 4.0, remove the line below:}
              Ans:=ReadKey;
              Ans:=UpCase(Ans);
          UNTIL (Ans IN['A','B']);
          WriteLn(Ans);
          WriteLn;
          NameFile(FName);
          ClrScr;
          Escape:=False;
          WHILE ( ((Escape=False) AND (WhereY<25)) OR
            ((Escape=False) AND (WhereY=25) AND (WhereX<80)) ) DO
                BEGIN {while}
          {To use this program with Turbo Pascal versions prior
             to 4.0, add the line below:}
                  { Read(KBD,Ch); }

          {To use this program with Turbo Pascal versions prior
             to 4.0, remove the line below:}
                  Ch:=ReadKey;

                  IF (Ch IN[#8,#10,#13,#32..#127]) THEN Write(Ch)
                      ELSE Escape:=((Ch=#27) AND
                                     (KeyPressed=False));
              END;  {while}
          IF (Ans='A') THEN ImageRecord(FName)
              ELSE TextRecord(FName);
      END.  {simple screen generator program 1}
```

Test Program 8.1: A simple screen-generator program.

After the program calls the NameFile procedure to get the file name, it calls either the ImageRecord or TextRecord procedure to record the screen to a file.

> **NOTE:** If you issue a line feed (press Ctrl-Enter) from line 25 while using the simple screen-generator program, the top line will scroll off the screen.

REDISPLAYING SCREENS

After you have designed a screen and saved it, you will need to recall it. Screens recorded as procedures in text files can be redisplayed by simply using an include directive referencing that file and calling the procedure. Files of captured images must be read and transferred to video RAM for display.

REDISPLAYING CAPTURED-IMAGE SCREENS

The ShowScrn procedure, shown as Tool 8.4, uses the same file and record format to reproduce screens as the ImageRecord procedure used to originally capture them.

The procedure requires two parameters be passed to it: ScrnFileName to indicate the file name for the screen file to be opened, and ScrnNo to indicate the record number of the screen to be displayed. Given this information, the ShowScrn procedure opens the file, reads the appropriate record, and then transfers the data directly to video RAM to instantly reproduce the screen.

Here's how the ShowScrn procedure works:

- Attempt to open the file named in the parameter ScrnFileName.
- If the file is not found, display a message and halt the program.
- Read the screen record number in the parameter ScrnNo.
- Determine the video RAM base address.
- Move the screen image read from the file (in the variable Screen) to video RAM and display it on the screen.

```
PROCEDURE ShowScrn(ScrnFileName:Str255; ScrnNo:Integer);

    TYPE
        ScreenRec = RECORD
                ScreenArray :ARRAY[0..3999] OF Byte;
        END;

    VAR
        Screen                  :ScreenRec;
        ScreenFile              :FILE OF ScreenRec;

    {To use this procedure with versions of Turbo Pascal
        prior to 4.0, change the type declaration of
        ScrAddr from Word to Integer.}

        ScrAddr                 :Word;

    BEGIN {display captured screen}
        Assign(ScreenFile,ScrnFileName);
        {$I-} Reset(ScreenFile); {$I+}
        IF (IOResult<>0) THEN
            BEGIN {file not found}
                WriteLn(#7,'>> SCREEN FILE NOT FOUND <<');
                Halt;
            END;   {file not found}
        Seek(ScreenFile,ScrnNo);
        Read(ScreenFile,Screen);
        IF ((Mem[0000:1040] AND 48) <> 48) THEN
            ScrAddr:=$B800
                ELSE ScrAddr:=$B000;
        Move(Screen,Mem[ScrAddr:0000],4000);
    END;   {display captured screen}
```

Tool 8.4: Procedure ShowScrn to redisplay screens in a file of captured images.

TESTING THE REDISPLAY OF SCREENS

Test Program 8.2 demonstrates the use of the ShowScrn procedure to display captured-image screens, as well as the use of the procedure written to a text file by the TextRecord procedure (Tool 8.3) to display text file screens.

> **NOTE:** For demonstrating the redisplay of a screen recorded in a text file, the test program assumes that an include file named TestScrn.Inc was created with the TextRecord procedure. If you have a screen file with another name, use that name instead of TestScrn for the included procedure ({$I *Procedure*.Inc.}).

The program begins by asking the user which type of screen display is to take place so that the proper procedure may be called. If the screen display is to be reproduced by the procedure created with TextRecord, procedure TestScrn is called.

```pascal
PROGRAM DemoScreenDisplay;

     {To use this program with Turbo Pascal versions prior to
         4.0, remove the Uses statement below.}

     Uses DOS,CRT;

     TYPE
         Str255 = STRING[255];

     VAR
         Ch          :Char;
         FName       :STRING[65];
         RecNum      :Integer;

     {-----------------------------------------------------------}
     { This program displays a screen produced with the          }
     { ImageRecord procedure by using the ShowScrn procedure.    }
     {-----------------------------------------------------------}

     {$I ShowScrn.Inc}

     {-----------------------------------------------------------}
     { This program is also intended to demonstrate a screen     }
     { produced by the procedure written by the TextRecord       }
     { procedure in Tool 8.3.  Therefore, the procedure          }
     { created to produce a screen must be included in this      }
     { program.  The test program will assume that the file      }
     { created with TextRecord was named TestScrn.Inc and        }
     { the procedure created was named TestScrn.                 }
     {-----------------------------------------------------------}

     {$I TestScrn.Inc}

     BEGIN {program}
         ClrScr;
         WriteLn('Reproduce screen created by:');
         Write('  <T>extRecord  <I>mageRecord  (T/I) ');
         REPEAT

         {To use this program with Turbo Pascal versions prior
             to 4.0, add the line below:}
             { Read(KBD,Ch); }

         {To use this program with Turbo Pascal versions prior
             to 4.0, remove the line below:}
             Ch:=ReadKey;
             Ch:=UpCase(Ch);
         UNTIL (Ch IN['T','I']);
         WriteLn(Ch);
         IF (Ch='T') THEN TestScrn
             ELSE
                 BEGIN
                     Write('Screen file name: ');
                     ReadLn(FName);
                     Write('Screen number: ');
                     ReadLn(RecNum);
                     ShowScrn(FName,RecNum);
                 END;
         Delay(2500);
     END.  {program}
```

Test Program 8.2: Using procedures ShowScrn and TextRecord in a program.

If the screen display is to be reproduced from a file of screens created by the ImageRecord procedure, the user is asked to supply the screen file name and the screen number (that is, record number) for the display. The ShowScrn procedure is called, and the parameters just supplied by the user (for the file name and record number) are passed to it.

ADDING ENHANCEMENTS TO THE SIMPLE SCREEN GENERATOR

The simple screen-generator program presented earlier can save you time in creating screens for your programs. However, there is a lot of room for improvement in this rudimentary generator. For example, you could design a screen generator that accepts Ctrl-key combinations, uses extended graphics codes, and reproduces some screen effects. The actual enhancements that you make depend on the particular program that will use the generated screens. This section suggests some enhancements that you may find useful.

USING CURSOR-MOVEMENT KEYS AND OTHER SPECIAL KEYSTROKES

You may want to design a keyboard input procedure that will allow the cursor keys and certain other key combinations to be used with your screen-generator program. The obvious advantage is that the cursor-movement keys will facilitate movement around the screen. Accepting and interpreting special keystrokes, such as Ctrl-key combinations, can be even more useful.

> **NOTE:** Allowing interpretation of the cursor keys and other selected key combinations can facilitate broad and easy movement around the screen being generated; however, all cursor movement should be handled directly by the program or by the procedure interpreting the keystrokes to ensure proper cursor placement. This involves writing directly to video RAM rather than using the Turbo Pascal Write statement (because the Write statement also moves the cursor), which we'll discuss later in this section.

A great array of options can be made available to your screen generator through a *translation table*, which translates the return code of special keystrokes. (In fact, a program may have several translation tables which operate under different conditions.) A translation table, when presented with the return code from the special key or key combination, can establish certain characteristics within the program itself or cause different characters to be printed than those actually on the keys pressed. For example, pressing Ctrl-R will generate the keyboard return code 18. The screen-generator program could use this as an on/off switch for reverse video. Each time the program receives the return code 18, the attribute byte would have the characteristics reversed for foreground and background to produce reverse video or, if reverse video was active, to produce normal video. For another example, pressing Ctrl-A might activate a translation table that will produce an alternate character set. We'll expand on the idea of using the attribute byte to produce interesting screen effects later in the chapter, when we discuss writing directly to video RAM. You'll also see an example of a translation table (in Tool 8.8).

LIMITED GRAPHICS

A number of the standard ASCII character codes and the extended graphics codes available on the IBM PC and compatible computers are quite useful in designing screens. The characters 185, 186, 187, 188, 200, 201, 202, 203, 204, 205, and 206, for example, can be used together to construct box figures on the screen with double-line characters. The characters 179, 180, 191, 192, 193, 194, 195, 196, 197, 217, and 218 form a box from single-line characters. You can use lines and boxes produced by these characters to offset screen areas, and even to create pictures. Table 8.1 lists the ASCII and extended graphics codes.

WRITING DIRECTLY TO VIDEO RAM

The simple screen generator in Test Program 8.1 uses the Turbo Pascal Write statement to place characters on the screen. With this statement, it is impossible to write the eightieth character of the twenty-fifth line without

Table 8.1:
ASCII and Extended Graphics Codes

ASCII Value	Character	Control Character	ASCII Value	Character
000	(null)	NUL	032	(space)
001	☺	SOH	033	!
002	●	STX	034	"
003	♥	ETX	035	#
004	♦	EOT	036	$
005	♣	ENQ	037	%
006	♠	ACK	038	&
007	(beep)	BEL	039	'
008	▪	BS	040	(
009	(tab)	HT	041	)
010	(line feed)	LF	042	★
011	(home)	VT	043	+
012	(form feed)	FF	044	,
013	(carriage return)	CR	045	-
014	♫	SO	046	.
015	☼	SI	047	/
016	►	DLE	048	0
017	◄	DC1	049	1
018	↕	DC2	050	2
019	‼	DC3	051	3
020	¶	DC4	052	4
021	§	NAK	053	5
022	▬	SYN	054	6
023	↨	ETB	055	7
024	↑	CAN	056	8
025	↓	EM	057	9
026	→	SUB	058	:
027	←	ESC	059	;
028	(cursor right)	FS	060	<
029	(cursor left)	GS	061	=
030	(cursor up)	RS	062	>
031	(cursor down)	US	063	?

Table 8.1:

ASCII and Extended Graphics Codes (continued)

ASCII Value	Character	ASCII Value	Character
064	@	096	
065	A	097	a
066	B	098	b
067	C	099	c
068	D	100	d
069	E	101	e
070	F	102	f
071	G	103	g
072	H	104	h
073	I	105	i
074	J	106	j
075	K	107	k
076	L	108	l
077	M	109	m
078	N	110	n
079	O	111	o
080	P	112	p
081	Q	113	q
082	R	114	r
083	S	115	s
084	T	116	t
085	U	117	u
086	V	118	v
087	W	119	w
088	X	120	x
089	Y	121	y
090	Z	122	z
091	[	123	{
092	\	124		
093	]	125	}
094	^	126	~
095	–	127	⌂

Table 8.1:
ASCII and Extended Graphics Codes (continued)

ASCII Value	Character	ASCII Value	Character
128	Ç	160	á
129	ü	161	í
130	é	162	ó
131	â	163	ú
132	ä	164	ñ
133	à	165	Ñ
134	å	166	ª
135	ç	167	º
136	ê	168	¿
137	ë	169	⌐
138	è	170	¬
139	ï	171	½
140	î	172	¼
141	ì	173	¡
142	Ä	174	«
143	Å	175	»
144	É	176	░
145	æ	177	▒
146	Æ	178	▓
147	ô	179	│
148	ö	180	┤
149	ò	181	╡
150	û	182	╢
151	ù	183	╖
152	ÿ	184	╕
153	Ö	185	╣
154	Ü	186	║
155	¢	187	╗
156	£	188	╝
157	¥	189	╜
158	Pt	190	╛
159	ƒ	191	┐

Table 8.1:
ASCII and Extended Graphics Codes (continued)

ASCII Value	Character	ASCII Value	Character
192	⌞	224	α
193	⊥	225	β
194	⊤	226	Γ
195	⊦	227	π
196	—	228	Σ
197	+	229	σ
198	⊨	230	μ
199	⊩	231	τ
200	⌞	232	Φ
201	⌐	233	θ
202	⊥	234	Ω
203	⊤	235	δ
204	⊩	236	∞
205	=	237	$\emptyset$
206	⊹	238	$\in$
207	⊥	239	$\cap$
208	⊥	240	$\equiv$
209	⊤	241	$\pm$
210	⊤	242	$\geq$
211	⊔	243	$\leq$
212	⊢	244	$\lceil$
213	⊨	245	$\rfloor$
214	⊓	246	$\div$
215	⧻	247	$\approx$
216	∓	248	°
217	⌟	249	•
218	⌜	250	·
219	■	251	$\sqrt{}$
220	▬	252	n
221	▮	253	^{2}
222	▮	254	▣
223	▬	255	(blank 'FF')

scrolling the screen and losing the top line. However, if you use a procedure to write directly to video RAM instead of the Write statement, it is possible to write to this screen position without scrolling the screen. Note that writing directly to screen memory will not move the cursor, so your program will have to relocate the cursor after each character is written.

Procedure WriteChar, shown in Tool 8.5, writes characters directly to video RAM. To use WriteChar, your screen-generator program should obtain the following information:

- The base address of video RAM (using the CheckForColor procedure, Tool 7.1, for example), to be passed as the word (or integer in Turbo Pascal versions prior to 4.0) parameter ScrAddr.
- The column and row of the current cursor position, to be passed as the integer parameters Col and Row.
- The ASCII value of the character to be displayed, to be passed as the integer parameter Character.
- The attribute byte of the screen cell, to be passed as the integer Attribute parameter.

Each time that the program reads a character from the keyboard that is to be written to the screen, it could call WriteChar, and then relocate the cursor after the character is displayed on the screen.

```
PROCEDURE WriteChar(ScrAddr:Word;
                    Col,Row,Character,Attribute:Integer);

        {To use this procedure with versions of Turbo Pascal
            prior to 4.0, change the type declaration of
            ScrAddr from Word to Integer.}

        VAR
            X,Y  :Integer;

        BEGIN {write character and attribute to video RAM}
            X:=((Col-1)*2);
            Y:=((Row-1)*160);
            Mem[ScrAddr:X+Y]:=Character;
            Mem[ScrAddr:X+Y+1]:=Attribute;
        END;  {write character and attribute to video RAM}
```

Tool 8.5: Procedure WriteChar to write characters directly to video RAM.

Here's how the WriteChar procedure works:

- Receive the base video RAM address as a parameter from the host program.
- Calculate the offset in video RAM for the current cursor position from the Col and Row parameters passed by the program.
- Set the memory location calculated for the character byte to the character value passed as a parameter.
- Set the memory location calculated for the attribute byte for the same screen cell to the value of the attribute passed as a parameter.

See Chapter 7 for more information about determining and setting the character and attribute bytes in video RAM.

When writing directly to video RAM, as described above, you can adjust the attribute byte to produce other screen effects. You can design screens that have a great deal of visual impact for the user and, often more importantly, for the prospective purchaser.

Some of the easiest screen effects to program are reverse-video, high-intensity, low-intensity, and blinking characters. You may even want to add colors to the screens. As discussed earlier, by setting up a translation table, you can have certain Ctrl-key combinations signal your screen-generator program to set the attribute of the characters entered.

MAKING A GRID FOR SCREEN DESIGN

Usually, on a blank or relatively blank screen, it is difficult to determine the cursor's exact position and place a character in a special place, such as in the center of the screen. A grid of dots on the screen that overlays all unused positions can be very helpful in screen design.

Procedure DoGrid, shown as Tool 8.6, will either construct or remove a grid, without interfering with other characters being placed on the screen. This procedure requires that the screen first be initialized to all zero values. This can be accomplished through the InitScrn procedure, presented as Tool 8.7. The InitScrn procedure simply sets all characters and attributes in video RAM to zero.

```
PROCEDURE DoGrid(VAR GridOn:Boolean);

    VAR

    {To use this procedure with versions of Turbo Pascal
        prior to 4.0, change the type declaration of
        ScrAddr from Word to Integer.}

        ScrAddr          :Word;
        Col, Row         :Integer;

    BEGIN {make or remove grid}
        IF ((Mem[0000:1040] AND 48) <> 48) THEN
            ScrAddr:=$B800
                ELSE ScrAddr:=$B000;
        FOR Col:=0 TO 79 DO
            FOR Row:=0 TO 24 DO
                BEGIN {check each screen cell}
                    IF NOT GridOn THEN {make a grid}
                    IF (Mem[ScrAddr:((Row*160)+(Col*2)+1)]=0) THEN
                        BEGIN
                            Mem[ScrAddr:((Row*160)+(Col*2)+1)]:=23;
                            Mem[ScrAddr:((Row*160)+(Col*2))]:=46;
                        END;
                    IF GridOn THEN {remove grid}
                    IF ((Mem[ScrAddr:((Row*160)+(Col*2)+1)]=23) AND
                        (Mem[ScrAddr:((Row*160)+(Col*2))]=46)) THEN
                        BEGIN
                            Mem[ScrAddr:((Row*160)+(Col*2)+1)]:=0;
                            Mem[ScrAddr:((Row*160)+(Col*2))]:=0;
                        END;
                END; {check each screen cell}
        GridOn:=NOT GridOn;
    END;  {make or remove grid}
```

Tool 8.6: Procedure DoGrid to place a grid on the screen.

```
PROCEDURE InitScrn;

    VAR

    {To use this procedure with versions of Turbo Pascal
        prior to 4.0, change the type declaration of
        ScrAddr from Word to Integer.}
        ScrAddr     :Word;
        X           :Integer;

    BEGIN {initialize screen}
        IF ((Mem[0000:1040] AND 48) <> 48) THEN
            ScrAddr:=$B800
                ELSE ScrAddr:=$B000;
        FOR X:=0 TO 3999 DO Mem[ScrAddr:X]:=0;
    END:  {initialize screen}
```

Tool 8.7: Procedure InitScrn to initialize the screen to zero values.

NOTE: Because the attribute is zero, the cursor will be "invisible" when located on any of these screen positions.

Here's how the DoGrid procedure works:

- Determine the base address of video RAM.
- Set up a loop within a loop to ensure that each screen cell is checked (columns 0 through 79 of rows 0 through 24).
- If the grid is presently on, as indicated by the parameter GridOn, then remove it; if the grid is off, construct it.
- Check video RAM for each screen position.
- To construct a grid, assume that the screen is initialized to all zero values. If a value is still zero, a character has never been written to it, so use it for the grid. If a character has been written to a screen position, do not disturb that position. Write a period to the screen and set an unusual attribute: white foreground and blue background (attribute 23).
- To remove a grid, reinitialize any cells that still have a character 46 (period) and an attribute of 23 to values of zero, and set zero for the character and attribute.
- Switch the variable parameter GridOn to its opposite state to track the presence or absence of the grid on the screen. Return this parameter to the host program so it can be passed back in its correct state whenever the grid procedure is called again.

When you use the DoGrid procedure, no screen cell that has been written to with the screen generator will become a part of the grid display. This is because each used cell will have a character value and attribute value other than the possible grid combinations of 0,0 or 46,23.

PUTTING SOME ENHANCEMENTS TOGETHER

The KeyTranslation procedure, shown as Tool 8.8, demonstrates some techniques for enhancing a simple screen generator (Test Program 8.1). The KeyTranslation calls the WriteChar procedure for actual screen output, as well as the DoGrid and InitScrn procedures (Tools 8.6 and 8.7).

```
PROCEDURE KeyTranslation;

     VAR
          Ch                                    :CHAR;
     {To use this procedure with versions of Turbo Pascal
          prior to 4.0, change the type declaration of
          ScrAddr from Word to Integer.}

          ScrAddr                               :Word;

          Col, Row, ChNo, Attrib          :Integer;
          Escape, EscapeSeq, DoWrite, Grid,
            TranslateA, Reverse, Blink,
            Intense                             :Boolean;

               {---------------------------------------------------}
               { The following additional procedures are necessary }
               { for this procedure to operate:                    }
               { WriteChr.Inc  InitScrn.Inc   DoGrid.Inc           }
               {---------------------------------------------------}

     PROCEDURE MoveCursor;

               {---------------------------------------------------}
               { This procedure prevents the screen from scrolling }
               { by controlling the cursor position and "wrapping" }
               { the cursor position from the right side of the    }
               { screen to then left, left to right, top to bottom,}
               { and bottom to top.                                }
               {---------------------------------------------------}

               BEGIN {move cursor to new position}
                    IF (Col<1) THEN
                         BEGIN
                              Col:=80;
                              Row:=Row-1;
                         END;
                    IF (Col>80) THEN
                         BEGIN
                              Col:=1;
                              Row:=Row+1;
                         END;
                    IF (Row<1) THEN Row:=25;
                    IF (Row>25) THEN Row:=1;
                    GotoXY(Col,Row);
               END;  {move cursor to new position}


     PROCEDURE HandleEscapeSeq;

               {----------------------------------------------------}
               { This procedure presently handles only cursor keys. }
               { You may wish to enhance it to handle other extended }
               { scan codes/escape sequences. See the table of char- }
               { acter return codes in Chapter 3, Table 3.2 or 3.3.  }
               {----------------------------------------------------}

               BEGIN {handle escape sequence character}

               {To use this program with Turbo Pascal versions prior
                    to 4.0, add the line below:}
                    { Read(KBD,Ch); }
```

Tool 8.8: Procedure KeyTranslation to add enhancements to a simple screen generator.

```
             {To use this program with Turbo Pascal versions prior
                to 4.0, remove the line below:}
             Ch:=ReadKey;

             CASE ORD(Ch) OF
               75:  {left arrow}
                      Col:=Col-1;
               77: {right arrow}
                      Col:=Col+1;
               72: {up arrow}
                      Row:=Row-1;
               80: {down arrow}
                      Row:=Row+1;
            END;  {case ch of}
          END;  {handle escape sequence character}

        PROCEDURE TableA(VAR CharNum:Integer);

             {-----------------------------------------------------}
             { This procedure translates a keystroke from a        }
             { character key so that it becomes a graphic          }
             { character when written to screen.                   }
             {-----------------------------------------------------}


             BEGIN {translation table}
                CASE CharNum OF
                    51:     CharNum:=201; {3}
                    52:     CharNum:=203; {4}
                    53:     CharNum:=187; {5}
                    69,101:CharNum:=186; {E,e}
                    82,114:CharNum:=205; {R,r}
                    83,115:CharNum:=204; {S,s}
                    68,100:CharNum:=206; {D,d}
                    70,102:CharNum:=185; {F,f}
                    88,120:CharNum:=200; {X,x}
                    67,99: CharNum:=202; {C,c}
                    86,118:CharNum:=188; {V,v}
                  END;  {case statement}
                END;  {translation table}


             BEGIN {receive and translate keystrokes}
                InitScrn;
                Escape:=False;
                TranslateA:=False;
                Reverse:=False;
                Blink:=False;
                Intense:=False;
                Grid:=False;
                GotoXY(1,1);
                Col:=1;
                Row:=1;
                Attrib:=7;
                IF ((Mem[0000:1040] AND 48) <> 48) THEN
                     ScrAddr:=$B800
                          ELSE ScrAddr:=$B000;
                REPEAT  {until escape}
```

Tool 8.8: Procedure KeyTranslation to add enhancements to a simple screen generator. (continued)

```
                {To use this program with Turbo Pascal versions prior
                    to 4.0, add the line below:}
                   { Read(KBD,Ch); }

                {To use this program with Turbo Pascal versions prior
                    to 4.0, remove the line below:}
                    Ch:=ReadKey;

                    DoWrite:=(Ch IN[#32..#127]);

                {To use this program with Turbo Pascal versions prior
                    to 4.0, add the line below:}
                   { EscapeSeq:=((Ch=#27) AND (KeyPressed)); }

                {To use this program with Turbo Pascal versions prior
                    to 4.0, remove the line below:}
                    EscapeSeq:=((Ch=#0) AND (KeyPressed));

                    IF EscapeSeq THEN HandleEscapeSeq
                        ELSE CASE ORD(Ch) OF {handle char}


                {-----------------------------------------------------}
                { Note that only a few of the 32 possible Ctrl-key    }
                { returns are handled here; the rest are ignored.     }
                { Many more enhancements may be handled by            }
                { recognizing other return codes.                     }
                {-----------------------------------------------------}

        {Ctrl-A}            1:  TranslateA:=NOT TranslateA;
        {Ctrl-B}            2:  Blink:=NOT Blink;
        {Ctrl-G}            7:  DoGrid(Grid);
        {Backspace}         8:  Col:=Col-1;
        {Ctrl-I}            9:  Intense:=NOT Intense;
        {Enter}            13:  Begin
                                    Row:=Row+1; Col:=1;
                                End;
        {Ctrl-R}           18:  Reverse:=NOT Reverse;
        {Escape}           27:  Escape:=True;
                END;  {handle char}
              ChNo:=ORD(Ch);
              IF TranslateA THEN TableA(ChNo);
              IF Reverse THEN Attrib:=112 ELSE Attrib:=7;
              IF Blink THEN Attrib:=(Attrib OR 128)
                  ELSE Attrib:=(Attrib AND NOT 128);
              IF Intense THEN Attrib:=(Attrib OR 8)
                  ELSE Attrib:=(Attrib AND NOT 8);
              IF DoWrite THEN
                 BEGIN
                    WriteChar(ScrAddr,Col,Row,ChNo,Attrib);
                    Col:=Col+1;
                 END;
              MoveCursor;
          UNTIL Escape;
      END;  {receive and translate keystrokes}
```

Tool 8.8: Procedure KeyTranslation to add enhancements to a simple screen generator. (continued)

The KeyTranslation procedure provides the following enhancements over the simple screen generator:

- The design can use the full screen (80 by 25), including column 80 of row 25.

- Users can press the cursor-movement keys for movement on the screen and the Enter key for line feed.

- The designer can use screen attributes to display high- and low-intensity characters, blinking characters, and reverse-video characters.

- Backspacing will take the user to the previous line.

- The top line cannot scroll off the screen.

- A graphic character set in a translation table will produce line drawings with double-line characters.

- A grid may be produced for placement of items on the screen.

You could use this procedure as a part of your own screen generator, or you could enhance it further to make a much more complex screen generator.

The KeyTranslation procedure contains three subprocedures: Move-Cursor, HandleEscapeSeq, and TableA. The MoveCursor procedure checks the present column and row values. If the column value is beyond the end of the screen, it is set to the first position on the opposite side of the screen and the row is either incremented or decremented, depending on the direction of cursor movement (right or left). If the column value is below the bottom or above the top of the screen, it is set to the opposite of its last position (that is, if it's at the top and moved up, it goes to the bottom of the screen). The cursor is moved to the new position.

The HandleEscapeSeq procedure is called when an extended scan code (Turbo Pascal 4.0 and 5.0) or escape sequence (earlier versions) is read and another character is waiting; this condition indicates that an extended scan code or escape sequence was entered. The second character of the extended scan code or escape sequence is read and acted upon. Depending on the cursor-movement key read, the column or row position is incremented or decremented, as appropriate. This procedure handles only the codes read from the cursor-movement (arrow) keys; any other codes are ignored. You could enhance the procedure to handle other combinations.

The TableA procedure is a translation table. If the Boolean variable TranslateA has been set to true by pressing Ctrl-A, then subsequent characters entered at the keyboard will be passed through this translation table. For this table, I chose a logical key set that can be used to create line drawings. The logical key set is four rows of two or three keys each: 3, 4, 5, E, R, S, D, F, X, C, and V.

LINE DRAWING WITH PROCEDURE KEYTRANSLATION

When translated, the keys in the TableA subprocedure will produce the following characters:

3	4	5	=	┌	┬	┐
	E	R	=		│	─
S	D	F	=	├	┼	┤
X	C	V	=	└	┴	┘

Here's how the KeyTranslation procedure works:

- Initialize the screen, set the initial cursor position and variables, and determine the base video RAM address.

- Enter a repeat loop, which will continue until the Escape key is pressed. The loop will continuously read characters from the keyboard, interpret those characters, and respond appropriately.

- Read a keystroke. If the keystroke is printable, the Boolean variable DoWrite is true. If the keystroke is part of an extended scan code or escape sequence, the Boolean variable EscapeSeq is true.

- If EscapeSeq is true, call the HandleEscapeSeq procedure; otherwise, inspect the character by a CASE statement.

- Through the CASE statement, handle the following characters: Ctrl-A, Ctrl-B, Ctrl-G, Backspace, Ctrl-I, Enter, Ctrl-R, and Escape. Ignore any other characters. The Ctrl-key combinations work with Boolean "switches" to turn screen attributes on or off. Each time a given Ctrl-key sequence is entered, the associated switch moves to its opposite state. Note that Ctrl-H produces the same return code as Backspace, so a Ctrl-H entered from the keyboard functions like a Backspace entry.

- Assign the ASCII value of the character (Ch) to the integer variable Ch#.

- Set the attribute byte according to the various switches controlling it and their present settings.

- If the character is printable, write it to the screen through the WriteChar procedure and increment the cursor position.

- Call the MoveCursor procedure to move the cursor after the character is written to the screen.

NOTE: If you want to use Ctrl-C as one of the valid characters that may be entered from the keyboard, your program must issue a compiler directive to prevent the Ctrl-C sequence from halting the program.

A BETTER SCREEN GENERATOR

Test Program 8.3 is a somewhat better and more comprehensive screen-generator program than the one presented in Test Program 8.1. The ScreenGen2 program uses the WriteChar, InitScrn, DoGrid, and Key-Translation procedures. This demonstration program will only produce screen files of captured-screen images.

MORE ENHANCEMENT SUGGESTIONS

Here are some other enhancements that you may want to make to your screen-generator program:

- Establish two control character sequences that will allow the deletion and insertion of whole, blank lines into the screen. This is accomplished easily by identifying the control characters to

```
PROGRAM ScreenGen2;

    {To use this program with Turbo Pascal versions prior to
        4.0, remove the Uses statement below.}

    Uses DOS,CRT;

    {$V-}      {relaxed parameter type checking}

    TYPE
        Str255 = STRING[255];

    VAR
        FName         :STRING[65];

    {$I NameFile.Inc}
    {$I ImageRec.Inc}
    {$I WriteChr.Inc}
    {$I InitScrn.Inc}
    {$I DoGrid.Inc}
    {$I KeyTrans.Inc}

    BEGIN {program}
        NameFile(FName);
        KeyTranslation;
        ImageRecord(FName);
    END.  {program}
```

Test Program 8.3: A better screen generator.

signal the program to perform the operation and using Turbo Pascal's DelLine and InsLine statements to perform the work.

- Use the return codes from the Insert and Delete keys to allow insertion and deletion of characters on a line. After the keyboard return code is recognized, simply calculate all cells from the right side of the row to the cursor position and set each equal to the previous one; the line moves one character to the right from the cursor and a space is inserted. For character deletion, move from the cursor to the end of the line and let the last cell of the line be a zero character with a zero attribute.

- Identify various control characters as a signal to produce specified colors in order to add color to the screen generator. After the character is read, either set the attribute to the proper combination for the desired color or use the Turbo Pascal TextColor and TextBackground statements to set the color.

PROGRAMMING A COMPLETE SCREEN GENERATOR

After you have tried working with a screen generator and discovered its benefits, you may decide to write a complete program. One of the first steps in designing a complete screen generator is putting together a menu of operations and incorporating several related tasks within the screen-generator program itself. This section suggests some helpful tasks that could be on your screen generator's menu of operations.

SAMPLE MENU FOR A SCREEN-GENERATOR PROGRAM

MENU

Create New Screen
Modify Existing Screen
Copy Existing Screen & Modify
Display Screens in File
Delete Screen from File
Make Template for a Screen
Revise Template for a Screen
Print Template Data
Delete Template for a Screen

REVISING EXISTING SCREENS

As sure as a screen is designed, there will be changes in it. Without too much difficulty, your complete screen-generator program can incorporate a procedure to read an existing screen file, pick out an existing screen, and display it for revision. After the revisions are made, the recording and filing process would be the same, except that the revised screen would be filed as the same record, thereby replacing the original screen with the revised version.

COPYING AND MODIFYING EXISTING SCREENS

Very often, a large portion of one screen can be used in the construction of another. This is particularly true in programs where the same screen format is to be used throughout. After the first screen is created, the basic pattern can be copied and modified for all of the screens in the program. To facilitate such operations, you can have your screen generator read a given screen from a file and bring it up for display and revision. Instead of filing this screen as a revision of the original, however, just have it added to the end of the screen file as a new screen.

DISPLAYING ALL THE SCREENS IN A FILE

It is often convenient to be able to look over all the screens in a file that have been created for a program. To do this, include the ShowScrn procedure (Tool 8.4) as a menu option, and produce a loop to show all the screens in file, pausing between screens and waiting for a key to be pressed to continue the display.

REMOVING SCREENS FROM A FILE

Occasionally, you may create screens which are never used. One of your menu options could be to remove a screen from a file. This can be accomplished by rewriting the file record for record, but omitting the screen record that is to be deleted.

USING A TEMPLATE MAKER FOR THE GENERATED SCREENS

If you plan to use data-entry or display templates (as discussed in Chapter 3), you can include an automated template creation facility in your screen-generator program. When creating screens, use a specified character (for example, the underline, ASCII #95) for data-entry areas. Have your template-making procedure identify these data-entry areas and automatically determine the column and row where they begin and the number of characters for input or display. Then the procedure needs only to ask the user pertinent questions about the data type of each area and write the records to the template file.

CHECKING CRITICAL ITEMS ON THE SCREEN

You've seen how you can save a great deal of programming time and code space by using a screen generator to create a file of screens and then simply open the screen file, read the data for a specific screen, and transfer that data to video RAM to instantly reproduce the screen. The price for this convenience, however, is that such screens are relatively easy to tamper with, and screen legends or copyrights could be changed. One way to control such tampering is to read a portion of each screen when it is displayed and compare this portion against a model contained in the program (usually a key line is sufficient). If the comparison does not match, this would indicate that the screen has been changed, and then the program can refuse to operate further.

CHECKING THE SCREEN AGAINST A MODEL

The ChekScrn procedure, shown as Tool 8.9, can be called to check a portion of the currently displayed screen against a "model" passed to the procedure. Col and Row indicate the beginning screen position to be checked, and NumChars indicates the number of consecutive screen positions to be checked. For example, if you want to check screen row 5

```
PROCEDURE ChekScrn(Col, Row, NumChars :Integer;
                   CompareAgainst:Str255;
                   VAR ResultCode:Integer);

    VAR
        OK                         :Boolean;
        ChekString                 :STRING[80];
        X, Offset, ScreenAddress :Integer;

    {To use this procedure with versions of Turbo Pascal prior
to 4.0, change the type declaration of ScreenAddress from Word to
Integer.}
    BEGIN   {check screen}
        IF (Mem[0000:1040] AND 48) <> 48 THEN
            ScreenAddress:=$B800
                ELSE ScreenAddress:=$B000;
        ChekString:='';
        FOR X:=1 TO NumChars DO
            BEGIN
                Offset:=((Row-1)*160)+((Col-2+X)*2);
                ChekString:=ChekString+
                    CHR(Mem[ScreenAddress:Offset]);
            END;
        OK:=(ChekString=CompareAgainst);
        IF OK THEN ResultCode:=0
            ELSE ResultCode:=1;
    END;    {check screen}
```

Tool 8.9: Procedure ChekScrn to check the screen against a model.

beginning at column 10 for the legend *Copyright (C) 1987 by*, the number of positions to be checked (NumChars) would be 21. The character string to be checked for is the CompareAgainst parameter. In our example, CompareAgainst would be 'Copyright (C) 1987 by'.

The ChekScrn procedure will return the ResultCode parameter to the host program. The result returned is 0 if the model (CompareAgainst) appears at the designated place on screen, or 1 if the screen does not display an exact copy of the model in the given location. Col, Row, NumChars, and ResultCode are integers; CompareAgainst is a string.

Here's how the ChekScrn procedure works:

- Determine the base address of video RAM.
- Initialize the ChekString as null.
- Establish a loop to repeat as many times as there are characters to be checked.
- Calculate the character offset for the position to be checked.
- Read the character at the position to be checked and add it to ChekString.
- When the loop is completed, ChekString is completed. Check it against the string parameter passed for comparison.
- If ChekString matched the comparison string, set a result code of zero; otherwise, set a result code of one. Return the result code to the program.

Test Program 8.4 illustrates the use of the ChekScrn procedure in a program. It establishes a pattern string, clears the screen, and displays the pattern string on screen. Five rows are checked for the pattern string. It will be found on only one of them. After each check, the result is reported on screen. There is a delay prior to the next check.

```
PROGRAM DemoProg1;

     (To use this program with Turbo Pascal versions prior to
         4.0, remove the Uses statement below.

     Uses DOS,CRT;

     TYPE
          Str255 = STRING[255];

     VAR
          X, Result        :Integer;
          Pattern          :Str255;
          Ch               :Char;

     {$I ChekScrn.Inc}

     BEGIN {demo program}
          Pattern:='Check this phrase.';
          ClrScr;
          GotoXY(1,10);
          WriteLn(Pattern);
          FOR X:=8 TO 12 DO
               BEGIN
                    GotoXY(1,20);
                    ClrEol;
                    Write('Checking at 1,',X,' for phrase.  ');
                    ChekScrn(1,X,18,Pattern,Result);
                    IF Result=1 THEN Write('NOT ');
                    Write('FOUND!');
                    Delay(1000);
               END;
     END.  {demo program}
```

Test Program 8.4: Using procedure ChekScrn in a program.

CHAPTER 9
SPECIAL CHARACTERS AND SCREEN EFFECTS

··
··
··
··
··
··
··
··
··
··
··
··
··
··
··
··
··
··
··
··
··
··
··
··

In this chapter, you will find procedures for producing extra large characters; active characters, which slide, spin, and push across the screen; and reverse-video characters. You can use them to make your program title screens a bit more unusual or in other screens that you want to make more attention-getting. Changing the size of the cursor can also make your program screen displays distinctive, and this chapter includes a procedure for making the cursor larger or smaller than the default size. Another way to add visual interest to a program is to have it display a bar graph of input values. The final procedure in the chapter will generate a simple horizontal bar graph.

GENERATING LARGE CHARACTERS

In IBM PCs and most compatible computers, the character set for display in text modes is stored in a table in ROM. You can use the patterns in this table to create much larger characters for screen display.

THE CHARACTER SHAPE TABLE

The ROM character shape table begins at memory address 61440:64110 ($F000:$FA6E hex). It contains the patterns of pixels that will produce each character in a screen cell. A character is stored in 8 consecutive bytes, and each byte has the bits set to correspond to the pixels that will be illuminated. This means that each character has a map of 8 (bytes) by 8 (bits) pixels, which may be illuminated in any combination.

You can manipulate the shape of any character by finding and capturing its pattern. You know where the table begins and that each character follows the last, so you can find a character's pixel map by calculating its offset from the base address. With this information, you can display large characters, as well as upside down, backwards, and reverse-video characters, from the regular character set.

DISPLAYING LARGE CHARACTERS

Procedure LgChar, shown as Tool 9.1, uses the ROM character shape table to generate the same character patterns in a larger format. Instead of 8-by-8 pixels, this procedure uses 8-by-8 screen cells to display the characters.

The LgChar procedure requires the following integer parameters be passed to it:

- The Col and Row parameters, which are where this particular character will begin on the screen
- The ToPrint parameter, which is the ASCII character number of the character to be displayed (for example, $A = 65$ and $a = 97$)
- The ChNo parameter, which is the ASCII character number of the character to be printed in each screen cell used to form the character pattern

```
PROCEDURE LgChar(Col,Row,ToPrint,ChNo:Integer);

    TYPE
        CharDesign = ARRAY[1..8] OF Byte;

    VAR
        Table                :ARRAY[0..255] OF CharDesign
                                    ABSOLUTE $F000:$FA6E;
        X, Y                 :Integer;
        Pattern              :CharDesign;

    BEGIN {display large character on screen}
        Pattern:=Table[ToPrint];
        FOR X:=1 TO 8 DO
            FOR Y:=7 DOWNTO 0 DO
                BEGIN
                    GotoXY((Col-1)+8-Y,(Row-1)+X);
                    IF (Odd(Pattern[X] Shr Y)) THEN
        {----------------------------------------------------}
        { Want some really unusual effects?                  }
        { For upside down and backwards letters use:         }
        {     GotoXY((Col-1)+Y,(Row-1)+8-X);                 }
        { For backwards letters use:                         }
        {     GotoXY((Col-1)+Y,(Row-1)+X);                   }
        { For reverse-video use:                             }
        {     IF NOT (Odd(Pattern[X] Shr Y)) THEN            }
        {----------------------------------------------------}
                        Write(Chr(ChNo));
                END;
    END;  {display large character on screen}
```

Tool 9.1: Procedure LgChar to display large characters from the regular character set.

For ChNo you could use the graphic block characters (ASCII #176 through #178), an asterisk (ASCII#42), or one of the smiling-face or card-suit characters (ASCII #1 through #6).

You can modify the procedure to produce upside down, backwards, or reverse-video characters. The changes for these variations are noted in comments within the procedure.

Here's how the LgChar procedure works:

- Declare the patterns for the characters as an array beginning at the appropriate address in ROM.
- Load a pattern for the character to be displayed, specified in the parameter ToPrint, into the array Pattern.
- Initiate a loop within a loop to read each bit of each byte of the Pattern array.

- As each bit is read, print a character to the appropriate screen cell or skip it, depending on whether the bit is set or not.

Test Program 9.1 uses the LgChar procedure to display an enlarged version of the alphabet in a row across the screen, first in uppercase letters, and then in lowercase.

```
PROGRAM TestLgChar;

     {To use this program with Turbo Pascal versions prior to
        4.0, remove the Uses statement below.}

     Uses DOS,CRT;

     VAR
          X,Col,Row      :Integer;


     {$I LgChar.Inc}

BEGIN {program}
     ClrScr;
     Col:=1; Row:=1;
     FOR X:=1 TO 26 DO
          BEGIN
               LgChar(Col,Row,64+X,178);
               Col:=Col+8;
               IF (Col>80) THEN
                    BEGIN
                         Col:=1; Row:=Row+8;
                    END;
          END;
     Delay(2000);
     ClrScr;
     Col:=1; Row:=1;
     FOR X:=1 TO 26 DO
          BEGIN
               LgChar(Col,Row,96+X,178);
               Col:=Col+8;
               IF (Col>80) THEN
                    BEGIN
                         Col:=1; Row:=Row+8;
                    END;
          END;
END.   {program}
```

Test Program 9.1: Using procedure LgChar in a program.

The program begins by clearing the screen and initializing the column and row positions. After entering a 26-cycle loop to produce each alphabetic character, the program calls the LgChar procedure and displays an uppercase letter, formed with one of the graphic block characters (ASCII #178). The character number to be displayed is incremented through each loop cycle. The column and row positions are recalculated after each character is displayed in order to display the next character in an adjacent position or, if necessary, begin a new row. After the twenty-sixth cycle, the program repeats the whole procedure to display the lowercase letters.

PRINTING LARGE CHARACTERS

The LgChar procedure may also be used in conjunction with a printer to produce large characters on paper. Procedure PrLgChar, shown as Tool 9.2, will produce large characters in either a vertical or horizontal format.

Like the LgChar procedure, PrLgChar requires the integer parameters ToPrint and ChNo be passed to it, except ChNo is the number of the printer character to be used to form the character. The procedure also requires a Direction parameter to indicate the direction of the printing. V is for vertical printing, and H is for horizontal (if anything other than H is specified, the printing will be vertical).

The procedure is designed to use a sheet of paper for each character printed vertically and nearly as much for horizontal characters. You may want to make some alterations to give the characters a somewhat different proportion.

Here's how the PrLgChar procedure works:

- Declare the patterns for the characters as an array beginning at the appropriate address in ROM.
- Ensure that the Direction parameter is an uppercase letter.
- Load a pattern for the character to be displayed, specified in the parameter ToPrint, into the array Pattern.
- If the character is to be printed horizontally, the GOTO statement directs the procedure to that label; otherwise, the character is printed vertically.
- Initiate a loop within a loop to read each bit of each byte of the Pattern array.
- As each bit is read, print a character or a space, depending on whether the bit is set or not.

```
PROCEDURE PrLgChar(ToPrint,ChNo:Integer;
                   Direction :Char);

    LABEL
        Horizontal, Finished;

    TYPE
        CharDesign = ARRAY[1..8] OF Byte;

    VAR
        Table                    :ARRAY[0..255] OF CharDesign
                                     ABSOLUTE $F000:$FA6E;
        PatternRow, PatternCol,
            Count, PgLines       :Integer;
        Pattern                  :CharDesign;

    BEGIN {print large character on printer}
        Direction:=UpCase(Direction);
        Pattern:=Table[ToPrint];
        IF (Direction='H') THEN GOTO Horizontal;
        FOR PatternRow:=1 TO 8 DO
            FOR PgLines:=1 TO 8 DO
                BEGIN {for pglines}
                    Write(LST,'        ');   {8 spaces}
                    FOR PatternCol:=7 DOWNTO 0 DO
                        BEGIN {for patterncol}
                            IF (Odd(Pattern[PatternRow]
                               Shr PatternCol)) THEN
                                FOR Count:=1 TO 8 DO
                                    Write(Lst,Ccr(ChNo))
                            ELSE
                                FOR Count:=1 TO 8 DO
                                    Write(LST,#32);
                        END;  {for patterncol}
                    WriteLn(Lst);
                END;  {for pglines}
        GOTO Finished;
        Horizontal:
        FOR PatternCol:=7 DOWNTO 0 DO
            FOR PgLines:=1 TO 5 DO
                BEGIN {for pglines}
                    Write(LST,'        ');   {8 spaces}
                    FOR PatternRow:=8 DOWNTO 1 DO
                        BEGIN {for patternrow}
                            IF (Odd(Pattern[PatternRow]
                               Shr PatternCol)) THEN
                                FOR Count:=1 TO 8 DO
                                    Write(Lst,Chr(ChNo))
                            ELSE
                                FOR Count:=1 TO 8 DO
                                    Write(Lst,#32);
                        END;  {for patternrow}
                    WriteLn(LST);
                END;  {for pglines}
    Finished:
END;  {print large character on printer}
```

Tool 9.2: Procedure PrLgChar to print large characters on paper.

- Repeat a pattern five times for horizontal characters or eight times for vertical characters as the printing proceeds down the page. Repeat the pattern eight times for each bit as the printer proceeds across the page.

Test Program 9.2 illustrates the use of the PrLgChar procedure. After the user enters a character to be printed, the printer character to be used, and the direction of print, the program calls the PrLgChar procedure. The single character will be printed as specified.

DISPLAYING ACTIVE CHARACTERS

The procedures presented in this section can give a little action to your screens. Your program can display sliding, spinning, or "pushing" characters. These procedures will handle a whole line, character by character, starting it at one side of the screen and moving it to the other.

SLIDING RIGHT CHARACTERS

The SlideRt procedure, presented as Tool 9.3, starts each character in a string at the left side of the screen and slides it to the right. There is sufficient delay to make the sliding motion apparent.

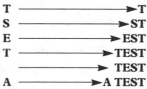

ACTION OF A SLIDING STRING

If the character string furnished to the SlideRt procedure was *A TEST*, the action would be:

```
T ──────────────►T
S ──────────────►ST
E ──────────────► EST
T ──────────────►TEST
  ──────────────►  TEST
A ──────────────►A TEST
```

```
PROGRAM TestPrLgChar;

     {To use this program with Turbo Pascal versions prior to
        4.0, remove the Uses statement below.}

     Uses DOS,CRT,Printer;

     VAR
         ChNo,PrintCh      :Integer;
         Ch, VorH          :Char;

     {$I PrLgChar.Inc}

BEGIN {program}
     ClrScr;
     WriteLn('Print large characters to printer.');
     WriteLn;
     Write('Character to print: ');

          {To use this program with Turbo Pascal versions prior
             to 4.0, add the line below:}
     { Read(KBD,Ch); }

          {To use this program with Turbo Pascal versions prior
             to 4.0, remove the line below:}
     Ch:=ReadKey;

     WriteLn(Ch);
     ChNo:=ORD(Ch);
     Write('Print <V>ertically or <H>orizontally? : ');
     REPEAT

          {To use this program with Turbo Pascal versions prior
             to 4.0, add the line below:}
       { Read(KBD,VorH); }

          {To use this program with Turbo Pascal versions prior
             to 4.0, remove the line below:}
       VorH:=ReadKey;

       VorH:=UpCase(VorH);
     UNTIL (VorH IN['V','H']);
     WriteLn(VorH);
     WriteLn('ASCII code (number) for character to use on printer');
     Write('to reproduce the character you selected (33..247) :');
     REPEAT
        ReadLn(PrintCh);
     UNTIL (PrintCh IN[33..247]);
     PrLgChar(ChNo,PrintCh,VorH);
  END.   {program}
```

Test Program 9.2: Using procedure PrLgChar in a program.

The SlideRt procedure must be furnished integer parameters for Col
and Row, which indicate the position of the first character of the string to
be placed on the screen. Note that this is actually the *last* character in the
string itself. In the example above, the procedure would need the column

```
PROCEDURE SlideRt(Col,Row:Integer; InString:Str255);

    VAR
    {To use this procedure with versions of Turbo Pascal
        prior to 4.0, change the type declaration of ScrAddr
        from Word to Integer.}
    ScrAddr            :Word;
    Offset, X, Y       :Integer;

    BEGIN {slide right}
        Col:=Col+LengthInString);         (*1*)
        IF (Mem[0000:1040] AND 48) <> 48 THEN ScrAddr:=$B800
            ELSE ScrAddr:=$B000;
   {-----------------------------------------------------------}
   { To make characters slide left, instead of right,         }
   {     make the following changes:                          }
   {                                                          }
   {   Delete:                                                }
   {      Col:=Col+Length(InString);                  (*1*)  }
   {   Change:                                                }
   {      Offset:=( ((Row-1)*160) + ((79)*2) );       (*2*)  }
   {      Mem[ScrAddr:Offset]:=ORD(InString[X]);      (*3*)  }
   {      FOR Y:=78 DOWNTO Col-1+X DO                 (*4*)  }
   {      Mem[ScrAddr:Offset]:=Mem[ScrAddr:Offset+2]; (*5*)  }
   {      Mem[ScrAddr:Offset+2]:=0;                   (*6*)  }
   {-----------------------------------------------------------}
        FOR X:=1 TO Length(InString) DO
            BEGIN {for x}
(*2*)           Offset:=( ((Row-1)*160) + ((0)*2) );
   {-----------------------------------------------------------}
   {        For spinning characters, add line here:           }
   {            SpinEm(ScrAddr,Offset);                        }
   {-----------------------------------------------------------}
(*3*)           Mem[ScrAddr:Offset]:=
                    ORD(InString[Length(InString)+1-X]);
(*4*)           FOR Y:=1 TO Col-X DO
                    BEGIN {for y}
                        Offset:=( ((Row-1)*160) + (Y*2) );
(*5*)                   Mem[ScrAddr:Offset]:=
                            Mem[ScrAddr:Offset-2];
(*6*)                   Mem[ScrAddr:Offset-2]:=0;
                        Delay(3);
                    END;   {for y}
            END;   {for x}
    END;   {slide right}
```

Tool 9.3: Procedure SlideRt to display sliding characters.

and row of the final *T* in *A TEST*. The SlideRt procedure is also passed a string to be displayed on the screen.

Here's how the SlideRt procedure works:

- Determine the base address of video RAM.
- Set up a loop for the length of the string (passed as a parameter).

- Calculate the offset to the base address of video RAM for the beginning of the screen row on which the line will be displayed.

- If the spinning-character procedure (presented next) is added, call it here to produce characters that appear to be spinning before they slide.

- Set the character to be displayed next into position at the end of the row.

- Initiate a loop to move the character from the end of the row to its final position on the screen. The move is made one screen cell at a time, with a delay between moves so that it will be slow enough to be seen.

NOTE: Because of differing processor speeds (that is, clock speeds) on various computers, you may need to adjust the delay period in the SlideRt procedure.

You can modify the SlideRt procedure to send characters from the right side of the screen to the left side. The changes necessary to make the procedure work in the opposite direction are noted in comments within the procedure.

SPINNING CHARACTERS

If you want to display even more active characters, you can have them spin before they move. Prior to sliding across the screen, the characters could appear to be spinning, as if they were shooting out of a wheel on the side of the screen. The SpinEm procedure, presented as Tool 9.4, used in conjunction with the SlideLft procedure, can produce this effect.

The SpinEm procedure must be called from the appropriate place within the SlideRt procedure, as noted in comments in the SlideRt procedure. The procedure requires the screen base address and proper offset; these positions are already in use within the SlideRt procedure and can be passed to SpinEm when it is called.

```
PROCEDURE SpinEm(ScrAddr:Word; Offset:Integer);

        {To use this procedure with versions of Turbo Pascal
         prior to 4.0, change the type declaration of
         ScrAddr from Word to Integer.}

        VAR
            W, Z    :Integer;

        BEGIN {spinem}
            FOR Z:=1 TO 6 DO
                BEGIN {z}
                    CASE Z OF
                        1: W:=124;
                        2: W:=47;
                        3: W:=92;
                        4: W:=124;
                        5: W:=47;
                        6: W:=92;
                    END;  {case statement}
                    Mem[ScrAddr:Offset]:=w;
                    Delay(30);
                END; {z}
        END;   {spinem}
```

Tool 9.4: Procedure SpinEm for spinning characters.

Here's how the SpinEm procedure works:

- Receive the proper video RAM address as a parameter.
- Set up a loop in which the following characters are specified and displayed, in turn, with a delay between, to give the visual impression of spinning: | (ASCII #124), /(ASCII #47), and \(ASCII #92).

PUSHING CHARACTERS

The PushLft procedure, presented as Tool 9.5, is another variation of the SlideRt procedure. With PushLft, however, the characters have a little different action. This time each character seems to "bump," or push, the preceding character across the screen.

The PushLft procedure is used in the same manner as the SlideRt procedure and requires the same parameters. As with SlideRt, the PushLft procedure may be made to operate from the opposite direction. The necessary

---

ACTION OF A PUSHING STRING

If the character string furnished to the PushLft procedure was *A TEST*,
the action would be:

A

A

A T

A TE

A TES

A TEST

---

statement changes to accomplish this are noted as comments within the procedure. You could also use the SpinEm procedure with PushLft to create spinning and pushing characters, as noted in the PushLft procedure.

Here's how the PushLft procedure works:

- Determine the base video RAM address.

- Pad the string supplied as a parameter so it will reach the desired
  starting column by being pushed with spaces when the string
  itself ends.

- Set up a loop for the length of the string passed as a parameter.

- Calculate the offset to the base address of video RAM for the end
  of the screen row on which the line will be displayed.

- If the spinning character procedure is added, it falls at this point
  and produces characters that appear to be spinning before they
  are pushed.

- Set the character to be displayed next into position at the end of
  the row.

- Initiate a loop to move all characters presently displayed over one
  screen cell. There is a delay between moves so that the action
  will be slow enough to be seen. As with the SlideRt procedure,
  you may have to adjust this delay for certain computer systems.

```
PROCEDURE PushLft(Col,Row:Integer; InString:Str255);

    VAR
    {To use this procedure with versions of Turbo Pascal
        prior to 4.0, change the type declaration of
        ScrAddr from Word to Integer.}

      ScrAddr       :Word;
      Offset, X, Y  :Integer;

    BEGIN {push left}
        IF (Mem[0000:1040] AND 48) <> 48 THEN ScrAddr:=$B800
            ELSE ScrAddr:=$B000;
        WHILE (Col+Length(InString)<80) DO          (*1*)
            InString:=InString+' ';
        {---------------------------------------------------}
        { To make characters push right, instead of left,   }
        {     make the following changes:                   }
        {                                                   }
        {   Delete:                                         }
        {       WHILE (Col+Length(InString)<80) DO   (*1*) }
        {           InString:=InString+' ';                }
        {   Add:                                     (*2*) }
        {       FOR X:=1 TO (Col-1) DO Insert(' ',InString,1); }
        {   Change:                                         }
        {       FOR X:=0 TO (Length(InString)-1) DO   (*3*) }
        {       Offset:=( ((Row-1)*160) + ((0)*2) );  (*4*) }
        {       Mem[ScrAddr:Offset]:=                 (*5*) }
        {       ORD(InString[Length(InString)-X]);          }
        {       FOR Y:=1+X DOWNTO 0 DO                (*6*) }
        {       Mem[ScrAddr:Offset]:=Mem[ScrAddr:Offset-2];(*7*)}
        {       Mem[ScrAddr:Offset-2]:=0;            (*8*) }
        {---------------------------------------------------}
        (*2*)
        FOR X:=1 TO Length(InString) DO         (*3*)
            BEGIN {for x}
(*4*)           Offset:=( ((Row-1)*160) + ((79)*2) );
        {---------------------------------------------------}
        { For spinning characters, add line here:           }
        {           SpinEm(ScrAddr,Offset);                 }
        {---------------------------------------------------}
(*5*)           Mem[ScrAddr:Offset]:=ORD(InString[X]);
(*6*)           FOR Y:=78-X TO 78 DO
                    BEGIN {for y}
                        Offset:=( ((Row-1)*160) + (Y*2) );
(*7*)                   Mem[ScrAddr:Offset]:=
                            Mem[ScrAddr:Offset+2];
(*8*)                   Mem[ScrAddr:Offset+2]:=0;
                        Delay(3);
                    END;   {for y}
            END;  {for x}
    END;  {push left}
```

Tool 9.5: Procedure PushLft to display "pushing" characters.

SLIDING LARGE CHARACTERS

A final variation on these attention-getting screen character techniques is to produce the large characters from the LgChar procedure and display them with the SlideRt procedure so that a large character, with more visual impact, appears to be sliding across the screen. The SlideBig procedure, presented as Tool 9.6, slides the large characters right to left across the screen. This procedure also can be modified to slide the characters in the opposite direction.

```
PROCEDURE SlideBig(Col,Row,ToPrint,ChNo:Integer);

    TYPE
        CharDesign = ARRAY[1..8] OF Byte;

    VAR
        Table                :ARRAY[0..255] OF CharDesign
                                  ABSOLUTE $F000:$FA6E;
        X,Y,Z,Bit,Bite,Ch,
             Offset          :Integer;
        Pattern              :CharDesign;

    {To use this procedure with versions of Turbo Pascal
     prior to 4.0, change the type declaration of
     ScrAddr from Word to Integer.}

        ScrAddr              :Word;

BEGIN {slide big chars}
     IF (Mem[0000:1040] AND 48) <> 48 THEN ScrAddr:=$B800
        ELSE ScrAddr:=$B000;
     Pattern:=Table[ToPrint];
     FOR Bit:=7 DOWNTO 0 DO
        FOR Bite:=1 TO 8 DO
            BEGIN {for bite}
                 IF (Odd(Pattern[Bite] Shr Bit)) THEN
                     Ch:=ChNo
                         ELSE Ch:=32;
                 Offset:=(((Row-2+Bite)*160)+((79-Bit)*2));
                 Mem[ScrAddr:Offset]:=Ch;
            END;  {for bite}
         FOR X:=70 DOWNTO Col DO
            FOR Y:=1 TO 8 DO {cols}
                BEGIN {for y}
                     FOR Z:=1 TO 8 DO {rows}
                        BEGIN {for z}
                            Offset:=((Row-2+Z)*160)+((X+Y)*2);
                            Mem[ScrAddr:Offset]:=
                                  Mem[ScrAddr:Offset+2];
                        END;  {for z}
                     Mem[ScrAddr:Offset+2]:=0;
                END;  {for y}
     END;  {slide big chars}
```

Tool 9.6: Procedure SlideBig to display large sliding characters.

Here's how the SlideBig procedure works:

- Derive the pattern for the character from the ROM character shape table, as described earlier in the chapter.
- Examine the character pattern one column at a time. After a column is examined, print it to the screen in eight rows. Then examine the next column and move it to the screen while the first column has been moved over one cell. Continue the process until all eight pattern columns have been examined and moved to the screen. This process entails examining the bits of each of the 8 pattern bytes in rotation; the sequence is byte 1, bit 7; byte 2, bit 7; through byte 8, bit 7; then byte 1, bit 6; byte 2, bit 6; through byte 8, bit 6; etc., through byte 8, bit 0.
- Beginning from the column immediately left of the first column (of the 8 columns) of the big character, move all columns and rows of a character one cell to the left; repeat the process until the character has been gradually moved to the desired screen position.

Because there are so many moves taking place in this procedure, a delay to add visual impact is not necessary.

USING THE ACTIVE CHARACTER PROCEDURES IN A PROGRAM

Test Program 9.3 demonstrates the use of the sliding and pushing character procedures. The SpinEm procedure is not demonstrated, but to make it appear in the program, simply add the SpinEm call statement to one of the procedures, as noted in the procedure comments.

The TestSlideChars program begins by clearing the screen and asking the user to enter a test line. The test line is padded so that it will be approximately in the center of the screen, and then displayed first as pushing characters and next as sliding ones. To demonstrate SlideBig, the program requests the user to enter up to nine characters, which are displayed as large sliding characters.

```
Program SlideChars;

     {To use this program with Turbo Pascal versions prior to
       4.0, remove the Uses statement below.}

     Uses DOS,CRT;

     TYPE
          Str255  =  STRING[255];


     VAR
          Line       :STRING[80];
          Center,X   :Integer;
     {$I SpinEm.Inc}
     {$I SlideRt.Inc}
     {$I PushLft.Inc}
     {$I SlideBig.Inc}

     BEGIN {program}
          ClrScr;
          WriteLn('Enter test line below:');
          ReadLn(Line);
          Center:=80-Length(Line);
          Center:=Center DIV 2;
          FOR X:=1 TO Center DO Insert(' ',Line,1);
          PushLft(1,4,Line);
          SlideRt(1,6,Line);
          GotoXY(1,8);
          Write('Enter up to 9 characters to display: ');
          ReadLn(Line);
          IF (Length(Line)>9) THEN Line[0]:=Chr(10);
          FOR X:=1 TO Length(Line) DO
               SlideBig(((X*8)-8),10,ORD(Line[X]),178);
     END.  {program}
```

Test Program 9.3: Using procedures SlideRt, PushLft, and SlideBig in a program.

DISPLAYING REVERSE-VIDEO AND BLINKING CHARACTERS

Turbo Pascal provides three commands for controlling the appearance of characters on the screen: HighVideo, LowVideo, and NormVideo. The language also has a structure that produces blinking characters. However, it does not have a command to display characters in reverse video. You can include the next procedure for such displays.

REVERSE-VIDEO CHARACTERS

Procedure ReverseVideo, shown as Tool 9.7, will display all items written to the screen after calling it in reverse video. To return to normal-video display, use the Turbo Pascal command NormVideo for high-intensity characters or LowVideo for characters of standard brightness.

```
PROCEDURE ReverseVideo;
    BEGIN
        TextColor(0);
        TextBackGround(7);
    END;
```

Tool 9.7: Procedure ReverseVideo to display reverse-video characters.

The operation of the procedure is simple. No parameters are required; you just need to invoke the procedure name. The normal foreground and background attributes are reversed from 7,0 to 0,7.

BLINKING CHARACTERS

For more eye-catching screen displays, you can have characters blink. One way to do this is to add the predefined value Blink to the color selected in the TextColor command. The statement

TextColor(7 + Blink);

will produce blinking characters.

CONTROLLING THE SIZE OF THE CURSOR

In text mode, the cursor you usually see is one or two blinking lines of pixels at the bottom of a screen cell position. You can control the form and size of this cursor through DOS interrupt 16 (10 hex), ROM BIOS service 1.

DISPLAY PARAMETERS

You modify the size of the cursor by changing the number of lines of pixels to be displayed. With a CGA display adapter, you can use up to 8 lines (numbered 0 through 7); the monochrome and EGA adapters have 14 available lines (numbered 0 through 13).

You specify the number of lines by setting the starting and ending line numbers for display. The CGA default cursor's starting line number is 6, and its ending one is 7. For the monochrome adapter, the default cursor starts with line 12 and ends with line 13. You can adjust these settings to make the cursor larger or smaller, and even to make it disappear entirely.

SETTING THE CURSOR'S SIZE

The SetCursor procedure, shown as Tool 9.8, will change the settings for the cursor's size as indicated by the Top and Bottom parameters passed

```
PROCEDURE SetCursor(Top,Bottom:Integer);

{If this procedure is to be used with Turbo Pascal versions
    prior to 4.0, the following declaration must be included:

    TYPE
        Registers = RECORD CASE Integer OF
                1: (AX,BX,CX,DX,BP,SI,DI,DS,ES,Flags :Integer);
                2: (AL,AH,BL,BH,CL,CH,DL,DH            :Byte);
        END;}

    VAR
        Regs                            :Registers;
        Color                           :Boolean;

BEGIN  {set cursor}
    Regs.AH:=1;
    Regs.AL:=0;
    IF ((Top=0) AND (Bottom=0)) THEN
            BEGIN {hidden cursor}
                Regs.CH:=32;
            END    {hidden cursor}
                ELSE
                    BEGIN {set cursor}
                        Regs.CH:=Top;
                        Regs.CL:=Bottom;
                    END;  {set cursor}
    Intr(16,Regs);
    END;  {set cursor}
```

Tool 9.8: Procedure SetCursor to set the cursor's size.

to it. These two integer parameters represent the cursor's top and bottom lines. If both are zero, the procedure sets a hidden cursor.

The procedure uses DOS interrupt 16, service 1 to set the cursor. This operates in the same manner as a function call to interrupt 33 (see Chapter 1 for details). Register AH is set to 1; register AL should be zero; and registers CH and CL contain the starting and ending pixel line numbers for the cursor, respectively. If the cursor is to disappear, bit 5 of register CH should be set (register CH is 32).

Here's how the SetCursor procedure works:

- Set register AH to 1 and register AL to 0 to indicate the service number desired.
- If an invisible cursor is indicated (both positions are set to zero), set register CH to 32 (set bit 5).
- If other positions are given in the parameters, set the appropriate registers with those values.
- Call the Turbo Pascal Intr procedure to access interrupt 16, furnishing the registers record as the parameter.

Test Program 9.4 uses the SetCursor procedure to demonstrate cursor control within a program. It first checks to see if it is on a color or monochrome computer. If it finds color, the CGA card is assumed to be in use. The program displays the cursor set in a variety of combinations, with a screen message denoting each. A delay allows time for viewing the cursor in each setting. The last setting is the default cursor.

DISPLAYING
BAR GRAPHS

A bar graph displayed on the screen can help a program user to compare numerical data quickly. It also is much more eye-catching than a table of numbers. The next procedure will produce a horizontal bar graph in your program. This procedure uses the extended ASCII graphics characters available on all IBM compatible computers and, therefore, can operate on systems with either a color or monochrome screen and any type of display adapter card.

```
PROGRAM TryCursor;

    {To use this program with Turbo Pascal versions prior to
        4.0, remove the Uses statement below.}

    Uses DOS,CRT;

    VAR
        X, Y     :Integer;
        Color    :Boolean;

    {$I SetCurs.Inc}

    BEGIN {program}
        ClrScr;
        Color:=NOT (48 AND Mem[0000:1040]=48);
        IF Color THEN Y:=7 ELSE Y:=13;
        FOR X:=0 TO Y-1 DO
            BEGIN
                Write('Cursor ',X,X+1:4);
                SetCursor(X,X+1);
                Delay(1500);
                WriteLn;
            END;
        Write('Cursor Hidden');
        SetCursor(0,0);
        Delay(1500);
        WriteLn;
        Write('Half-Cell Cursor ');
        SetCursor(0,(Y DIV 2));
        Delay(1500);
        WriteLn;
        Write('Half-Cell Cursor ');
        SetCursor((Y DIV 2),Y);
        Delay(1500);
        WriteLn;
        Write('Normal Cursor ');
        SetCursor((Y-1),Y);
        Delay(1500);
        WriteLn;
    END.   {program}
```

Test Program 9.4: Using procedure SetCursor in a program.

A SIMPLE BAR GRAPH

Procedure BarGraph, shown as Tool 9.9, will display a bar graph of user-specified values. The procedure first builds a display screen by issuing a ClrScr command, writing a heading or title line centered at the top of the screen, and then framing an area on the screen for the horizontal bars of the graph. The Frame procedure from Chapter 7 (Tool 7.2) is used to produce the frame.

```
PROCEDURE BarGraph(GraphData:GraphRec);

{ This procedure requires the following declaration in the
  host program for the data record being passed as a
  parameter:
    TYPE
        GraphRec = RECORD
            Heading             :STRING[80];
            Values              :ARRAY[1..18] OF Real;
            Labels              :ARRAY[1..18] OF STRING[12];
        END; }



    VAR
        X, Y, Times                          :Integer;
        Largest, Smallest, Range, UnitSize,
            Multiplier, Amount               :Real;

    BEGIN {procedure to produce horizontal bar graph}
        ClrScr;
        GotoXY(1,1);
        X:=Length(GraphData.Heading);
        X:=80-X;
        IF (X>0) THEN X:=X DIV 2;
        Write(' ':X);
        Write(GraphData.Heading);
        Frame(13,3,80,22);
        FOR X:=1 TO 18 DO
            BEGIN   {for x}
                GotoXY(1,3+X);
                Write(GraphData.Labels[X]);
            END;    {for x}
        Largest:=0.0;
        Smallest:=0.0;
        FOR X:=1 TO 18 DO
            BEGIN {for x}
                IF (GraphData.Values[X]<0.0) THEN
                    GraphData.Values[X]:=0.0;
                IF (Smallest=0.0) THEN
                    Smallest:=GraphData.Values[X];
                IF (GraphData.Values[X]>Largest) THEN
                    Largest:=GraphData.Values[X];
                IF ((GraphData.Values[X]>0.0) AND
                    (GraphData.Values[X]<Smallest)) THEN
                        Smallest:=GraphData.Values[X];
            END;    {for x}
        Range:=Largest-Smallest;
        UnitSize:=Range/64;
        IF (UnitSize>1) THEN UnitSize:=((Int(UnitSize))+1);
        IF (UnitSize<0.25) THEN UnitSize:=0.25;
        IF ((UnitSize<0.5) AND (UnitSize>0.25))
            THEN UnitSize:=0.5;
        IF ((UnitSize<0.75) AND (UnitSize>0.5))
            THEN UnitSize:=1.0;
        Multiplier:=0.0;
        IF (UnitSize>100) THEN
            REPEAT
                IF (Multiplier=0.0) THEN Multiplier:=10
                    ELSE Multiplier:=Multiplier*10;
```

Tool 9.9: Procedure BarGraph to display a simple bar graph.

```
     UNTIL ((UnitSize/Multiplier)<100);
GotoXY(1,25);
Write('Each graph unit = ',Unitsize:5:3);
GotoXY(14,22);
FOR X:=14 TO 79 DO
    IF (X MOD 2 =0) THEN Write(#220)
       ELSE Write(#32);
GotoXY(14,23);
FOR X:=14 TO 79 DO
    IF (X In[14,24,34,44,54,64,74]) THEN Write(#24)
       ELSE Write(#32);
IF (Multiplier>0.0) THEN
    BEGIN {if multiplier>0}
        GotoXY(1,24);
        Write('x',Multiplier:2:0,#26);
    END;  {if multiplier>0}
GotoXY(13,24);
IF (Multiplier>0.0) THEN Write(Smallest/Multiplier:4:2)
    ELSE Write(Smallest:4:2);
FOR X:=24 TO 79 DO
    IF (X In[24,34,44,54,64,74]) THEN
        BEGIN {if x in}
            Amount:=X-14;
            Amount:=Amount*UnitSize;
            Amount:=Amount+Smallest;
            IF (Multiplier>0.0) THEN
                Amount:=Amount/Multiplier;
            GotoXY(X-1,24);
            Write(Amount:4:2);
        END;  {if x in}
FOR X:=1 TO 18 DO
    BEGIN {for x}
        IF (UnitSize>1) THEN
            Times:=Round((GraphData.Values[X]-
                        Smallest)/UnitSize)
            ELSE Times:=Round((GraphData.Values[X]-
                        Smallest)/UnitSize);
        Times:=Times+1;
        GotoXY(14,3+X);
        FOR Y:=1 TO Times DO Write(#220);
        IF (Times<56) THEN Write(' ',GraphData.Values[X]:3:2);
    END;  {for x}
END;  {procedure to produce horizontal bar graph}
```

Tool 9.9: Procedure BarGraph to display a simple bar graph. (continued)

The framed area allows 18 lines (horizontal bars) with 66 spaces or graph cells to each line. To the left of the framed area, the procedure will place 18 labels of up to 12 characters each (one for each available horizontal graph line). The bottom of the frame is replaced by an alternating series of ASCII characters #220 and #32 to form a line of alternating graph characters and blank spaces. This makes it easier to determine the exact width (and thus the represented numerical value) of each horizontal bar displayed on the screen.

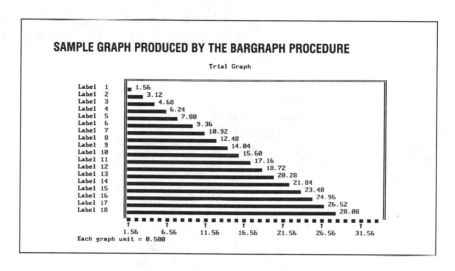

Beneath the frame, arrows (ASCII #24) are placed under the first and every tenth following cell. The procedure displays a number below each arrow to indicate the exact value of that particular cell on the graph. Depending on the range of values to be displayed on the graph, the numbers beneath the arrows may be the actual values or multipliers. If the numbers are multipliers, the display includes a notation indicating the multiplier values. This is placed on the left side of the screen, on the same line as the bar graph values. On the final line, a notation indicating the value of each screen cell in the graph (a scale value) is displayed:

Each graph unit = *nnn.nn*

If sufficient space remains at the end of the line (more than ten remaining spaces on that line) after a bar graph line is produced, the procedure will display a number representing the value of the bar.

The graph works with any numbers. The procedure determines the range of the numbers being displayed and, through division, the amount to be represented by each screen cell. This is accomplished by taking the largest number and subtracting the smallest number to determine the range, and then dividing the range by 64 (the number of graph cells available).

The graph procedure requires a record parameter to be passed to it. The record structure must be declared within your program prior to calling the procedure, and the data in the record must be set with the bar graph values by your program in order for the procedure to work properly. The record structure is:

```
TYPE
  GraphRec = RECORD
    Heading :STRING[80];
    Values :ARRAY[1..18] OF Real;
    Labels :ARRAY[1..18] OF STRING[12];
  END;
```

Here's how the BarGraph procedure works:

- Clear the screen.
- Determine the length of the heading line and number of spaces required to center it. Write the blank spaces followed by the heading or title of the graph.
- Call the Frame procedure to produce a frame for the horizontal bars.
- Write the label for each horizontal bar, in turn, down the left side of the screen.
- Determine the largest and smallest values to be represented on the graph, calculate the range (largest to smallest), and calculate the unit size.
- If the unit size is large enough (greater than 100), determine the multiplier to be used on the line where values are to be displayed. Display the unit size on line 25.
- Replace the bottom line of the frame with alternating ASCII #220 and #32 (graph characters and spaces).
- Place ASCII #24 (an up arrow character) at the first graph cell and every tenth cell thereafter.
- If a multiplier is being used, show its value on line 24.
- Place a value under each arrow which is calculated by the cell position of the arrow relative to the first cell position (number of cells displayed at that point on the screen) times the unit value and divided by the multiplier.

- Display each horizontal bar based on the value contained in the record passed as a parameter. If there are ten or more spaces available on the screen after displaying the bar, print the value of that bar on the screen also.

Test Program 9.5 demonstrates the use of the BarGraph procedure. It begins by asking the user to supply a base value. The values of each bar are set by simply multiplying the base value supplied by 1 through 18. The labels for each bar are set by using the word *Label* followed by the number of the bar it is labeling. The heading is simply *Trial Graph*. After the values are assigned to the record, the BarGraph procedure is called to produce a graph on the screen.

```
PROGRAM TryBarGraph;

     {To use this program with Turbo Pascal versions prior to
        4.0, remove the Uses statement below.}

     Uses DOS,CRT;

TYPE
     GraphRec = RECORD
         Heading                :STRING[80];
         Values                 :ARRAY[1..18] OF Real;
         Labels                 :ARRAY[1..18] OF STRING[12];
     END;

VAR
     GraphData :GraphRec;
     X          :Integer;
     BaseVal    :Real;
     S          :STRING[2];

{$I Frame.Inc}
{$I BarGraph.Inc}


BEGIN  {program to test bar graph procedure}
     ClrScr;
     Write('Enter a BASE VALUE (real number) for the graph: ');
     ReadLn(BaseVal);
     WITH GraphData DO
         BEGIN
             Heading:='Trial Graph';
             FOR X:=1 TO 18 DO Values[X]:=(X*BaseVal);
             FOR X:=1 TO 18 DO
                 BEGIN {for x}
                     Str(X:2,S);
                     Labels[X]:='Label '+S;
                 END;  {for x}
         END;
     BarGraph(GraphData);
END.   {program to test bar graph procedure}
```

Test Program 9.5: Using procedure BarGraph in a program.

CHAPTER 10
MISCELLANEOUS TOOLS

....
....
....
....
....
....
....
....
....
....
....
....
....
....
....
....
....
....
....
....
....
....
....
....
....
....
....
....
....
....
....
....
....

This chapter deals with several miscellaneous operations that can be quite handy in your programs. Among the many procedures presented here, you will find those for displaying prompts, manipulating string data, obtaining hardware information from DOS, working with the printer, and preserving data-file integrity.

PROMPTS

Programs that interact with users typically display many prompts. Having the more common prompts already written as procedures saves time and program code. Even those prompts that must be unique to a specific area can usually be prewritten to fit virtually all circumstances. The next three procedures are examples of prompts that you can use throughout your programs.

THE Y/N PROMPT

The YesNo function, shown as Tool 10.1, produces a small but handy prompt. You can save a number of lines of program code by using the function to display this common choice (Y/N). Your program can display the specific question on the screen, and then call YesNo to obtain the yes or no answer. It will return a Y or N from the user. The function forces an answer in the range of Y or N and always returns the answer in uppercase.

THE PRESS ANY KEY TO CONTINUE PROMPT

Another often-used prompt tells the user to "Press any key to continue" the program after it has been suspended for some reason. The PressKey procedure, shown as Tool 10.2, will handle this simple prompt and save some lines of program code every time it is used. Note that it first clears the screen to the end of the line prior to displaying the prompt. This is so that it will not inadvertently overwrite part of a preceding line and display a confusing message.

A UNIVERSAL PROMPT

You can use the Prompt procedure, shown as Tool 10.3, to display your prompt message in normal or reverse video anywhere on the screen. For this procedure, you specify the location of the prompt through the Column and Row integer parameters. Typically, you would place it on your program's prompt line, where all other brief instructions appear.

Note that the prompt does not have to appear in reverse video. After receiving the Column and Row parameters, the Prompt procedure looks

```
FUNCTION YesNo:Char;

     VAR
          Ch  :Char;

     BEGIN {yes no}
          Write(' (Y/N) ');
          REPEAT

          {To use this program with Turbo Pascal versions prior
               to 4.0, add the line below:}
             { Read(KBD,Ch); }

          {To use this program with Turbo Pascal versions prior
               to 4.0, remove the line below:}
             Ch:=ReadKey;

             Ch:=UpCase(Ch);
          UNTIL (Ch IN['Y','N']);
          Write(Ch);
          YesNo:=Ch;
     END;  {yes no}
```

Tool 10.1: Function Yes/No to display a Y/N prompt.

```
PROCEDURE PressKey;

     VAR
          Ch  :Char;

     BEGIN {press key}
          ClrEol;
          Write(' Press any key to continue...');

          {To use this program with Turbo Pascal versions prior
               to 4.0, add the line below:}
          { Read(KBD,Ch); }

          {To use this program with Turbo Pascal versions prior
               to 4.0, remove the line below:}
          Ch:=ReadKey;

     END;  {press key}
```

Tool 10.2: Procedure PressKey to display a Press any key to continue prompt.

for the character R as the next parameter. If an R follows, the procedure will display the prompt in reverse video, and then reset normal video. Any character other than an R in this parameter position will have no effect. The final parameter is the prompt string itself—the message that you want to appear as a prompt. Like the PressKey procedure, the

Prompt procedure first clears the screen to the end of the line prior to displaying the prompt so that it will not inadvertently overwrite part of a preceding message.

```
PROCEDURE Prompt(Col,Row:Integer; ReverseVideo:Char;
                 PromptString:Str255);

    BEGIN {prompt}
        GotoXY(Col,Row);
        IF (ReverseVideo='R') THEN
            BEGIN
                TextColor(0); TextBackground(7);
            END;
        ClrEol;
        Write(PromptString);
        IF (ReverseVideo='R') THEN NormVideo;
    END;  {prompt}
```

Tool 10.3: Procedure Prompt to display any message in normal or reverse video, in the specified screen position.

USING A PROMPT ARRAY

When I write a program, I normally construct a list of the prompts that will be used in the program and define a constant array containing all these prompts. Frequently, a number of the same prompt lines will be repeated in several locations throughout the program. It is faster, easier, and saves code space to predefine the prompts and call them with the prompt array element number. This strategy will also work well with the Prompt procedure (Tool 10.3).

STRING HANDLING

Sometimes a program must deal with string data that are not in the preferred format for the operation at hand. For example, you may need a string that is centered, padded with extra spaces, or in all uppercase letters. In these cases, a procedure to make the necessary adjustments can be very handy.

ADJUSTING THE FORMAT OF STRING DATA

The FixString procedure, shown as Tool 10.4, will make any of several modifications to a string passed to it as a parameter. The procedure requires the character parameter Operation to indicate the desired adjustment and the integer parameter Width to specify the number of spaces involved. The possible modifications and their associated parameters are summarized below.

```
PROCEDURE FixString(Operation:Char;
                    Width:Integer;
                    VAR StringVar:Str255);
    VAR
        LEN, PAD, X       :Integer;

    BEGIN {procedure fix string}
        Operation:=UpCase(Operation);
        CASE Operation OF
          'C':BEGIN {center the string}
             WHILE ((Length(StringVar)>1) AND
                    (StringVar[1]=#32)) DO
                 Delete(StringVar,1,1);
             LEN:=Length(StringVar);  PAD:=Width-LEN;
             FOR X:=1 TO (PAD DIV 2) DO
                 Insert(#32,StringVar,1);
             WHILE (Length(StringVar)<Width) DO
                 StringVar:=StringVar+' ';
             END;
          'L':BEGIN {left justify - remove leading spaces}
             WHILE ((Length(StringVar)>1) AND
                    (StringVar[1]=#32)) DO
                 Delete(StringVar,1,1);
             WHILE (Length(StringVar)<Width) DO
                 StringVar:=StringVar+' ';
             END;
          'P':BEGIN {pad with spaces to right side of string}
             WHILE (Length(StringVar)<Width) DO
                 StringVar:=StringVar+' ';
             END;
          'R':BEGIN {right justify}
             WHILE ((Length(StringVar)>1) AND
                    (StringVar[Length(StringVar)]=#32)) DO
                 Delete(StringVar,Length(StringVar),1);
             WHILE (Length(StringVar)<Width) DO
                 Insert(' ',StringVar,1);
             END;
          'U':BEGIN {convert to uppercase}
             FOR X:=1 TO Length(StringVar) DO
                 StringVar[X]:=UpCase(StringVar[X]);
             END;
          'D':BEGIN {"downcase" - convert to lowercase}
             FOR X:=1 TO Length(StringVar) DO
                 IF (ORD(StringVar[X]) IN[65..90]) THEN
                     StringVar[X]:=CHR(ORD(StringVar[X])+32);
             END;
```

Tool 10.4: Procedure FixString to adjust the format of string data.

```
          'S':BEGIN {strip leading spaces}
              FOR X:=1 TO Length(StringVar) DO
                  IF (StringVar[1]=#32) THEN
                      Delete(StringVar,1,1);
              END;
          'T':BEGIN {strip trailing spaces}
              FOR X:=1 TO Length(StringVar) DO
                  IF (StringVar[Length(StringVar)]=#32) THEN
                      Delete(StringVar,Length(StringVar),1);
              END;
          'N':BEGIN {construct a null string}
              StringVar:=#0;
              WHILE (Length(StringVar)<Width) DO
                  StringVar:=StringVar+#0;
              END;
        END; {case statement}
    END;   {procedure fix string}
```

Tool 10.4: Procedure FixString to adjust the format of string data. (continued)

Modification	Operation Parameter	Width Parameter
Center the string in a specified field, padding it with spaces on both sides	C	A number from 3 through 255 indicating how many character spaces to center the string within
Left-justify the string, removing leading spaces and padding the right side with spaces	L	A number from 3 through 255 indicating the width of the field
Right-justify the string, removing trailing spaces and padding the left side with spaces	R	A number from 3 through 255 indicating the width of the field
Pad the right side of the string	P	A number from 3 through 255 indicating the width of the field
Convert all string characters to uppercase	U	0 (as a dummy number)

Modification	Operation Parameter	Width Parameter
Convert all string characters to lowercase	D	0
Strip all leading spaces (ASCII #32) from the string	S	0
Strip all trailing spaces from the string	T	0
Construct a string of nulls (ASCII #0)	N	A number from 3 to 255 indicating the desired string length (how many nulls)

Note that the Width parameter does not apply to all operations; a zero is listed above, but you can use any Width integer for those modifications. Here's how the FixString procedure works:

- Through a CASE statement, select the processing which will be done to the target string, based on the Operation parameter received.

- For centering, strip the string of any leading blanks and then center it in the desired width (indicated by the Width parameter) by adding leading and trailing blanks.

- For left justification, strip the target of leading blanks and pad it with trailing blanks to the desired length.

- For a padding operating, add spaces to the right side of the string until it reaches the specified width.

- For the right justification operation, first strip any trailing spaces and then pad the string with spaces to the left of the first string character.

- For the uppercase and lowercase conversion operations, examine each string character and convert it to the proper case. For uppercase conversions, use the Turbo Pascal UpCase function.

Handle conversion to lowercase by program statements (Turbo Pascal does not provide this utility).

- For stripping leading or trailing spaces, examine the beginning or end of the string for spaces and remove them.

- For the null-string creation operation, initialize the string at a single null (ASCII #0), and then continue adding null characters until the string reaches the value specified in the Width parameter.

USING THE PROMPT AND STRING-HANDLING PROCEDURES IN A PROGRAM

Test Program 10.1 illustrates the use of the prompt function YesNo and procedures PressKey and Prompt and the string-handling procedure FixString in a program.

For the demonstration, 13 of the 14 messages to be displayed with the Prompt procedure are first declared as an array of constants. Then the Prompt procedure writes all messages to the screen, and the YesNo procedure asks if the user wishes to continue the demonstration; if not, it is halted. Next, the program requests that the user enter a string. The string is modified by the FixString procedure and displayed after each action. The original string is always acted upon so that the cumulative effect of the operations does not affect the presentation of the altered original string. Finally, the PressKey procedure is demonstrated, and the program ends.

FILE SIZE

Many times, it would be useful for a program to check the size of a file in bytes. For example, if a program is copying files, having it check the file size, as well as the available disk space (with a procedure such as Disk-FreeSpc, Tool 1.7), would ensure that a successful file-copy operation can take place.

```
PROGRAM StringAndPromptDemo;

     {To use this program with Turbo Pascal versions prior to
        4.0, remove the Uses statement below.}

     Uses DOS,CRT;

     {$V-}    {relaxed parameter type checking}

     TYPE
          Str255 = STRING[255];

     VAR
          Ans                    :Char;
          TestString, WorkString :STRING[80];

     CONST
          Prompts  :ARRAY[1..13] OF STRING[79] =
                  (' All messages are displayed by "Prompt". ',
                   ' This is how the YesNo function works... ',
                   'Do you want to continue ? ',
                   ' This is a demonstration of FixString... ',
                   'Enter a string below: (Max. 70 characters)',
                   ' String centered 78 cols. enclosed by quotes: ',
                   ' String right justified 78 cols.: ',
                   ' String left justified 78 cols.: ',
                   ' String converted to uppercase: ',
                   ' String converted to lowercase: ',
                   ' String stripped of leading spaces: ',
                   ' String stripped of trailing spaces: ',
                   ' String padded to right to 78 spaces length: ');

     {$I YesNo.Inc}
     {$I PressKey.Inc}
     {$I Prompt.Inc}
     {$I FixStrng.Inc}

     BEGIN {program}
          ClrScr;
          Prompt(1,1,'R',Prompts[1]);
          Prompt(1,3,'R',Prompts[2]);
          Prompt(1,4,'x',Prompts[3]);
          Ans:=YesNo;
          IF (Ans='N') THEN Halt;
          Prompt(1,6,'R',Prompts[4]);
          Prompt(1,7,'x',Prompts[5]);
          WriteLn;
          ReadLn(TestString);
          WorkString:=TestString;
          Prompt(1,9,'R',Prompts[6]);
          FixString('C',78,WorkString);
          GotoXY(1,10);
          Write('"',WorkString,'"');
          WorkString:=TestString;
          Prompt(1,11,'R',Prompts[7]);
          FixString('R',78,WorkString);
          GotoXY(1,12);
```

Test Program 10.1: Using procedures PressKey, Prompt, and FixString and function
YesNo in a program.

```
                Write('"',WorkString,'"');
                WorkString:=TestString;
                Prompt(1,13,'R',Prompts[8]);
                FixString('L',78,WorkString);
                GotoXY(1,14);
                Write('"',WorkString,'"');
                WorkString:=TestString;
                Prompt(1,15,'R',Prompts[9]);
                FixString('U',78,WorkString);
                GotoXY(1,16);
                Write('"',WorkString,'"');
                WorkString:=TestString;
                Prompt(1,17,'R',Prompts[10]);
                FixString('D',78,WorkString);
                GotoXY(1,18);
                Write('"',WorkString,'"');
                WorkString:=TestString;
                Prompt(1,19,'R',Prompts[11]);
                FixString('S',78,WorkString);
                GotoXY(1,20);
                Write('"',WorkString,'"');
                WorkString:=TestString;
                Prompt(1,21,'R',Prompts[12]);
                FixString('T',78,WorkString);
                GotoXY(1,22);
                Write('"',WorkString,'"');
                WorkString:=TestString;
                Prompt(1,23,'R',Prompts[13]);
                FixString('P',78,WorkString);
                GotoXY(1,24);
                Write('"',WorkString,'"');
                GotoXY(1,25);
                PressKey;
                WriteLn; WriteLn; WriteLn;
                Prompt(1,24,'x',' >> Demonstration complete! ');
        END.   {program}
```

Test Program 10.1: Using procedures PressKey, Prompt, and FixString and function
YesNo in a program. (continued)

CHECKING THE FILE SIZE IN BYTES

Function FileBytes, shown as Tool 10.5, returns a real number containing the number of bytes in the file specified.

Here's how the FileBytes function works:

- After assigning the file name passed as a parameter, attempt to open the file.

- Check I/OResult and, if satisfactory, determine the size using the Turbo Pascal LongFileSize function.

```
FUNCTION FileBytes(FileName:Str255):Real;

    VAR
            TextFile :FILE OF Byte;
            Result   :Integer;
            Size     :Real;

    BEGIN {file bytes}
            Assign(TextFile,FileName);
            {$I-} Reset(TextFile); {$I+}
            Result:=IOResult;

            {To use this program with Turbo Pascal versions prior
                to 4.0, add the line below:}
            { IF (Result=0) THEN Size:=LongFileSize(TextFile)
                ELSE Size:=0.0; }

            {To use this program with Turbo Pascal versions prior
                to 4.0, remove the line below:}
            IF (Result=0) THEN Size:=FileSize(TextFile)
                ELSE Size:=0.0;

            {$I-} Close(TextFile); {$I+}
            Result:=IOResult;
            FileBytes:=Size;
    END;   {file bytes}
```

Tool 10.5: Function FileBytes to get the size of a file in bytes.

- Close the file. Make another call to I/OResult in order to prevent it from holding an error code that would lock up other I/O procedures.

The use of the FileBytes function in a program is demonstrated in Test Program 10.2. In this program, the user is asked to supply a file name, and then the file size in bytes is obtained.

COMPUTER EQUIPMENT AND MEMORY REPORTS

Among the data items stored by BIOS into a low memory area of RAM during bootup is information concerning the computer hardware available. Memory location 0000:1040 contains a bit map that provides several useful pieces of information. In fact, you've already seen many procedures that make use of some of these data. The procedures in this book that

```
PROGRAM TestFileBytes;

     {To use this program with Turbo Pascal versions prior to
         4.0, remove the Uses statement below.}

     Uses DOS;

     {$V-}  {relaxed parameter type checking}

     TYPE
          Str255 = STRING[255];

     VAR
          FName     :STRING[65];
          Size      :Real;

     {$I FileByte.Inc}

     BEGIN {program}
          WriteLn;
          Write('Enter name of file to check: ');
          ReadLn(FName);
          Size:=FileBytes(FName);
          WriteLn;
          WriteLn('File size is ',Size:7:0,' bytes.');
     END.   {program}
```

Test Program 10.2: Using function FileBytes in a program.

directly manipulate video RAM check the data on the video mode (color or monochrome), stored in 2 bits of this 2-byte configuration. Table 10.1 shows a bit map of the memory location.

GETTING USEFUL BIOS EQUIPMENT INFORMATION

Tool 10.6 presents four functions to report the more useful data items stored by the BIOS: functions Drives, Color80Col, Printers, and SerialPrinter. Each function examines specific bits of the appropriate byte for the desired information. If your program needs other information from this memory area, such as game adapter data, you can use the functions here as a guide for designing your own.

The Drives function reports the diskette drives (not hard drives). If such drives are present, the function obtains the number by reading the 2 bits with this information (bits 6 and 7) and adding 1 to that value.

The Color80Col function reports true or false that the startup video mode is for 80-column color. It uses the AND operator to determine if the bit is set to indicate a monochrome configuration, and then uses the

Table 10.1:
Bit Map of DOS Equipment List Bytes

Byte at 1041								Byte at 1040								Indication
15	14	13	12	11	10	9	8	7	6	5	4	3	2	1	0	
X	X	_	_	_	_	_	_	_	_	_	_	_	_	_	_	Number printers
_	_	1	_	_	_	_	_	_	_	_	_	_	_	_	_	Serial printer
_	_	_	1	_	_	_	_	_	_	_	_	_	_	_	_	Game adapter
_	_	_	_	X	X	X	_	_	_	_	_	_	_	_	_	Number RS-232 ports
_	_	_	_	_	_	_	0	_	_	_	_	_	_	_	_	0 = DMA installed
_	_	_	_	_	_	_	_	X	X	_	_	_	_	_	_	Number diskette drives (00 = 1, 01 = 2, 10 = 3, 11 = 4)
_	_	_	_	_	_	_	_	_	_	X	X	_	_	_	_	Initial video mode (10 = 80 column color, 11 = 80 column monochrome)
_	_	_	_	_	_	_	_	_	_	_	_	X	X	_	_	System board RAM (11 = 64K = normal)
_	_	_	_	_	_	_	_	_	_	_	_	_	_	0	_	Not used
_	_	_	_	_	_	_	_	_	_	_	_	_	_	_	1	Disk drive present

NOT operator to apply that information to the truth of the presence of a color card.

The Printers function reports the number of printers installed. It reads the 2 bits indicating the number of printers and reports the number back to the host program.

The SerialPrinter reports true or false that a serial printer is installed. It uses the AND operator to determine if the bit is set to indicate the presence of a serial printer.

GETTING THE SYSTEM RAM

Another useful data item stored by BIOS during bootup is the system RAM. Function RAMSize, shown as Tool 10.7, returns an integer indicating

```
FUNCTION Drives:Integer;

     VAR
        X:Integer;

     BEGIN {report number drives present}
          X:=0;
          IF (1 AND Mem[0000:1040]=1) THEN {drive is present}
               BEGIN
                    X:=Mem[0000:1040] SHR 6;
                    X:=X+1;
               END;
          Drives:=X;
     END;   {report number drives present}

FUNCTION Color80Col:Boolean;

     BEGIN {report if initial mode is 80-column color,}
           {if not, it is 80-column monochrome       }
           Color80Col:=NOT (48 AND Mem[0000:1040]=48);
     END;

FUNCTION Printers:Integer;

     BEGIN {report number printers installed}
          Printers:=Mem[0000:1041] SHR 6;
     END;   {report number printers installed}

FUNCTION SerialPrinter:Boolean;

     BEGIN {is a serial printer installed?}
          SerialPrinter:=(32 AND Mem[0000:1041]=32);
     END;   {is a serial printer installed?}
```

Tool 10.6: Functions Drives, Color80Col, Printers, and SerialPrinter to obtain useful BIOS information.

```
FUNCTION RAMSize:Integer;

     BEGIN {get system RAM in Kb}
          RAMSize:=MemW[0000:1043];
     END;   {get system RAM in Kb}
```

Tool 10.7: Function RAMSize to get the system RAM in kilobytes.

the system RAM in kilobytes (1024 bytes = 1 kilobyte). The RAMSize function reads a 2-byte word from memory where the size of the system RAM is stored at bootup and returns the number to the host program.

USING THE SYSTEM INFORMATION FUNCTIONS IN A PROGRAM

Test Program 10.3 illustrates the use of the functions RAMSize, Color80Col, SerialPrinter, Printers, and Drives. It obtains the system information and displays it on the screen.

```
PROGRAM SysInfo;

    {To use this program with Turbo Pascal versions prior to
     4.0, remove the Uses statement below.}

Uses DOS,CRT;

{$I RAMSize.Inc}
{$I Color80.Inc}
{$I SerPrntr.Inc}
{$I Printers.Inc}
{$I Drives.Inc}

BEGIN {program}
    ClrScr;
    WriteLn('System RAM is: ',RAMSize,' Kb.');
    WriteLn('System is 80 column color: ',Color80Col);
    WriteLn('There is a serial printer installed: ',
            SerialPrinter);
    WriteLn('There is (are) ',Printers,
            ' printer(s) installed.');
    WriteLn('There is/are ',Drives,' diskette drives.');
END.    {program}
```

Test Program 10.3: Using functions RAMSize, Color80Col, SerialPrinter, and Printers in a program.

WORKING WITH PRINTERS

Although Turbo Pascal provides the necessary structures for working with printers, you can use certain other services available through DOS to add a more professional touch to your programs. They also can provide a little extra help in preventing printing problems. For example, most programs offer some report printing capabilities and, when the user requests such a report, just begin sending data to the printer. If the user has neglected to turn the printer on or load it with paper, an error occurs and is reported by

DOS. Aside from the inconvenience, this can play havoc with the appearance of a screen. Using the procedures and functions presented in this section, your program can check to see if the printer is ready to operate, as well as obtain other useful printer status information.

DOS PRINTER SERVICES

The printer services available through DOS' ROM BIOS use interrupt 23 (17 hex). The following services are available:

- Service 0: Send 1 byte to the printer
- Service 1: Initialize the printer port
- Service 2: Get the printer status

The service that is probably the most useful is the one that provides information about printer status (service 2).

You can use these services in the same way that the DOS functions are accessed through interrupt 33 (see Chapter 1) and the cursor-setting service is accessed through interrupt 16 (Tool 9.7). When requesting printer services, specify the printer number in register DX (because DOS allows multiple printers). The default printer is zero.

Service 0: Send 1 Byte to the Printer

To use service 0, set register AH to the service number (zero) and set register AL to the byte to be sent to the printer. Register DX is set to the printer number to be reported upon. After sending a byte to the printer, register AH is set to report the printer status in order to determine the success of the operation. It may be read just as if service 2 had been called.

Service 1: Initialize the Printer Port

To use service 1, set register AH to the service number (1) and set register AL to zero. Register DX is set to the printer number to be initialized. This service sends two control codes to the printer control port: 8 and 12 (08 and 0C hex). After returning, the printer status is reported in register AH and may be read just as if service 2 had been called.

Service 2: Get the Printer Status

To use service 2, set register AH to the service number (2) and set AL to zero. Register DX is set to the printer number to be reported upon. When the service returns, register AH contains the printer status.

The Printer Status Byte

The printer status byte is bit-mapped with each bit representing a specific piece of information. Table 10.2 shows the information contained in the printer status byte.

Table 10.2:
Bit Map of the DOS BIOS Printer Status Byte

7	6	5	4	3	2	1	0	**Meaning**
1	_	_	_	_	_	_	_	Printer not busy (0 indicates busy)
_	1	_	_	_	_	_	_	Acknowledgment from printer
_	_	1	_	_	_	_	_	Paper empty
_	_	_	1	_	_	_	_	Selected (0 indicates deselected)
_	_	_	_	1	_	_	_	I/O error
_	_	_	_	_	X	X	_	Not used
_	_	_	_	_	_	_	1	Time out

ASKING FOR PRINTER STATUS

Function PrintStat, presented as Tool 10.8, uses interrupt 23, service 2 to obtain the printer status. The printer status is returned as a byte, which then must be examined (the next procedure does this). The function must be passed the number of the printer on which it is to check. The default printer is zero.

Here's how the PrintStat function works:

- Set register AH to 2 (the service number) and register DX to the printer number passed as a parameter.

```
FUNCTION PrintStat(WhichPrinter:Integer):Integer;

{If this procedure is to be used with Turbo Pascal versions
    prior to 4.0, the following declaration must be included:

   TYPE
        Registers = RECORD CASE Integer OF
                1: (AX,BX,CX,DX,BP,SI,DI,DS,ES,Flags :Integer);
                2: (AL,AH,BL,BH,CL,CH,DL,DH            :Byte);
        END;}

   VAR
        Regs                      :Registers;

   BEGIN {get printer status}
        Regs.AH:=2;
        Regs.AL:=0;
        Regs.DX:=WhichPrinter;
        Intr(23,Regs);
        PrintStat:=Regs.AH;
   END;   {get printer status}
```

Tool 10.8: Function PrintStat to ask for printer status.

- Call the Turbo Pascal Intr procedure and furnish it with interrupt number 23 and Registers as a record parameter.

- Upon return from the interrupt, pass the value of register AH, which contains the printer status, to the calling program.

CHECKING PRINTER STATUS

The PrinterError procedure, presented as Tool 10.9, interprets the printer status byte returned by any of the three DOS printer services. It returns an integer number code to tell the host program what error occurred, as well as a literal string to describe the error.

Here's how the PrinterError procedure works:

- Receive the printer StatusByte returned by any of the three services for checking.

- Initialize ErrorCode at zero (no error).

- Check the StatusByte for error conditions, and if one is found, set the ErrorCode. A value of 1 for ErrorCode indicates the printer is off line, and 2 indicates the printer paper supply is empty.

```
PROCEDURE PrinterError(StatusByte:Integer;
                       VAR ErrorCode:Integer;
                       VAR ErrorReturn:Str255);

    VAR
        X       :Integer;

    CONST
        Error :ARRAY[0..2] OF STRING[10] =
        ('No error',
        'Off Line',
        'Paper Out');

    BEGIN {decode error from printer}
        ErrorCode:=0;
        IF ((16 AND StatusByte=0) OR (8 AND StatusByte>0))
            THEN ErrorCode:=1;
        IF (32 AND StatusByte>0) THEN ErrorCode:=2;
        ErrorReturn:=Error[ErrorCode];
    END;  {decode error from printer}
```

Tool 10.9: Procedure PrinterError to check the printer status.

- Load the ErrorReturn string with the literal representing the error code being returned.

INITIALIZING THE PRINTER

Function InitPrnt, shown as Tool 10.10, uses interrupt 23, service 1 to initialize the printer port. As with function PrintStat, the printer status is returned as a byte in register AH, and then returned to the host program by the function. The function must be passed the number of the printer which it is to initialize.

SENDING A BYTE TO THE PRINTER

Interrupt 23, service 0 allows you to send a byte to the printer. Although you could handle this through the Turbo Pascal command for a normal Write operation to the printer, function SendByte, presented as Tool 10.11, uses this alternative method. The function requires a parameter indicating the printer to which the byte should be sent and an ASCII code byte for the character being sent.

```
FUNCTION InitPrnt(WhichPrinter:Integer):Integer;

{If this procedure is to be used with Turbo Pascal versions
     prior to 4.0, the following declaration must be included:

     TYPE
          Registers = RECORD CASE Integer OF
               1: (AX,BX,CX,DX,BP,SI,DI,DS,ES,Flags :Integer);
               2: (AL,AH,BL,BH,CL,CH,DL,DH          :Byte);
          END;}

     VAR
          Regs                    :Registers;

     BEGIN {initialize printer}
          Regs.AH:=1;
          Regs.AL:=0;
          Regs.DX:=WhichPrinter;
          Intr(23,Regs);
          InitPrnt:=Regs.AH;
     END;   {initialize printer}
```

Tool 10.10: Function InitPrnt to initialize the printer port.

Here's how the SendByte function works:

- Set the registers. Register AH is set to the service number (0), register AL to the ASCII code that will be sent to the printer, and register DX to the printer number.
- Call the Turbo Pascal Intr procedure.
- After returning from the interrupt, return the value in register AH, which contains the status byte from the printer, to the calling program.

USING THE PRINTER FUNCTIONS IN A PROGRAM

Test Program 10.4 demonstrates the use of the printer functions and procedure presented in this section. Note that although the demonstration program allows characters to be fed to the printer for printing, they usually will not be printed immediately. Generally, the printer will store the characters in its buffer until a carriage return is received, and then print a line.

The program works with printer zero, the default printer. It first goes into a repeat loop to check printer status so that the printer may be turned on, off, deselected, etc., to test the varying results. Next, it offers the option

```
FUNCTION SendByte(WhichPrinter:Integer;Code:Integer):Integer;

{If this procedure is to be used with Turbo Pascal versions
    prior to 4.0, the following declaration must be included:

    TYPE
        Registers = RECORD CASE Integer OF
              1: (AX,BX,CX,DX,BP,SI,DI,DS,ES,Flags :Integer);
              2: (AL,AH,BL,BH,CL,CH,DL,DH           :Byte);
        END;}

    VAR
        Regs                    :Registers;

    BEGIN {send byte to printer}
        Regs.AH:=0;
        Regs.AL:=Code;
        Regs.DX:=WhichPrinter;
        Intr(23,Regs);
        SendByte:=Regs.AH;
    END;  {send byte to printer}
```

Tool 10.11: Function SendByte for sending a byte to the printer.

of initializing the printer port; if approved, the initialization takes place. Finally, the program goes into a repeat loop to send characters to the printer. Any time an error is encountered in the various functions, it is reported.

PRESERVING DATA-FILE INTEGRITY

Most programs use data files and rely upon them to have complete integrity. Good programming practices can maintain complete control of the data files and ensure that the data reaches them properly and are always correct (subject always, of course, to operator error). However, the best software cannot control hardware failures, accidental shutdown of equipment, power failures, and other such situations. When a program is in the midst of a long file-handling procedure and disaster strikes, the integrity of all files involved is compromised. Some may have been updated with new information, while others may not have had appropriate data added to them. In these cases, the user must resort to restoration of data files with their most recent backup copies.

```
PROGRAM TestPrnt;

    {To use this program with Turbo Pascal versions prior to
        4.0, remove the Uses statement below.}

    Uses DOS,CRT;

    {$V-}  {relaxed parameter type checking}

    TYPE
        Str255 = STRING[255];

    VAR
        B,X             :Integer;
        Ch              :Char;
        Error           :STRING[10];

    {$I SendByte.Inc}
    {$I InitPrnt.Inc}
    {$I PrntErr.Inc}
    {$I PrntStat.Inc}

    BEGIN {program}
        ClrScr;
        WriteLn('Check printer status.');
        REPEAT
            B:=PrintStat(0);
            PrinterError(B,X,Error);
            WriteLn('     Printer error = ',X,' = ',Error);
            Write('Check again? (Y/N) ');

        {To use this program with Turbo Pascal versions prior
            to 4.0, add the line below:}
            { Read(KBD,Ch); }

        {To use this program with Turbo Pascal versions prior
            to 4.0, remove the line below:}
            Ch:=ReadKey;

            WriteLn(Ch);
        UNTIL (Ch IN['N','n']);
        WriteLn;
        Write('Initialize printer ?  (Y/N)  ');



        {To use this program with Turbo Pascal versions prior
            to 4.0, add the line below:}
        { Read(KBD,Ch); }

        {To use this program with Turbo Pascal versions prior
            to 4.0, remove the line below:}
        Ch:=ReadKey;
        WriteLn(Ch);
        IF (Ch IN['Y','y']) THEN
            BEGIN
                B:=InitPrnt(0);
                PrinterError(B,X,Error);
                WriteLn('     Printer error = ',X,' = ',Error);
            END;
```

Test Program 10.4: Using functions SendByte, InitPrnt, and PrintStat and procedure PrinterError in a program.

```
          WriteLn;
          WriteLn('Send characters to printer until a ',
                  'period (.) is entered.');
          WriteLn('>  Must enter <CR> to actually print line.');
          WriteLn;
          Write('>>>>>  ENTER CHARACTERS TO PRINT, . TO STOP:');
          REPEAT

       {To use this program with Turbo Pascal versions prior
             to 4.0, add the line below:}
             { Read(KBD,Ch); }

       {To use this program with Turbo Pascal versions prior
             to 4.0, remove the line below:}
             Ch:=ReadKey;

             Write(Ch);
             B:=SendByte(0,ORD(Ch));
             PrinterError(B,X,Error);
             IF (X<>0) THEN
                    Write('  Printer error = ',X,' = ',Error);
          UNTIL (Ch='.');
          B:=SendByte(0,10);
          B:=SendByte(0,13);
  END.   {program}
```

Test Program 10.4: Using functions SendByte, InitPrnt, and PrintStat and procedure PrinterError in a program. (continued)

While you cannot guard against calamity completely, you can take measures to greatly reduce the risk of file corruption. The following procedures work together to help guard data-file integrity within your programs. Although these procedures will slow down some operations in your program, they effectively minimize the time during which files can be damaged should disaster strike.

AN OVERVIEW OF THE FILE-PROTECTION TECHNIQUE

The file-protection technique uses three procedures:

- The FileSafe1 procedure is used at the beginning of a program to see if there is an indication that the program was last terminated during file activity that probably resulted in incomplete data processing. If such a scenario is apparent, FileSafe1 offers to restore all the affected data files.

- The FileSafe2 procedure is used within a program immediately prior to file activity. It is given the names of all data files to which operations are to be performed. Prior to any file activity, each of these files is quickly duplicated, and a list of the affected files is placed in another special file.

- The FileSafe3 procedure is called immediately following the complete sequence of file activity and destroys the duplicate files and the file referencing the duplicated files.

If a failure occurs between the time FileSafe2 is called and the time File-Safe3 removes the duplicate files, the only data lost are those worked with during that specific file-access period. FileSafe1 will restore the files to their previous state when the program is again invoked. Data-file vulnerability is reduced to the time it takes to remove the FileSafe duplicate files.

The FileSafe procedures require the use of several other procedures presented in this book: Exist or Exist4 (depending upon the Turbo Pascal version in use), FileByte, and DiskFreeSpc. The description of each FileSafe procedure illustrates the manner in which these procedures may be most effectively employed within your programs. Even though the FileSafe1 procedure should always be used at the very beginning of the program, it is described last in order to clarify the manner in which the procedures operate in conjunction with one another.

BEGINNING THE FILE-PROTECTION PROCESS

Procedure FileSafe2, presented as Tool 10.12, begins the file-protection process. When this procedure is called, it is passed one or more file names. Each of these files is duplicated, and the duplicate copy is named FILE-SAFE. The copy is given, as a unique file-name extension, a three-digit series number in the range of 001 to 020. Theoretically, up to 999 files could be duplicated, but the procedure has a built-in limit of 20 files.

This procedure should be called in a program that is updating a number of files with related information or a single file with a lot of information. These operations are lengthy enough to allow time for a hardware failure, which could result in partially completed data transfer.

The FileSafe2 procedure is simple to call. It must be passed a string containing the names of the files which are involved in the transaction to be protected. The files must all be existing files, not ones created during the

```
PROCEDURE FileSafe2(FileSpecs:Str255);

    CONST
        RecordSize          = 128;
        RecsToRead          = 80; {reads up to 10 Kb at a time}

    VAR
        SizeOfFileToCopy, TS, TF        :Real;
        BPS,SPC,AC,TC,RecsRead, X, FN :Integer;
        File1, File2                    :FILE;
        FileBuffer                      :ARRAY[1..RecordSize,
                                            1..RecsToRead] OF Byte;
        FileNames                       :Text;
        FName                           :ARRAY[1..20] OF STRING[64];
        WorkLine                        :Str255;
        S                               :STRING[3];
        FileToCopy                      :STRING[64];

    PROCEDURE Notify;
        BEGIN {notify that file not found and halt}
            Write(#7#7);
            WriteLn; WriteLn;
            WriteLn(FName[FN],' file not found.  Program Halts.');
            Write(#7#7);
            Halt;
        END;  {notify that file not found and halt}

    PROCEDURE Notify2;

        VAR
            X  :Integer;

        BEGIN {notify of insufficient disk space}
            Write(#7#7);
            WriteLn; WriteLn;
            WriteLn('Insufficient disk space.  Program Halts.');
            {destroy any files already copied and the control
                file so that it does not appear program
                terminated inproperly}
            Assign(File1,'FILESAFE.000');
            Erase(File1);
            FOR X:=1 TO 20 DO
                BEGIN {for x}
                    Str(X:3,S);
                    IF NOT (S[1] In['1'..'9']) THEN S[1]:='0';
                    IF NOT (S[2] In['1'..'9']) THEN S[2]:='0';
                    Assign(File1,'FILESAFE.'+S);

        {To use this program with Turbo Pascal versions prior
            to 4.0, add the line below:}
                { IF (Exist('FILESAGE.'+S)) THEN Erase(File1);}

        {To use this program with Turbo Pascal versions prior
            to 4.0, remove the line below:}
                IF (Exist4('FILESAFE.'+S)) THEN Erase(File1);

                END;  {for x}
```

Tool 10.12: Procedure FileSafe2 to begin the file-protection process.

```
            Write(#7#7);
            Halt;
        END;  {notify of insufficient disk space}


BEGIN {procedure filesafe 2}
    WorkLine:=FileSpecs;
    FOR FN:=1 TO 20 DO FName[FN]:='';
    FN:=1;
    WHILE (Length(WorkLine)>0) DO
        BEGIN {separate file names + check existence}
            X:=Pos(' ',WorkLine);
            FName[FN]:=Copy(WorkLine,1,X-1);
            Delete(WorkLine,1,X);

        {To use this program with Turbo Pascal versions prior
            to 4.0, add the line below:}
            { IF NOT Exist(FName[FN]) THEN Notify; }

        {To use this program with Turbo Pascal versions prior
            to 4.0, remove the line below:}
            IF NOT Exist4(FName[FN]) THEN Notify;

            FN:=FN+1;
            IF (FN>20) THEN WorkLine:='';
        END;  {separate file names + check existence}
    {set up FILESAFE.000}
    Assign(FileNames,'FILESAFE.000');
    Rewrite(FileNames);
    FOR FN:=1 TO 20 DO IF (FName[FN]<>'') THEN
        BEGIN {make a copy of each file}
            {get file size}
            FileToCopy:=FName[FN];
            SizeOfFileToCopy:=FileBytes(FileToCopy);
            DiskFreeSpc('0',BPS,SPC,AC,TC,TS,TF);
            IF (SizeOfFileToCopy>TF) THEN Notify2;
            Assign(File1,FileToCopy);
            Str(FN:3,S);
            IF NOT (S[1] In['1'..'9']) THEN S[1]:='0';
            IF NOT (S[2] In['1'..'9']) THEN S[2]:='0';
            Assign(File2,'FILESAFE.'+S);
            Reset(File1);
            Rewrite(File2);
            REPEAT
                BlockRead(File1,FileBuffer,RecsToRead,RecsRead);
                BlockWrite(File2,FileBuffer,RecsRead);
            UNTIL (RecsRead=0);
            Close(File1);
            Close(File2);
            WriteLn(FileNames,FName[FN]);
        END; {make a copy of each file}
    Close(FileNames);
END;  {procedure filesafe 2}
```

Tool 10.12: Procedure FileSafe2 to begin the file-protection process. (continued)

transaction. File names are to be separated with a space within the string and can contain drive specifiers and paths. All file names must be specific—wild-card characters cannot be used. The FileSafe2 procedure should be called immediately prior to the actual processing of the files or as near (but prior) to this time as possible. All affected files must be closed at the time FileSafe2 is called.

The procedure reads the string of file names passed as a parameter and assigns each file name to an element of an array of file names used by the procedure. As each file name is extracted from the string, a check is made to determine that the file actually exists. If any file does not exist, a

File not found

message is displayed, and program execution stops immediately. Next, the procedure creates its own special file, named FILESAFE.000, to track and identify all files being duplicated. Each of the files to be duplicated is checked for file size. The remaining space on the default drive, where the file duplication will be made, is also checked to determine if it is sufficient for the copy to be made. If disk space is insufficient, the procedure displays a message and stops program execution immediately.

There must always be sufficient disk space for duplication of all affected files. If there is not enough space, the duplicate files that have already been made and the FILESAFE.000 file are erased so that it will not appear that the program terminated improperly the next time it is invoked. Assuming that there is sufficient space for the file copy to proceed, a duplicate file is made, and the file name is added to FILESAFE.000. Each duplicate file is assigned the primary name FILESAFE and a sequential extension. For example, the first file to be duplicated has the extension .001, the second has .002, and so on. When all files specified in the parameter string have been copied, the procedure ends.

If a failure occurred during the time FileSafe2 was duplicating files, no actual files would have been compromised. Now, since duplicates are in place, if a failure occurs, the only loss will be of the data that are about to be exchanged in the various file operations that will be undertaken prior to calling the FileSafe3 procedure, described next. If the program is unexpectedly terminated prior to completing these operations, all the files that were duplicated by FileSafe2 are available for data restoration.

COMPLETING THE FILE-PROTECTION PROCESS

After your program has performed all its file operations and closed all files, it is time to call FileSafe3, presented as Tool 10.13. The FileSafe3 procedure simply erases control file FILESAFE.000 and all duplicate files (FILESAFE.001 through FILESAFE.020). As soon as the control file has been erased, the FileSafe system of procedures will know that the program has not terminated abnormally during file transactions.

```
PROCEDURE FileSafe3;

    VAR
        WF1         :Text;
        X           :Integer;
        S           :STRING[3];

    BEGIN {procedure filesafe 3}
        Assign(WF1,'FILESAFE.000');
        Erase(WF1);
        FOR X:=1 TO 20 DO
            BEGIN {for x}
                Str(X:3,S);
                IF NOT (S[1] In['1'..'9']) THEN S[1]:='0';
                IF NOT (S[2] In['1'..'9']) THEN S[2]:='0';
                Assign(WF1,'FILESAFE.'+S);

        {To use this program with Turbo Pascal versions prior
            to 4.0, add the line below:}
            {IF (Exist('FILESAFE.'+S)) THEN Erase(WF1);}

        {To use this program with Turbo Pascal versions prior
            to 4.0, remove the line below:}
            IF (Exist4('FILESAFE.'+S)) THEN Erase(WF1);

            END;  {for x}
        END;   {procedure filesafe 3}
```

Tool 10.13: Procedure FileSafe3 to complete the file-protection process.

The FileSafe3 procedure is called by simply invoking the name of the procedure; it does not require any parameters.

BEGINNING A PROGRAM THAT USES THE FILE-PROTECTION PROCESS

The FileSafe1 procedure, shown as Tool 10.14, should be called at the very beginning of a program. We know that FileSafe2 created a control file containing the names of the files it was duplicating. If the program terminated abruptly, the control file and duplicate files will still exist because the

```
PROCEDURE FileSafe1;

    VAR
        FileNames, WF1, WF2     :Text;
        FName                   :ARRAY[1..20] OF STRING[64];
        Action                  :Char;
        X                       :Integer;
        S                       :STRING[3];
        There1, There2          :Boolean;

    PROCEDURE Assignment;
        BEGIN {assign filenames}
            Assign(WF1,FName[X]);
            Str(X:3,S);
            IF NOT (S[1] In['1'..'9']) THEN S[1]:='0';
            IF NOT (S[2] In['1'..'9']) THEN S[2]:='0';
            Assign(WF2,'FILESAFE.'+S);
        END;  {assign filenames}

    PROCEDURE Notify;
        BEGIN {notify that file not found and halt}
            Write(#7#7);
            WriteLn; WriteLn;
            WriteLn('Needed file not found.  Program halts now.');
            Write(#7#7);
            Halt;
        END;  {notify that file not found and halt}

    BEGIN {procedure filesafe 1}
        Assign(FileNames,'FILESAFE.000');
        {$I-} Reset(FileNames); {$I+}
        IF (IOResult=0) THEN
            BEGIN {files must be restored}
                ClrScr;
                GotoXY(1,4);
                WriteLn('>>> ATTENTION:',#7);
                WriteLn;
                WriteLn('Apparent system failure during last ',
                        'use of this program.');
                WriteLn;
                WriteLn('Now ready to restore data files as ',
                        'before failure.');
                WriteLn;
                WriteLn('Choose action to be taken:');
                WriteLn;
                WriteLn('<R>estore files');
                WriteLn('<D>estroy FileSafe files - ',
                        'DO NOT RESTORE');
                WriteLn('<H>alt program now - Take no action');
                WriteLn;
                TextColor(0); TextBackground(7);
                WriteLn(' If uncertain about action - ',
                        'Choose <H>alt! ');
                TextColor(7); TextBackGround(0);
                WriteLn;
                Write('Choice of action ?  ( R, D, H)  ');

                {To use this procedure with Turbo Pascal versions
                    prior to 4.0, add the line below.}
                { Read(KBD,Action); }
```

Tool 10.14: Procedure FileSafe1 to begin a program that uses the file-protection process.

```
                    {To use this procedure with Turbo Pascal versions
                       prior to 4.0, remove the line below.}
                    Action:=ReadKey;

                    Action:=UpCase(Action);
                    WriteLn(Action);
                    CASE Action OF
                      'R': BEGIN {restore}
                               WriteLn('Restoring files...');
                               FOR X:=1 TO 20 DO FName[X]:='';
                               X:=1;
                               WHILE NOT EOF(FileNames) DO
                                  BEGIN {while not eof}
                                     ReadLn(FileNames,FName[X]);
                                     IF (FName[X]<>'') THEN
                                        BEGIN {if}
                                        Assignment;

          {To use this program with Turbo Pascal versions prior
             to 4.0, add the 2 lines below:}
                                        {There1:=Exist(FName[X]);}
                                        {There2:=Exist('FILESAFE.'+S);}

          {To use this program with Turbo Pascal versions prior
             to 4.0, remove the 2 lines below:}
                                        There1:=Exist4(FName[X]);
                                        There2:=Exist4('FILESAFE.'+S);

                                        IF NOT (There1 AND There2) THEN
                                             Notify;
                                        END;  {if}
                                     X:=X+1;
                                  END;  {while not eof}
                               FOR X:=1 TO 20 DO IF (FName[X]<>'') THEN
                                  BEGIN {for x}
                                     Assignment;
                                     WriteLn('> Erase: ',FName[X]);
                                     Erase(WF1);
                                     WriteLn('  Rename FILESAFE.',S,
                                            ' as above file.');
                                     Rename(WF2,FName[X]);
                                  END;  {for x}
                               Close(FileNames);
                               Erase(FileNames);
                         END;  {restore}
                      'D': BEGIN {destroy}
                               WriteLn('Destroying FileSafe files...');
                               FOR X:=1 TO 20 DO
                                  BEGIN {for x}
                                     Str(X:3,S);
                                     IF NOT (S[1] In['1'..'9']) THEN
                                          S[1]:='0';
                                     IF NOT (S[2] In['1'..'9']) THEN
                                          S[2]:='0';
                                     Assign(WF1,'FILESAFE.'+S);

          {To use this program with Turbo Pascal versions prior
             to 4.0, add the line below:}
                                     {IF (Exist('FILESAFE.'+S)) THEN
                                          Erase(WF1);}
```

Tool 10.14: Procedure FileSafe1 to begin a program that uses the file-protection process. (continued)

```
            {To use this program with Turbo Pascal versions prior
          to 4.0, remove the line below:}
                               IF (Exist4('FILESAFE.'+S)) THEN
                                 Erase(WF1);

                   END;  {for x}
                 Close(FileNames);
                 Erase(FileNames);
             END;   {destroy}
        'H': BEGIN {halt}
                 WriteLn('Program stops now!');
                 Close(FileNames);
                 Halt;
             END;   {halt}
        END;   {case statement}
        WriteLn('Finished!!');
        Delay(2000);
      END;   {files must be restored}
    {$I-} Close(FileNames); {$I+}
    IF IOResult<>0 THEN BEGIN     END;
END;   {procedure filesafe 1}
```

Tool 10.14: Procedure FileSafe1 to begin a program that uses the file-protection process. (continued)

FileSafe3 procedure would not have had the opportunity to erase them. The FileSafe1 procedure simply checks to see if the control file FILE-SAFE.000 exists. If it does, there was obviously a problem, and FileSafe1 takes further action (as described below); if not, FileSafe1 ends, and the program continues normally.

If the control file is spotted by FileSafe1, indicating an abnormal program termination, it displays a message that informs the user that the last time it was used, the program appears to have been terminated improperly. The procedure then offers the user a choice of three actions: to have FileSafe1 restore the files to their state prior to the apparent abnormal termination, to simply destroy all FileSafe files without making any restoration, or to just stop the program at this point without taking any action. If the latter choice is selected, the next time the program is invoked, FileSafe1 will again find the control file and offer these choices to the user. A message suggests that if the user is unsure about what to do, he or she should select the third option to stop the program before taking any action. Perhaps the proper action can be determined from instructions accompanying the software or from a support service.

If the file-restoration option is chosen, the FileSafe1 procedure will open its control file and obtain the names of all the files that were to be duplicated. A check is made to ensure that all of these files and each of the File-Safe series of files that were made are present. If it cannot find any of these files, the procedure displays a message, no further action is taken, and the program terminates. Assuming that all the files are found, the original program files are erased and the duplicate files made by FileSafe2 are renamed to replace the program files. Messages are displayed to indicate which files are being replaced.

If the user chooses not to restore files and, instead, wishes to destroy the FileSafe duplicate files, the procedure erases each of these files in turn.

USING THE FILESAFE PROCEDURES IN A PROGRAM

The FileSafe procedures are easily incorporated into your programs. The method of incorporation is illustrated in Test Program 10.5.

The program checks for the presence of a dummy file, and if it does not find the dummy file, it creates a set of nine dummy files. Regardless of the presence of the dummy file, the program constructs a string of the dummy file names for use as a parameter string with the procedure FileSafe2. After calling the FileSafe2 procedure, the demonstration program is at a point where the activity involving file input and output would normally take place and the time when a program is susceptible to damage from hardware failure. At this point, the program displays a message offering the user the opportunity to interrupt program execution to simulate hardware failure. If execution is interrupted, the FileSafe duplicate files will remain and be detected by FileSafe1 when the demonstration program is next invoked; if execution is not interrupted, the FileSafe3 procedure will remove the FileSafe files as it would with the normal termination of file-handling processes within an ordinary program.

AUTOMATED FILE BACKUPS

Although program users are expected to understand the process of making backups of data files and regularly do so, sometimes they are confused

```
PROGRAM TryFileSafe;

     {To use this program with Turbo Pascal versions prior to
        4.0, remove the Uses statement below.}

     Uses DOS,CRT;
TYPE
    Str255 = STRING[255];

VAR
    FNames     :Str255;
    DemoFile   :Text;
    X          :Integer;
    S          :STRING[3];
    Ch         :Char;


     {To use this program with Turbo Pascal versions prior to
        4.0, add the line below.}
(* {$I Exist.Inc} *)

     {To use this program with Turbo Pascal versions prior to
        4.0, remove the line below.}
{$I Exist4.Inc}

{$I FileByte.Inc}
{$I FreeSpc.Inc}
{$I FilSafe1.Inc}
{$I FilSafe2.Inc}
{$I FilSafe3.Inc}

BEGIN {program}
    FileSafe1;
    FNames:='';

          {To use this program with Turbo Pascal versions prior
             to 4.0, add the line below:}
    { IF NOT (Exist('DUMMY.001')) THEN }

          {To use this program with Turbo Pascal versions prior
             to 4.0, remove the line below:}
    IF NOT (Exist4('DUMMY.001')) THEN


       FOR X:=1 TO 9 DO
          BEGIN {create dummy files}
              Str(X:3,S);
              S[1]:='0';
              S[2]:='0';
              Assign(DemoFile,'DUMMY.'+S);
              Rewrite(DemoFile);
              WriteLn(DemoFile,'Demonstration line.');
              Close(DemoFile);
              FNames:=FNames+'DUMMY.'+S+' ';
          END;  {create dummy files}

          {To use this program with Turbo Pascal versions prior
             to 4.0, add the line below:}
    { IF (Exist('DUMMY.001')) THEN }
```

Test Program 10.5: Using procedures FileSafe1, FileSafe2, and FileSafe3 in a program.

```
                 {To use this program with Turbo Pascal versions prior
                    to 4.0, remove the line below:}
           IF (Exist4('DUMMY.001')) THEN

               FOR X:=1 TO 9 DO
                   BEGIN  {create file string}
                        Str(X:3,S);
                        S[1]:='0';
                        S[2]:='0';
                        FNames:=FNames+'DUMMY.'+S+' ';
                   END;   {create file string}
           FileSafe2(FNames);
           ClrScr;
           WriteLn('If program is interrupted now, it will simulate');
           WriteLn('a power failure in the midst of file activity.');
           WriteLn;
           WriteLn('To interrupt, enter   I');
           Write('To continue without interruption, press any key.');

           {To use this program with Turbo Pascal versions prior to
                4.0, add the line below.}
           { Read(KBD,Ch); }

           {To use this program with Turbo Pascal versions prior to
                4.0, remove the line below.}
           Ch:=ReadKey;

           IF (Ch In['I','i']) THEN Halt;
           FileSafe3;
        END.   {program}
```

Test Program 10.5: Using procedures FileSafe1, FileSafe2, and FileSafe3 in a program.
(continued)

about just which files to back up. It can be very helpful to the application program user to have a menu selection within the program itself which automatically selects the files for backing up and handles the basics of the process. The following procedure makes it easy for you to insert such an option within your program.

PROVIDING AUTOMATIC BACKUP

The AutoBackup procedure, presented as Tool 10.15, is a fairly simple one. It uses the FileBytes function, (Tool 10.5), to determine the size of the file to be backed up and the DiskFreeSpc procedure, presented in Chapter 1 (Tool 1.7), to determine if there is sufficient disk space remaining to accommodate the file to be backed up. Assuming that the file to be backed up is found and that there is sufficient disk space, the file copy is made and the procedure ends. If the file copy is not made, the procedure ends and returns a result code indicating the reason for failure.

```
PROCEDURE AutoBackup(DriveName:Char;
                     FileToCopy,CopyToFile:Str255;
                     VAR Result:Integer);

{ Result = 0 = Success }
{ Result = 1 = File not found }
{ Result = 2 = Disk not available (e.g. invalid drive) }
{ Result = 3 = File too large for disk }
{ Result = 4 = Insufficient disk space remaining }
{ Result = 5 = Other error }

CONST
     RecordSize         = 128;
     RecsToRead         = 80; {reads up to 10 Kb at a time}

VAR
     SizeOfFileToCopy, TS, TF   :Real;
     BPS,SPC,AC,TC,RecsRead     :Integer;
     File1, File2               :FILE;
     FileBuffer                 :ARRAY[1..RecordSize,
                                 1..RecsToRead] OF Byte;


BEGIN {automated backup procedure}
     Result:=0;
     {see if file is present, get file size}
     SizeOfFileToCopy:=FileBytes(FileToCopy);
     IF (SizeOfFileToCopy=0.0) THEN Result:=1;
     IF (Result=0) THEN
         BEGIN {check the disk, get disk size}
             DiskFreeSpc(DriveName,BPS,SPC,AC,TC,TS,TF);
             IF (SizeOfFileToCopy>TF) THEN Result:=4;
             IF (SizeOfFileToCopy>TS) THEN Result:=3;
             IF (TS=0.0) THEN Result:=2;
         END;   {check the disk, get disk size}
     IF (Result=0) THEN
         BEGIN  {if OK, do backup}
             {$I-}
             Assign(File1,FileToCopy);
             Assign(File2,DriveName+':'+CopyToFile);
             Reset(File1);
             IF (IOResult=0) THEN Rewrite(File2);
             IF (IOResult<>0) THEN Result:=5;
             {$I+}
             IF (Result=0) THEN
               BEGIN  {copy file}
                 REPEAT
                     BlockRead(File1,FileBuffer,RecsToRead,RecsRead);
                     BlockWrite(File2,FileBuffer,RecsRead);
                 UNTIL (RecsRead=0);
                 Close(File1);
                 Close(File2);
               END;   {copy file}
         END; {if OK, do backup}
     END; {automated backup procedure}
```

Tool 10.15: Procedure AutoBackup to provide automatic backup.

The following integer result codes are returned by the procedure:

    0 = Success
    1 = File not found
    2 = Disk not available (e.g., invalid drive)
    3 = File too large for disk (i.e., file is larger than disk capacity
        even if disk is blank)
    4 = Insufficient disk space remaining
    5 = Failed for other reason

The procedure requires three parameters to be passed to it: the drive name of the drive to which the backup file is to be written, the name (including path, if applicable) of the file to be backed up, and the name (including path, if applicable) of the backup file.

If a number of files are to be backed up, you can use the procedure in a loop within your program and call it for each file to be backed up.

Here's how the AutoBackup procedure works:

- Check to see if the file to be backed up exists and how large it is.
- Check the capacity of the disk to which the backup file is to be written and the amount of free space on that disk.
- Check that the overall disk capacity is sufficient for the file to be copied.
- Check that the remaining space on the disk to which the backup file is to be copied is sufficient to accommodate the file.
- If everything is okay, copy the file.

Test Program 10.6 illustrates the use of the AutoBackup procedure within a simple program. The program requests the user to enter the name of the file to be backed up, the drive the backup is to be copied to, and the name for the backup copy. After calling the AutoBackup procedure to attempt to make the backup copy, the program reports the result code returned and the meaning of the code.

```
Program TryAutoBackup;

        {To use this program with Turbo Pascal versions prior to
            4.0, remove the Uses statement below.}

        Uses DOS,CRT;
TYPE
        Str255 = String[255];

VAR
        FName1, FName2        :String[64];
        DestDrive             :Char;
        Result                :Integer;

{$I FileByte.Inc}
{$I FreeSpc.Inc}
{$I AutoBkUp.Inc}


BEGIN {program}
        ClrScr;
        Write('File to back up: ');
        ReadLn(FName1);
        Write('Drive to copy to: ');

        {To use this program with Turbo Pascal versions prior to
            4.0, add the line below.}
        { Read(KBD,DestDrive); }

        {To use this program with Turbo Pascal versions prior to
            4.0, remove the line below.}
        DestDrive:=ReadKey;

        WriteLn(DestDrive);
        Write('Backup to File Name: ');
        ReadLn(FName2);
        AutoBackup(DestDrive,FName1,FName2,Result);
        CASE Result OF
          0: Write('File copied successfully!');
          1: Write('Error 1 = File not found');
          2: Write('Error 2 = Disk not available (e.g., invalid drive)');
          3: Write('Error 3 = File too large for disk');
          4: Write('Error 4 = Insufficient disk space remaining');
          5: Write('Error 5 = Other error');
        END;  {case statement}
END.  {program}
```

Test Program 10.6: Using procedure AutoBackup in a program.

LIMITING PROGRAM LIFE

Sometimes it is convenient to have a program written so that it will be useful for only a limited period of time. After that time, the program will cease to function properly. This can be used as a method of copy protection or for demonstration programs that are useful for only a limited amount of time, which is sufficient for demonstration or trial purposes. As with any protection method, there are ways of defeating it, but often the cost of defeating copy protection outweighs the cost of getting a legitimate copy of a program. The next procedure offers a method of making a program inoperable after a specified date.

MAKING A PROGRAM INOPERABLE AFTER A SPECIFIED DATE

The KillDate procedure, shown as Tool 10.16, will make a program inoperable after a specified expiration date. This date must first be set. If a program is to have different versions, for which the expiration dates may vary from one compilation to the next, such as a version for demonstration and one that is permanent, the expiration date should be defined as a global constant at the beginning of the program. If defined in this manner, the expiration date is always easy to find and change.

The proper way of declaring the expiration date within a program when using the KillDate procedure is

```
CONST
PrgmExpires :STRING[3] = #12#31#88;
```

Each of the three characters within the declared string constitutes an element of the date. The date declared above is 12/31/88. The string of three characters should be declared with the first character representing the expiration month, the second representing the expiration day, and the final character defining the expiration year. The expiration date may be declared either within the procedure itself or within the program.

Generally, when a program begins, the system date will be checked and verified as correct. This is the first occasion within a program to make use of the KillDate procedure. When the correct system date is set, pass the date to the KillDate procedure for checking; if it is beyond the expiration date, the program will halt.

During the operation of a program, there may be various times when the current date must be entered or is referenced. This is another excellent

```
PROCEDURE KillDate(Month,Day,Year:Integer);

    {The expiration date of the program may be declared within
        this procedure or globally within the program.  It
        should be declared as:

        CONST
            PrgmExpires :STRING[3] = #12#31#88;

        where each of the 3 characters in the string represents
        a part of the expiration date; above = 12/31/88 }

    VAR
        Quit :Boolean;

    BEGIN {procedure killdate}
        Quit:=(Year>ORD(PrgmExpires[3]));
        IF NOT Quit THEN
            Quit:=((Year=ORD(PrgmExpires[3])) AND
                    (Month>ORD(PrgmExpires[1])));
        IF NOT Quit THEN
            Quit:=((Year=ORD(PrgmExpires[3])) AND
                    (Month=ORD(PrgmExpires[1])) AND
                    (Day>ORD(PrgmExpires[2])));
        IF Quit THEN
            BEGIN {program has expired}
                ClrScr;
                GotoXY(1,10);
                Write(#7);
                WriteLn('The expiration date of this program has',
                    ' been reached.  Program will quit now.');
                Write('Expiration date: ',ORD(PrgmExpires[1]),
                    '/',ORD(PrgmExpires[2]),'/',
                    ORD(PrgmExpires[3]));
                Halt;
            END; {program has expired}
    END;   {procedure killdate}
```

Tool 10.16: Procedure KillDate to make a program inoperable after a specified date.

time to call the KillDate procedure. If the procedure is brought into operation only when the program is begun, it will be easy enough for a user to defeat it by beginning the program with an older date and then correcting the date later in the program. If the KillDate procedure is called at various times within the program when it is essential that the correct date be used, a user will find it much more difficult to escape the consequences of having an expired program.

Note that care must be taken when passing a date to the KillDate procedure. Sometimes, dates within a program use the real year (e.g., 1988) as opposed to the abbreviated year (e.g., 88). The KillDate procedure looks for an abbreviated year because of the manner in which the expiration date string is declared.

NOTE: If a program is to be set as permanent (which will, in effect, make it impossible to stop the program), the expiration date should be set to 1/1/100 (#1#1#100).

Here's how the KillDate procedure works:

- Check each element of the date passed as a parameter against the expiration date. If the date passed as a parameter is greater than the expiration date, the Boolean variable Quit is true.
- If Quit is true, display a message indicating the expiration date and that the program has expired and will halt.

Test Program 10.7 demonstrates the use of the KillDate procedure in a program. First, the program sets the expiration date at 11/2/87. As the program begins, the current date is set to 11/1/87, and the KillDate procedure is called. Because this date is within the bounds of the expiration date, nothing happens—the program continues and displays a message stating that it is continuing. Next the program sets the current date to 11/3/87 and calls the KillDate procedure again. This time the expiration date has been passed, and KillDate halts the program and displays its message.

```
PROGRAM TryKillDate;

    {To use this program with Turbo Pascal versions prior to
        4.0, remove the Uses statement below.}

    Uses DOS,CRT;


    CONST
        PrgmExpires :String[3] = #11#2#87;

    VAR
        Mm, Dd, Yy  :Integer;

    {$I KillDate.Inc}

BEGIN {program}
    Mm:=11; Dd:=1; Yy:=87;
    KillDate(Mm,Dd,Yy);
    WriteLn('Program continues...');
    Delay(1500);
    Dd:=3;
    KillDate(Mm,Dd,Yy);
END.  {program}
```

Test Program 10.7: Using procedure KillDate in a program.

READING CHARACTERS
FROM THE SCREEN

BASIC provides a handy command for reading a character from any given position on screen. The following function accomplishes the same end.

GETTING THE CHARACTER AT A SPECIFIED SCREEN POSITION

When the ReadScrn function, presented as Tool 10.17, is called and passed the desired screen position to be read in the parameters Col and Row, it will return with the character which is at that screen position. The Col and Row parameters should use the same screen positions that would be used for locating the cursor with a GotoXY statement.

```
FUNCTION ReadScrn(Col,Row:Integer):Char;

    VAR

    {To use this procedure with versions of Turbo Pascal prior
to 4.0, change the type declaration of ScreenAddress from Word to
Integer.}
        ScreenAddress           :Word;
        Offset                  :Integer;

    BEGIN  {read screen location}
        IF (Mem[0000:1040] AND 48) <> 48 THEN
              ScreenAddress:=$B800
                     ELSE ScreenAddress:=$B000;
        Offset:=((Row-1)*160)+((Col-1)*2);
        ReadScrn:=CHR(Mem[ScreenAddress:Offset]);
    END;   {read screen location}
```

Tool 10.17: Function ReadScrn to read characters from the screen.

Here's how the ReadScrn function works:

- Determine the base address of video RAM.
- Determine the character offset for the position to be read from the parameters Col and Row, which have been passed to the procedure by the program.
- Read the appropriate screen memory position and pass the character at that location back to the program.

Test Program 10.8 illustrates the use of the ReadScrn procedure in a program. A loop is established to read seven consecutive screen positions and determine the character present at each. As each character is read, it is written to the screen. A delay is issued between each read so that the process will be more visually obvious.

```
PROGRAM DemoProg2;

     {To use this program with Turbo Pascal versions prior to
         4.0, remove the Uses statement below.}

     Uses DOS,CRT;

     TYPE
          Str255 = STRING[255];

     VAR
          X, Result      :Integer;
          Pattern        :Str255;
          Ch             :Char;

     {$I ReadScrn.Inc}

     BEGIN {demo program}
          Pattern:='Check this phrase.';
          ClrScr;
          GotoXY(1,10);
          WriteLn(Pattern);
          GotoXY(1,22);
          Write('Reading screen positions 1,10-7,10: ');
          FOR X:=1 TO 7 DO
               BEGIN
                    Ch:=ReadScrn(X,10);
                    Write(Ch);
                    Delay(500);
               END;
     END.   {demo program}
```

Test Program 10.8: Using function ReadScrn in a program.

APPENDIX A
INCORPORATING THE PROCEDURES AND FUNCTIONS INTO YOUR PROGRAMS

Incorporating a single procedure or function into your program is a simple matter. You can either key it into the program or place the source code in a separate file, and then include that file (using the Include compiler directive) when you compile the program. Any data types that are being used as parameters to the procedures and functions must be globally declared within your program. If they are not defined, a compiler error will result.

Note that although most of the procedures work by themselves, some require other procedures to work with them. Check the procedure before using it in your program to see if it calls other procedures. If so, be certain to include these in the program, as well.

In this appendix, the procedures, functions, and programs are referred to by name. See Appendix B for their tool and test program numbers and a brief summary of each one.

STAND-ALONE PROCEDURES

Most of the procedures presented in this book are stand alone; they work entirely by themselves and do not require the presence of other procedures. Table A.1 lists all the stand-alone procedures. To use any of these within your program, just be certain that the procedure appears before it is called by the program or that it is forward declared.

Table A.1:
Stand-Alone Procedures

Attribute	FixString	ReadBit2
BeginDirSearch	Frame	ReadBits
BitSet	GetDate	ReadKeyCode
CalendarDate	GetDTA	ReadScrn
CheckForColor	GetError	ReverseVideo
ChekScrn	GetFileName	SendByte
Color80Col	GetOffset	SerialPrinter
ContDirSearch	GetTime	SetBits
ConvertWords	GetVerify	SetCursor
CurrDrive	GetVersion	SetDate
CurntPath	InitPrnt	SetDTA
DecodeDateArray	InKey	SetTime
DecodeDateString	Julian	SetVerify
DiskFreeSpc	KillDate	SlideBig
Drives	LgChar	SpinEm
ElapsedTime	PressKey	Template
EncodeDateArray	Printers	WeekDayNo
EncodeDateString	PrLgChar	WindowOut
Exist	PrinterError	WindowIn
Exist4	PrintStat	YesNo
ExWindow	Prompt	
FileBytes	RAMSize	
Fiscal		

PROCEDURES THAT REQUIRE OTHER PROCEDURES

Table A.2 lists the procedures that require the presence of other procedures to operate correctly. The requisite accompanying procedures must, in all cases, either precede the procedure requiring its presence or be forward declared prior to the placement of that procedure. See Appendix B for the specific auxiliary procedures required for the procedures listed in Table A.2.

Table A.2:
Procedures that Require Other Procedures

AutoBackup	InpDate
BarGraph	InterpretDate
ChekDate	InterpretTime
CMenu	KbdCtrl
Directry	Menu
FileSafe1	PushLft
FileSafe2	SlideRt
FileSafe3	ValidDate
GetDirectory	

SPECIALIZED PROCEDURES AND PROGRAMS

There are a few procedures presented in the book that are not tools for general use in your programs; instead, they are designed to be used in specialized programs or as a group. Table A.3 lists the specialized procedures and programs.

USING UNITS WITH TURBO PASCAL VERSIONS 4.0 AND 5.0

Along with the procedures and functions in this book, you may have other special procedures and functions that you would like to include within

Table A.3:
Specialized Procedures and Programs

Data Entry and Display	Screen Generator	Keyboard Reading
DataDisp	DemoScreenDisplay	ShowCode
DataEntry	DoGrid	
EntrRev	ImageRecord	
MakeTemp	InitScrn	
ReadTemp	KeyTranslation	
	NameFile	
	ScreenGen2	
	ShowScrn	
	SimpleScreenGen1	
	TextRecord	
	WriteChar	

your application programs. You can place these into one or more *units*, and then use the Uses statement at the beginning of the Turbo Pascal 4.0 or 5.0 program to include the applicable units in that program, just as most of the programs presented in this book include the DOS and CRT units supplied with versions 4.0 and 5.0.

You can place all the procedures and functions in a single unit, or you can divide them among several units, based on the type of operations they perform. If you plan on using all the procedures and functions in the book, you will have to split them into at least two units because they will not fit into one.

Here is how you can construct two unit files for the tools in this book:

1. Make the unit shell as illustrated below. Note that if you are dividing the procedures and functions into two units, some of the procedures in the second unit will be using procedures in the first unit. In these cases, you must specify that the second unit uses the first unit. Do not make the type declarations again in the second unit; they will have already been defined in the first unit.

Redefining them will cause a type mismatch error when you reference the procedure in the first unit.

```
Unit TPTUnit1;
  Interface
    Uses DOS,CRT,Printer;
    TYPE
      Str255    =  STRING[255];
      Pointr    =  ^ Integer;
      Arr3      =  ARRAY[1..3] OF Byte;
      BoolArray =  ARRAY[0..15] OF Boolean;

      {headings of procedures/functions that will be
       contained in this unit}

    Implementation {of unit TPTUnit1}

    {list of include files containing the procedures and
     functions that will be in this unit}

    END. {of unit TPTUnit1}

Unit TPTUnit2;
  Interface
  Uses DOS,CRT,Printer,TPTUnit1;
  {headings of procedures/functions that will be
   contained in this unit}
  Implementation {of unit TPTUnit2}
    {list of include files containing the procedures and
     functions that will be in this unit}
  END. {of unit TPTUnit}
```

2. Remove the parameters from each procedure or function because these will be listed in the unit interface and need not be referenced again (as with a forward declaration).

3. Batch the files into units containing numerous procedures and functions, so the list of units used in your program will be shorter and less confusing.

4. When batching the files into units, remember that the procedures or functions that use other procedures or functions must appear following those procedures or functions.

The following procedures require only auxiliary assistance from the stand-alone procedures:

KbdCtrl	SlideRt
PushLft	ValidDate

The following procedures call other procedures which, in turn, call auxiliary procedures:

AutoBackup	FileSafe1
BarGraph	FileSafe2
CMenu	FileSafe3
ChekDate	GetDirectry
Directry	InpDate
	Menu

PUTTING THE PROCEDURES IN A LIBRARY AND USING OVERLAYS

If you have an earlier version of Turbo Pascal, you can use libraries instead of units. Rather than including a long list of procedures in each program you write, you can save space and time by batching all the procedures and functions you generally will be using into one or two library files. Then you can just include these files in the programs you are writing. When building a library, be certain that any procedures requiring the presence of auxiliary procedures are placed following those procedures.

It's possible that a complete library of procedures and functions that you plan to include in your programs may be near, or even exceed, the 64-kilobyte limit of versions of Turbo Pascal prior to 4.0. Also, regardless of the Turbo Pascal version in use, you may want to keep the RAM space occupied by your program to the minimum. The solution is to use overlay

files to build a large program that occupies a minimum of memory space.
Here is how you can construct library files and use overlays for the tools
in this book:

1. Insert OVERLAY in front of each procedure or function name
   using the Turbo Pascal editor. For example:

OVERLAY PROCEDURE Attribute

2. Batch the files into libraries containing numerous procedures and
   functions, so the list of include files in your program will be
   shorter and less confusing.

3. When batching the files into libraries, remember that two procedures or functions from the same overlay file cannot be in use at
   once. To avoid this problem, those procedures and functions that
   do not require other procedures or functions should be in the
   first overlay file (e.g., PROGRAM.000). If there is not enough
   room for all of them in a single overlay, divide them into two
   overlay files (e.g., PROGRAM.000 and PROGRAM.001). Any
   other of the program's procedures and functions that do not
   call other procedures or functions in the library files can also be
   included in the first overlay file.

4. Some of the procedures may require another procedure that also
   requires one or more auxiliary procedures. These procedures
   must be separated into two separate overlay files (e.g., PRO-
   GRAM.002 and PROGRAM.003 if PROGRAM.000 and
   PROGRAM.001 contain the library of stand-alone procedures
   and functions).

The following procedures require only auxiliary assistance from the
stand-alone procedures:

InpDate	PushLft
InterpretDate	SlideRt
InterpretTime	ValidDate
KbdCtrl	

The following procedures call other procedures which, in turn, call auxiliary procedures:

AutoBackup	FileSafe1
BarGraph	FileSafe2
ChekDate	FileSafe3
CMenu	GetDirectry
Directry	Menu

REQUIRED DECLARATIONS FOR YOUR PROGRAMS

Many of the procedures contained within this book require no special declarations within your application programs to operate correctly, but some do. Therefore, for the sake of simplicity, you can make the declarations discussed below globally within your program; they will suffice for every procedure contained within this text.

RELAXED PARAMETER TYPE CHECKING

The compiler should be issued the directive {$V-} at the beginning of the program to set relaxed parameter type checking. Most of the procedures that require passing string data use a string type declared as Str255 (STRING[255]), even though the actual string length that will be passed is substantially shorter. For these procedures to compile correctly, the parameter type checking must be relaxed.

REQUIRED DATA-TYPE DECLARATIONS

The following declaration for data types used within the procedures contained in this book should be made to ensure that all the procedures will compile without error when included in your programs.

```
TYPE
  Str255   = STRING[255];
  Pointr   = ^ Integer;
```

```
Arr3      = ARRAY[1..3] OF Byte;
BoolArray = ARRAY[0..15] OF Boolean;
```

The following declaration is necessary only if you are using the BarGraph procedure in your program:

```
TYPE
  GraphRec = RECORD
    Heading    :STRING[80];
    Values     :ARRAY[1..18] OF Real;
    Labels     :ARRAY[1..18] OF STRING[12];
  END;
```

If you are using the KillDate procedure in your program, the expiration date of the program can be declared within the KillDate procedure or globally within the program. It should be declared as

```
CONST
  PrgmExpires :STRING[3] = #12#31#88;
```

where each of the three characters in the string represents a part of the expiration date. In the example above, the date is 12/31/88.

FILE-NAME DECLARATION

When using the data-entry procedures described in Chapter 3, specifically when using templates, it is wise to name the template file as a global constant within your program, as in

```
CONST
  TemplateFile = 'PROGNAME.TEM';
```

Then you can just refer to that constant identifier when calling the template.

APPENDIX B
QUICK REFERENCE LIST

This appendix contains an alphabetical listing of all the programs, procedures, and functions presented in the book. It includes the following information:

- The name of the procedure, function, or program
- The tool or program number
- A file name reference (Most test programs use the Include compiler directive to incorporate the appropriate procedures; the file names are the names referenced by the directive. They are also the file names used on the source code diskette, which you can obtain by using the order form included at the end of the book.)
- The proper syntax for using the procedure or function within a program
- A brief description of the purpose of the procedure, function, or program
- Any required auxiliary procedures or functions
- The data types expected for the various parameters that may have to be passed
- The number of the page on which the discussion of the procedure, function, or program begins

.... **Attribute**

NUMBER

Tool 1.8

FILE NAME

ATTRIBUT.INC

SYNTAX

Attribute(Get_Set,FileName,FileAttribute,ErrorCode);

DESCRIPTION

Gets or sets the attribute of a disk file.

PARAMETERS

Char, Str255, Integer, Integer

PAGE NUMBER

30

.... **AutoBackup**

NUMBER

Tool 10.15

FILE NAME

AUTOBKUP.INC

SYNTAX

AutoBackup(DriveName,FileToCopy,CopyToFile,Result);

DESCRIPTION

Automatically backs up a file if free space on disk permits.

AUXILIARY PROCEDURES

DiskFreeSpc, FileBytes

PARAMETERS

Char, Str255, Str255, Integer

PAGE NUMBER

310

BarGraph

NUMBER

Tool 9.9

FILE NAME

BARGRAPH.INC

SYNTAX

BarGraph(GraphData);

DESCRIPTION

Constructs a horizontal bar graph using data passed in the record GraphData.

AUXILIARY PROCEDURE

Frame

PARAMETERS

GraphData is a record consisting of the fields: Heading :STRING[80]; Values :ARRAY[1..18] OF Real; Labels :ARRAY[1..18] OF STRING[12];

PAGE NUMBER

270

BeginDirSearch

NUMBER

Tool 2.1

FILE NAME

BEGSRCH.INC

SYNTAX

BeginDirSearch(FileSpec,Attribute,ErrorCode);

DESCRIPTION
Uses DOS function 78 to search for the specified file.

PARAMETERS
Str255, Integer, Integer

PAGE NUMBER
43

BitSet

NUMBER
Tool 6.2

FILE NAME
BITSET.INC

SYNTAX
T_or_F: = BitSet(Position,Flag);

DESCRIPTION
Returns true or false indicating whether the bit specified by position in the target flag integer is set (has a value of 1).

PARAMETERS
Integer, Integer

PAGE NUMBER
180

CalendarDate

NUMBER
Tool 4.4

FILE NAME
CALDATE.INC

SYNTAX

CalendarDate(JulianDate,Year,Month,Day);

DESCRIPTION

When passed the Julian date, returns the correct calendar month, day, and year.

PARAMETERS

Real, Integer, Integer, Integer

PAGE NUMBER

136

CheckForColor

NUMBER

Tool 7.1

FILE NAME

CHEKCOLR.INC

SYNTAX

CheckForColor(Color,ScreenAddress);

DESCRIPTION

Returns true or false depending on whether or not a color card is present; also returns the base address of video RAM.

PARAMETERS

Boolean, Word for versions 4.0 and 5.0, Integer for earlier version.

PAGE NUMBER

193

ChekDate

NUMBER

Tool 4.6

FILE NAME

CHEKDATE.INC

SYNTAX

ChekDate(Hours, Mins, Secs, Month, Day, Year);

DESCRIPTION

Sets up a screen that allows the user to accept the present system date and time as valid or to change it.

AUXILIARY PROCEDURES

InKey, GetDate, GetTime, SetDate, SetTime, ValidDate

PARAMETERS

All Words for versions 4.0and 5.0; all Integers for earlier versions

PAGE NUMBER

140

ChekScrn

NUMBER

Tool 8.9

FILE NAME

CHEKSCRN.INC

SYNTAX

ChekScrn(Col,Row,NumChars,Template,Result);

DESCRIPTION

Checks the individual screen cells beginning at Col and Row and continuing for NumChars to ascertain whether those cells contain the same characters as the Template. The Result parameter is either 0, meaning that the screen matches the template, or 1, meaning that the screen does not match the template.

PARAMETERS

Integer, Integer, Integer, Str255, Integer

PAGE NUMBER
247

CMenu

NUMBER
Tool 5.1

FILE NAME
CMENU.INC

SYNTAX
CMenu(MenuNumber,MenuFileName,MenuWidth,MenuLength,Choice);

DESCRIPTION
Saves the present screen, presents a menu centered in the screen of the width and length specified, and lists the heading and selections on the menu after reading them from the ASCII file MenuFileName, based on the MenuNumber specification. The user selects a menu choice, which is returned in the parameter Choice.

AUXILIARY PROCEDURES
KbdCtrl, WindowIn, WindowOut, BitSet, SetBits

PARAMETERS
Str255, Str255, Integer, Integer, Integer

PAGE NUMBER
157

Color80Col

NUMBER
Tool 10.6

FILE NAME
COLOR80.INC

SYNTAX

BoolVar: = Color80Col;

DESCRIPTION

Sets the value of the variable as true if a color video display card is present on the equipment list.

PAGE NUMBER

288

ContDirSearch

NUMBER

Tool 2.3

FILE NAME

CONTSRCH.INC

SYNTAX

ContDirSearch(Error);

DESCRIPTION

Continues with a directory search using DOS function 79 after the search has been initiated by the BeginDirSearch procedure using DOS function 78.

PARAMETER

Integer

PAGE NUMBER

47

ConvertWords

NUMBER

Tool 2.8

FILE NAME

CONVWORD.INC

SYNTAX
ConvertWords(DTASeg,DTAOfs,FileSize);

DESCRIPTION
Interprets the information returned to the DTA in the course of a directory search. Given the address of the DTA through DTASeg and DTAOfs, it reads the integer words containing the size of the file found and returns a real number with the number of bytes of space occupied by the file.

PARAMETERS
Integer, Integer, Real

PAGE NUMBER
57

CurntPath

NUMBER
Tool 1.3

FILE NAME
CURPATH.INC

SYNTAX
CurntPath(Drive,Path);

DESCRIPTION
Uses DOS function 71 to report the current path for the specified drive.

PARAMETERS
Char, Str255

PAGE NUMBER
12

CurrDrive

NUMBER
Tool 1.2

FILE NAME
CURDRIVE.INC

SYNTAX
CurrDrive(Drive);

DESCRIPTION
Returns the name (letter) of the current drive using DOS function 25.

PARAMETER
Char

PAGE NUMBER
11

DataDisp

NUMBER
Tool 3.8

FILE NAME
DATADISP.INC

SYNTAX
DataDisp(TopHeap,ItemNum,StrItem,IntItem,RealItem);

DESCRIPTION
Reads template records from dynamic memory (beginning at TopHeap), finds the template for the ItemNum to be displayed, and displays it according to the instructions contained in the template using the parameter of the appropriate type, which has been loaded with a StringItem, IntegerItem, or RealItem. This procedure is used in conjunction with the other procedures in Chapter 3 for data entry and display.

PARAMETERS
Pointr, Integer, Str255, LongInt (versions 4.0 and 5.0) or Integer (earlier versions), Real

PAGE NUMBER
118

DataEntry

NUMBER
Tool 3.4

FILE NAME
DATANTRY.INC

DESCRIPTION
Illustrates a data-entry and display loop.

AUXILIARY PROCEDURE
InKey

PAGE NUMBER
103

DecodeDateArray

NUMBER
Tool 4.1

FILE NAME
FIG_4_1.INC

SYNTAX
DecodeDateArray(DateArray);

DESCRIPTION
Illustrates the method of decoding a three-element array with a date.

PARAMETER
Arr3

PAGE NUMBER
131

DecodeDateString

NUMBER
Tool 4.1

FILE NAME
FIG_4_1.INC

SYNTAX
DecodeDateString(DateString,Month,Day,Year);

DESCRIPTION
Illustrates the method of decoding a three-character string with a date.

PARAMETERS
Str255, Integer, Integer, Integer

PAGE NUMBER
131

DemoProg1

NUMBER
Test Program 8.4

FILE NAME
DEMOPRG1.PAS

DESCRIPTION
Demonstrates the ChekScrn procedure.

PAGE NUMBER
248

DemoProg2

NUMBER
Test Program 10.8

FILE NAME
DEMOPRG2.PAS

DESCRIPTION
Demonstrates the ReadScrn procedure.

PAGE NUMBER
318

.... **DemoScreenDisplay**

NUMBER
Test Program 8.2

FILE NAME
DEMOSCRN.PAS

DESCRIPTION
Redisplays screens created and saved by the TextRecord procedure or by the ImageRecord procedure, using the ShowScrn procedure. This program expects a procedure created by the TextRecord procedure to be present and named TESTSCRN.INC.

PAGE NUMBER
226

.... **Directry**

NUMBER
Tool 2.11

FILE NAME
DIRECTRY.INC

SYNTAX
Directry(Level,Mask);

DESCRIPTION
Produces an ASCII file containing the specified directory. The directory is specified by a mask, which includes the drive, file specification, and path. The level indicates the extent of the directory search as follows: 1 = standard files in directory; 2 = standard files in directory and subdirectories; 3 = standard, hidden, and system files in directory; 4 = standard, hidden, and system files in directory and subdirectories.

AUXILIARY PROCEDURES

BeginDirSearch, ContDirSearch, GetDTA, SetDTA, InterpretTime, InterpretDate, ConvertWord, GetFileName, ReadBits, SetBits

PARAMETERS

Integer, Str255

PAGE NUMBER

62

DiskFreeSpc

NUMBER

Tool 1.7

FILE NAME

FREESPC.INC

SYNTAX

DiskFreeSpc(Drive,BytesPerSect,SectorsPerClust,AvailClust,TotClust,TotSpace,TotFree);

DESCRIPTION

Uses DOS function 54 to obtain information about the specified disk drive. It returns the bytes per sector, sectors per cluster, available clusters, total clusters, total disk space, and total free space on disk.

PARAMETERS

Char, Integer, Integer, Integer, Integer, Real, Real

PAGE NUMBER

25

DoGrid

NUMBER

Tool 8.6

FILE NAME

DOGRID.INC

SYNTAX

DoGrid(On_Off);

DESCRIPTION

Places or removes a grid of dots on the screen for use as reference points. This procedure is used in conjunction with other procedures in Chapter 8 for the creation of a screen generator.

PARAMETER

Boolean

PAGE NUMBER

235

Drives

NUMBER

Tool 10.6

FILE NAME

DRIVES.INC

SYNTAX

IntVar: = Drives;

DESCRIPTION

Sets the value of an integer variable to the number of drives present on the computer.

PAGE NUMBER

288

ElapsedTime

NUMBER

Tool 4.9

FILE NAME

ELAPSED.INC

SYNTAX

ElapsedTime(StHour,StMin,StSec,EndHour,EndMin,EndSec,ElHour,ElMin,ElSec,Time);

DESCRIPTION

When provided with the starting hour, minute, and seconds and the ending hour, minute, and seconds, returns the elapsed hours, minutes, and seconds and the time in hours with a decimal fraction of partial hours.

PARAMETERS

Integer, Integer, Integer, Integer, Integer, Integer, Integer, Integer, Integer, Real

PAGE NUMBER

149

EncodeDateArray

NUMBER

Tool 4.1

FILE NAME

FIG_4_1.INC

SYNTAX

EncodeDateArray(Month,Day,Year,DateArray);

DESCRIPTION

Demonstrates the method of encoding a three-element array with a date.

PARAMETERS

Integer, Integer, Integer, Arr3

PAGE NUMBER

131

EncodeDateString

NUMBER

Tool 4.1

FILE NAME

FIG_4_1.INC

SYNTAX

EncodeDateString(Month,Day,Year,DateString);

DESCRIPTION

Demonstrates the method of encoding a three-character string with a date.

PARAMETERS

Integer, Integer, Integer, Str255

PAGE NUMBER

131

EntrRev

NUMBER

Tool 3.9

FILE NAME

ENTRREV.INC

SYNTAX

EntrRev(TopHeap,ItemNum,StrItem,IntItem,RealItem,Result);

DESCRIPTION

Used along with other procedures presented in Chapter 3 for data input and display. This procedure positions the cursor and calls the InKey procedure to accept data entry. It reads template records from dynamic RAM to determine the position and type of keyboard entries to expect. TopHeap is the beginning of template records in RAM; ItemNum is the field number for which input is desired; StrItem, IntItem, and RealItem are for passing input data of the appropriate type back to the program; and Result tells the program how the input was handled, using the same return codes as the InKey procedure.

PARAMETERS
Pointr, Integer, Str255, Integer, Real, LongInt (versions 4.0 and 5.0) or
Integer (earlier versions)

AUXILIARY PROCEDURE
InKey

PAGE NUMBER
120

Exist or Exist4

NUMBER
Tool 2.2

FILE NAME
EXIST.INC

SYNTAX
T_or_F: = Exist4(FileName); {for versions 4.0 and 5.0}
T_or_F: = Exist(FileName); {for earlier versions}

DESCRIPTION
Boolean that uses DOS function 78 to report whether or not the specified
file exists.

PARAMETER
Str255

PAGE NUMBER
45

ExWindow

NUMBER
Tool 7.4

FILE NAME
EXWINDOW.INC

SYNTAX

ExWindow(TopL,TopRow,BotR,BotRow,CursorCol,CursorRow, DataPtr);

DESCRIPTION

Identical to the WindowIn procedure, except that it creates an "exploding window"—a windowing effect where the window seems to clear from the center outward and a corresponding sound is produced as the window appears.

PARAMETERS

Integer, Integer, Integer, Integer, Integer, Integer, Pointr

PAGE NUMBER

203

FileBytes

NUMBER

Tool 10.5

FILE NAME

FILEBYTE.INC

SYNTAX

RealVar: = FileBytes(FileName);

DESCRIPTION

Returns a real number indicating the size of the file FileName in bytes.

PARAMETER

Str255

PAGE NUMBER

286

FileSafe1

NUMBER

Tool 10.14

FILE NAME

FILSAFE1.INC

SYNTAX

FileSafe1;

DESCRIPTION

Checks to see if program appears to have terminated irregularly during its last use and during file-handling operations protected by the procedures FileSafe2 and FileSafe3, and restores files if necessary.

AUXILIARY PROCEDURE

Exist4 (or Exist for versions prior to 4.0)

PAGE NUMBER

304

FileSafe2

NUMBER

Tool 10.12

FILE NAME

FILSAFE2.INC

SYNTAX

FileSafe2(FileSpecs);

DESCRIPTION

Used prior to opening files for a series of file transactions. This procedure copies the files named in the parameter FileSpecs so that backup copies will be available for easy restoration if a hardware failure occurs during the file transactions between the use of the procedures FileSafe2 and File-Safe3. File names must be separated by a space and may include drive and path.

AUXILIARY PROCEDURES

Exist4 (or Exist for versions prior to 4.0), DiskFreeSpc, File Bytes

PARAMETER
Str255

PAGE NUMBER
300

FileSafe3

NUMBER
Tool 10.13

FILE NAME
FILSAFE3.INC

SYNTAX
FileSafe3;

DESCRIPTION
Used following a series of file transactions to erase the duplicate files created by FileSafe2.

AUXILIARY PROCEDURE
Exist4 (or Exist for versions prior to 4.0)

PAGE NUMBER
304

Fiscal

NUMBER
Tool 4.8

FILE NAME
FISCAL.INC

SYNTAX
Fiscal(StartFisYr,CalMo,CalYr,FisMo,FisYr);

DESCRIPTION

Calculates the current fiscal month and year when provided with the month that begins the fiscal year and the current calendar month and year.

PARAMETERS

All Integers

PAGE NUMBER

147

FixString

NUMBER

Tool 10.4

FILE NAME

FIXSTRNG.INC

SYNTAX

FixString(Operation,Width,StringVar);

DESCRIPTION

Operates upon the parameter StringVar according to the Operation parameter specified. As applicable, the Operation is carried out, and StringVar is returned with a string length as specified in the parameter Width. Operations are: C=Center, L=Left justify, P=Pad with spaces to right of string, R=Right justify, U=Convert to uppercase, D=Convert to lowercase, S=Strip leading spaces, T=Strip trailing spaces, and N=Return a string of nulls (ASCII # 0).

PARAMETERS

Char, Integer, Str255

PAGE NUMBER

281

Frame

NUMBER

Tool 7.6

FILE NAME
FRAME.INC

SYNTAX
Frame(TopLeftCol,TopRow,BotRightCol,BotRow);

DESCRIPTION
Produces a double-line frame between the coordinates passed as parameters; generally used to frame windows.

PARAMETERS
All Integers

PAGE NUMBER
209

GetDate

NUMBER
Tool 1.9

FILE NAME
GETDATE.INC

SYNTAX
GetDate(Month,Day,Year,WeekDay);

DESCRIPTION
Uses DOS function 42 to obtain the system date and weekday number.

PARAMETERS
All Integers

PAGE NUMBER
33

GetDirectory

NUMBER
Tool 2.10

FILE NAME
GETDIR.INC

SYNTAX
GetDirectory;

DESCRIPTION
Reads the directory for the current drive and path and writes each entry to the screen.

AUXILIARY PROCEDURES
GetDTA, SetDTA, BeginDirSearch, ContDirSearch, GetFileName

PAGE NUMBER
59

GetDTA

NUMBER
Tool 2.4

FILE NAME
GETDTA.INC

SYNTAX
GetDTA(DTASegment,DTAOffset);

DESCRIPTION
Uses DOS function 47 to obtain the current address of the DTA and returns the segment and offset of the address.

PARAMETERS
Both Integer

PAGE NUMBER
50

GetError

NUMBER

Tool 1.4

FILE NAME

GETERROR.INC

SYNTAX

GetError(Extended,Class,Action,Locus);

DESCRIPTION

Uses DOS function 89 to report the extended error codes when an error occurs under DOS 3.x.

PARAMETERS

All Integers

PAGE NUMBER

15

GetFileName

NUMBER

Tool 2.9

FILE NAME

GETFNAME.INC

SYNTAX

GetFileName(DTASeg,DTAOfs,FileName);

DESCRIPTION

Used when interpreting the information returned to the DTA in the course of a directory search. Given the address of the DTA through DTASeg and DTAOfs, it reads the ASCIIZ string containing the file name and returns the file name to the program.

PARAMETERS

Integer, Integer, Str255

PAGE NUMBER
58

GetOffset

NUMBER
Tool 7.2

FILE NAME
GETOFS.INC

SYNTAX
GetOffset(Col,Row,BaseAddress,CharOffset,AttributeOffset);

DESCRIPTION
Illustrates the method of determining the video RAM address of a particular character display cell on the screen. Given the screen column and row, the procedure will return the video RAM base address and the offsets for the character and attribute bytes.

PARAMETERS
All Integers

PAGE NUMBER
196

GetTime

NUMBER
Tool 1.11

FILE NAME
GETTIME.INC

SYNTAX
GetTime(Hour,Minute,Second);

DESCRIPTION
Uses DOS function 44 to obtain the system time.

PARAMETERS
All Integers

PAGE NUMBER
36

GetVerify

NUMBER
Tool 1.5

FILE NAME
GETVERIF.INC

SYNTAX
GetVerify(Verify);

DESCRIPTION
Obtains the present value of the verify switch using DOS function 84.

PARAMETER
Boolean

PAGE NUMBER
22

GetVersion

NUMBER
Tool 1.1

FILE NAME
GETVERS.INC

SYNTAX
GetVersion(DOSVersion);

DESCRIPTION
Uses DOS function 48 to return the version number of DOS in use.

PARAMETER
Real

PAGE NUMBER
9

ImageRecord

NUMBER

Tool 8.2

FILE NAME

IMAGEREC.INC

SYNTAX

ImageRecord(FileName);

DESCRIPTION

Captures the screen image and writes it to the file named in the parameter FileName. This procedure is used in conjunction with other procedures in Chapter 8 for the creation of a screen generator.

PARAMETER

Str255

PAGE NUMBER

219

InitPrnt

NUMBER

Tool 10.10

FILE NAME

INITPRNT.INC

SYNTAX

IntVar: = InitPrnt(WhichPrinter);

DESCRIPTION

Uses the printer services through DOS interrupt 23 to initialize the printer control port for the specified printer. It returns a status byte (i.e., IntVar = status byte), which may be passed on to the PrinterError procedure for interpretation.

PARAMETER

Integer

PAGE NUMBER
295

InitScrn

NUMBER
Tool 8.7

FILE NAME
INITSCRN.INC

SYNTAX
InitScrn;

DESCRIPTION
Initializes video RAM to zeroes so that all screen positions show no character and have no attribute. This procedure is used in conjunction with other procedures in Chapter 8 for the creation of a screen generator.

PAGE NUMBER
235

InKey

NUMBER
Tool 3.3

FILE NAME
INKEY.INC

SYNTAX
InKey(Col,Row,NumChars,TypeInput,Format,InString,InReal, Result);

DESCRIPTION
A keyboard data-entry procedure that moves the cursor to the specified column and row and accepts the specified number of valid keystrokes. Keystrokes are valid if they are the data type specified and in the appropriate format. The keyboard entry made by the user is returned in the

variable parameter InString or InReal, and the action terminating key-board input is reported by the Result parameter. Type input may be: B=Byte, I=Integer, R=Real, and S=String. The format for string input may be: A=As entered, U=Forced uppercase, L=Forced lowercase, and N=Numeric characters only. The format for real-number input is a character in the range of 0 through 9, indicating the allowable number of decimal places. All numeric input is returned in a real parameter, and for integer or byte data types, the returned number must be converted by a statement such as IntVariable: = Trunc(InReal). The result codes returned indicate: 0=Normal data input, 1=No data input, 2=User backspaced out of field, 3=Escape key pressed, and 4=User pressed Alt-H to request help.

PARAMETERS
Integer, Integer, Integer, Char, Char, Str255, Real, Integer

PAGE NUMBER
93

InpDate

NUMBER
Tool 4.7

FILE NAME
INPDATE.INC

SYNTAX
InpDate(Column,Row,mm,dd,yy,DayNo,Result);

DESCRIPTION
A keyboard-entry routine for dates that are to be input in the format mm/dd/yy. Column and Row position the cursor to the Month field, and entry continues from there. The weekday number is also returned to the program, and the Result codes are the same as those returned by the InKey procedure.

AUXILIARY PROCEDURES

InKey (for the actual keyboard input), ValidDate (to verify valid date entry)

PARAMETERS

All Integers

PAGE NUMBER

143

InterpretDate

NUMBER

Tool 2.7

FILE NAME

INTDATE.INC

SYNTAX

InterpretDate(DTASeg,DTAOfs,Month,Day,Year);

DESCRIPTION

Used when interpreting the information returned to the DTA in the course of a directory search. Given the address of the DTA through DTASeg and DTAOfs, it finds the encoded file-creation date and returns it as month, day, and year.

AUXILIARY PROCEDURES

ReadBits, SetBits

PARAMETERS

All Integers

PAGE NUMBER

55

InterpretTime

NUMBER

Tool 2.6

FILE NAME
  INTTIME.INC

SYNTAX
  InterpretTime(DTASeg,DTAOfs,Hour,Minute,Second);

DESCRIPTION
  Used when interpreting the information returned to the DTA in the course of a directory search. Given the address of the DTA through DTASeg and DTAOfs, it finds the encoded file-creation time and returns it as hours, minutes, and seconds.

AUXILIARY PROCEDURES
  ReadBits, SetBits

PARAMETERS
  All Integers

PAGE NUMBER
  53

Julian

NUMBER
  Tool 4.2

FILE NAME
  JULIAN.INC

SYNTAX
  JulianDate: = Julian(Year,Month,Day);

DESCRIPTION
  Returns the Julian date as a real number when provided the calendar month, day, and year.

PARAMETERS
  All Integers

PAGE NUMBER
  133

KbdCtrl

NUMBER

Tool 3.1

FILE NAME

KBDCTRL.INC

SYNTAX

KbdCtrl(Get_Set,Control,Setting,Result);

DESCRIPTION

Enables setting the Caps Lock, Num Lock, Scroll Lock, and Insert keys from within a program. Get_Set determines whether the procedure will obtain the present setting or set the appropriate control. Control specifies what is to be set: INS=Insert, SCR=Scroll Lock, CAP=Caps Lock, and NUM=Num Lock. Setting is either on or off. A zero result indicates success.

AUXILIARY PROCEDURES

BitSet, SetBits

PARAMETERS

Char, Str255, Str255, Integer

PAGE NUMBER

78

KeyTranslation

NUMBER

Tool 8.8

FILE NAME

KEYTRANS.INC

SYNTAX

KeyTranslation;

DESCRIPTION

Receives and translates keystrokes and takes appropriate action within the framework of the screen generator. This procedure is used in conjunction with other procedures in Chapter 8 for the creation of a screen generator.

PAGE NUMBER
237

KillDate

NUMBER
Tool 10.16

FILE NAME
KILLDATE.INC

SYNTAX
KillDate(Month,Day,Year);

DESCRIPTION
Checks the date passed as a parameter to see if it is beyond the expiration date of the program; if it is, the program is halted immediately.

PARAMETERS
All Integers

PAGE NUMBER
314

LgChar

NUMBER
Tool 9.1

FILE NAME
LGCHAR.INC

SYNTAX
LgChar(Col,Row,ToPrint,ChNo);

DESCRIPTION

Prints a large character on the screen from the character-pattern generator. Character's top-left corner is at Col and Row coordinates, as passed in the parameters. The character to be displayed is specified by ToPrint, and the character to use to make the pattern is specified by ChNo. See source code for upside down, backwards, and reverse-video character modifications.

PARAMETERS

All Integers

PAGE NUMBER

252

MakeTemp

NUMBER

Tool 3.6

FILE NAME

MAKETEMP.PAS

DESCRIPTION

A simple program for making a template file for use with the data-entry and display procedures in Chapter 3. The templates may be read with the ReadTemp procedure.

PAGE NUMBER

110

Menu

NUMBER

Tool 5.2

FILE NAME

MENU.INC

SYNTAX

Menu(MenuNumber,MenuFileName,TLCol,TLRow,MenuWidth, MenuLength,Choice);

DESCRIPTION

Saves the present screen, presents a menu on the screen of the width and length specified, and beginning at TLCol (top-left column) and TLRow (top-left row), lists the heading and selections on the menu after reading them from the ASCII file MenuFileName, based on the MenuNumber specification. The user selects a menu choice, which is returned in the parameter Choice.

AUXILIARY PROCEDURES

KbdCtrl, WindowIn, WindowOut, BitSet, SetBits.

PARAMETERS

Str255, Str255, Integer, Integer, Integer

PAGE NUMBER

168

NameFile

NUMBER

Tool 8.1

FILE NAME

NAMEFILE.INC

SYNTAX

NameFile(FileName);

DESCRIPTION

Determines if the screen file named exists and, if not, should be created. This procedure is used in conjunction with other procedures in Chapter 8 for the creation of a screen generator.

PARAMETER

Str255

PAGE NUMBER

217

PressKey

NUMBER
Tool 10.2

FILE NAME
PRESSKEY.INC

SYNTAX
PressKey;

DESCRIPTION
Issues a ClrEol statement, displays the message *Press any key to continue...*, and waits for a keystroke before returning to the program.

PAGE NUMBER
278

PrinterError

NUMBER
Tool 10.9

FILE NAME
PRNTERR.INC

SYNTAX
PrinterError(Status,ErrorNo,ErrorReturn);

DESCRIPTION
Furnished with the printer status byte returned by the PrintStat procedure, returns an error code indicating if a problem exists, as well as a literal ErrorReturn message specifying the problem.

PARAMETERS
Integer, Integer, Str255

PAGE NUMBER
294

················ ## Printers

NUMBER

Tool 10.6

FILE NAME

PRINTERS.INC

SYNTAX

IntVar: = Printers;

DESCRIPTION

Sets an integer variable to the number of parallel printers connected to the computer, according to the BIOS equipment list.

PAGE NUMBER

288

················ ## PrintStat

NUMBER

Tool 10.8

FILE NAME

PRNTSTAT.INC

SYNTAX

IntVar: = PrintStat(WhichPrinter);

DESCRIPTION

Returns a printer status code after using DOS interrupt 23. The status code is returned for the printer specified in the parameter WhichPrinter. This printer status code is then passed on to the PrinterError procedure for interpretation.

PARAMETER

Integer

PAGE NUMBER

293

PrLgChar

NUMBER

Tool 9.2

FILE NAME

PRLGCHAR.INC

SYNTAX

PrLgChar(ToPrint,ChNo,Direction);

DESCRIPTION

Applies the LgChar procedure to the printer and allows reproduction of a large character, specified by ToPrint, on the printer in either direction (vertically or horizontally). The character is printed using characters indicated by ChNo.

PARAMETERS

Integer, Integer, Char

PAGE NUMBER

255

Prompt

NUMBER

Tool 10.3

FILE NAME

PROMPT.INC

SYNTAX

Prompt(Col,Row,Video,PromptString);

DESCRIPTION

Writes the PromptString to the screen at Col and Row in either reverse video if Video=R, or normal video otherwise.

PARAMETERS

Integer, Integer, Char, Str255

PAGE NUMBER
278

PushLft

NUMBER
Tool 9.5

FILE NAME
PUSHLFT.INC

SYNTAX
PushLft(Col,Row,InString);

DESCRIPTION
Accepts a string of characters and displays them on the screen so that they appear to be pushing the previous characters to the left each time a new character appears. Display stops at the position indicated by Col and Row. See the source-code listing for modifications to make characters push to the right instead of the left.

AUXILIARY PROCEDURE
SpinEm (for characters that spin before moving)

PARAMETERS
Integer, Integer, Str255

PAGE NUMBER
261

RAMSize

NUMBER
Tool 10.7

FILE NAME
RAMSIZE.INC

SYNTAX
IntVar: = RAMSize;

DESCRIPTION
Sets the value of an integer variable to the size of RAM present on the computer in kilobytes.

PAGE NUMBER
289

ReadBit2

NUMBER
Tool 6.4

FILE NAME
READBIT2.INC

SYNTAX
ReadBit2(FlagInt,FlagArray);

DESCRIPTION
Reads the setting of each bit of the FlagInteger passed to it and sets the appropriate element of the Boolean array FlagArray to either true or false, depending on the setting of the bit read. FlagArray[0]=Bit 0 of FlagInt; FlagArray[15]=Bit 15 of FlagInt.

PARAMETERS
Integer, BoolArray

PAGE NUMBER
182

ReadBits

NUMBER
Tool 6.3

FILE NAME
  READBITS.INC

SYNTAX
  ReadBits(FlagInt,FlagString);

DESCRIPTION
  Takes the FlagInteger passed to it, reads the setting of each bit, and returns the settings as a series of ones or zeroes in the FlagString. FlagString[1]=Bit 0 of FlagInt; FlagString[16]=Bit 15 of FlagInt.

PARAMETERS
  Integer, Str255

PAGE NUMBER
  181

ReadKeyCode

NUMBER
  Tool 3.2

FILE NAME
  READKEY.INC

SYNTAX
  ReadKeyCode(Code,Standard);

DESCRIPTION
  Reads a keystroke and reports back the keyboard return code and whether it is a standard (printable) character (ASCII #32 through #126).

PARAMETERS
  Byte, Boolean

PAGE NUMBER
  90

ReadScrn

NUMBER
Tool 10.17

FILE NAME
READSCRN.INC

SYNTAX
CharVal: = ReadScrn(Col,Row);

DESCRIPTION
Returns the character that is displayed on the screen at the position indicated by the parameters Col and Row.

PARAMETERS
Both Integer

PAGE NUMBER
317

ReadTemp

NUMBER
Tool 3.7

FILE NAME
READTEMP.INC

SYNTAX
ReadTemp(FName,ScreenNum,TopHeap,NumberItems);

DESCRIPTION
Reads the template file created with the MakeTemp program. It is used in conjunction with the data-entry and display procedures in Chapter 3.

PARAMETERS
Integer, Integer, Pointr, Integer

PAGE NUMBER

115

ReverseVideo

NUMBER

Tool 9.7

FILE NAME

REVVIDEO.INC

SYNTAX

ReverseVideo;

DESCRIPTION

Causes reverse video to be displayed by reversing the normal monochrome foreground and background screen attributes.

PAGE NUMBER

267

ScreenGen2

NUMBER

Test Program 8.3

FILE NAME

SCRNGEN2.PAS

DESCRIPTION

A more complete screen generator than SimpleScreenGen1. Uses the
procedures NameFile, ImageRecord, WriteChar, InitScrn, DoGrid, and
KeyTranslation.

PAGE NUMBER

243

SendByte

NUMBER

Tool 10.11

FILE NAME

SENDBYTE.INC

SYNTAX

IntVar: = SendByte(WhichPrinter,ByteToSend);

DESCRIPTION

Uses DOS interrupt 23 to send the byte specified in the parameter Byte-ToSend to the printer specified by WhichPrinter. The status byte returned by the function to IntVar may be submitted to the PrinterError procedure to interpret which, if any, error has occurred.

PARAMETERS

Both Integer

PAGE NUMBER

295

SerialPrinter

NUMBER

Tool 10.6

FILE NAME

SERPRNTR.INC

SYNTAX

BoolVar: = SerialPrinter;

DESCRIPTION

Sets a Boolean variable to true if a serial printer is on the computer's equipment list; otherwise, it sets the variable to false.

PAGE NUMBER

288

SetBits

NUMBER

Tool 6.1

FILE NAME

SETBITS.INC

SYNTAX

SetBits(Operation,Position,Flag);

DESCRIPTION

Operates upon a bit in the specified Position of the FlagInteger and performs the specified operation. The operation may be: S=Set the bit to 1, U=Unset the bit to 0, or X=Change the bit to the opposite of its present state.

PARAMETERS

Char, Integer, Integer

PAGE NUMBER

179

SetCursor

NUMBER

Tool 9.8

FILE NAME

SETCURS.INC

SYNTAX

SetCursor(Top,Bottom);

DESCRIPTION

Using interrupt 16, sets the size of the cursor.

PARAMETERS

Both Integer

PAGE NUMBER
268

SetDate

NUMBER
Tool 1.10

FILE NAME
SETDATE.INC

SYNTAX
SetDate(Month,Day,Year);

DESCRIPTION
Uses DOS function 43 to set the system date.

PARAMETERS
All Integers

PAGE NUMBER
35

SetDTA

NUMBER
Tool 2.5

FILE NAME
SETDTA.INC

SYNTAX
SetDTA(DTASeg,DTAOfs);

DESCRIPTION
Uses DOS function 26 to reset the DTA to the address specified by DTASeg and DTAOfs.

PARAMETERS
Both Integer

PAGE NUMBER
51

SetTime

NUMBER
Tool 1.12

FILE NAME
SETTIME.INC

SYNTAX
SetTime(Hour,Minute,Second);

DESCRIPTION
Uses DOS function 45 to set the system time.

PARAMETERS
All Integers

PAGE NUMBER
37

SetVerify

NUMBER
Tool 1.6

FILE NAME
SETVERIF.INC

SYNTAX
SetVerify(Verify);

DESCRIPTION
Uses DOS function 46 to set the verify switch to the desired value.

PARAMETER
Boolean

PAGE NUMBER
23

ShowCode

NUMBER
No number—this program appears in Chapter 3 text

FILE NAME
SHOWCODE.PAS

DESCRIPTION
Program that displays return codes for keys pressed at the keyboard.

PAGE NUMBER
82

ShowScrn

NUMBER
Tool 8.4

FILE NAME
SHOWSCRN.INC

SYNTAX
ShowScrn(ScreenFileName,ScreenNo);

DESCRIPTION
Displays a screen image that has been captured and filed in a screen file. This procedure is used in conjunction with other procedures in Chapter 8 for the creation of a screen generator.

PARAMETERS
Str255, Integer

PAGE NUMBER

225

SimpleScreenGen1

NUMBER

Test Program 8.1

FILE NAME

SCRNGEN1.PAS

DESCRIPTION

A simple screen generator, which uses the procedures NameFile, ImageRecord, and TextRecord.

PAGE NUMBER

223

SlideBig

NUMBER

Tool 9.6

FILE NAME

SLIDEBIG.INC

SYNTAX

SlideBig(Col,Row,ToPrint,ChNo);

DESCRIPTION

Slides a large character across the screen. This procedure is a combination of the LgChar and SlideRt procedures.

PARAMETERS

All Integers

PAGE NUMBER

263

SlideChars

NUMBER

Test Program 9.3

FILE NAME

SLIDECHR.PAS

DESCRIPTION

Demonstrates the SlideRt, PushLft, and SlideBig procedures.

PAGE NUMBER

265

SlideRt

NUMBER

Tool 9.3

FILE NAME

SLIDERT.INC

SYNTAX

SlideRt(Col,Row,InString);

DESCRIPTION

Accepts a character string and causes it to appear to slide onto the screen from left to right and stop at the position specified by Col and Row. See the source code listing for modifications to slide characters from right to left.

AUXILIARY PROCEDURE

SpinEm (for characters that spin before moving)

PARAMETERS

Integer, Integer, Str255

PAGE NUMBER

257

....   **SpinEm**

NUMBER
Tool 9.4

FILE NAME
SPINEM.INC

SYNTAX
SpinEm(ScrAddr,Offset)

DESCRIPTION
Can be called by either the SlideRt or PushLft procedures to make the characters appear to be spinning at the side of the screen before moving across. ScrAddr and Offset have already been set in the SlideRt or PushLft procedures.

PARAMETERS
Word (versions 4.0 and 5.0) or Integer (earlier versions), Integer

PAGE NUMBER
260

....   **StringAndPromptDemo**

NUMBER
Test Program 10.1

FILE NAME
S&PDEMO.PAS

DESCRIPTION
Demonstrates the YesNo function, and the PressKey, Prompt, and FixString procedures.

PAGE NUMBER
284

SysInfo

NUMBER

Test Program 10.3

FILE NAME

SYSINFO.PAS

DESCRIPTION

Demonstrates the equipment list operations RAMSize, Color80Col, SerialPrinter, Printers, and Drives.

PAGE NUMBER

291

Template

NUMBER

Tool 6.5

FILE NAME

TEMPLATE.INC

SYNTAX

FlagInt: = Template(Pattern);

DESCRIPTION

Constructs an integer number equivalent to the bit map supplied by the parameter Pattern, which is a series of ones and zeroes.

PARAMETER

Str255

PAGE NUMBER

184

TestAttribute

NUMBER

Test Program 1.7

FILE NAME
TESTATTR.PAS

DESCRIPTION
Demonstrates the Attribute procedure.

PAGE NUMBER
32

TestBits

NUMBER
Test Program 6.1

FILE NAME
TESTBITS.PAS

DESCRIPTION
Demonstrates the procedures SetBits, BitSet, ReadBits, ReadBit2, and Template.

PAGE NUMBER
185

TestCurntPath

NUMBER
Test Program 1.3

FILE NAME
TESTCURP.PAS

DESCRIPTION
Demonstrates the CurntPath procedure.

PAGE NUMBER
14

TestCurrDrive

NUMBER
Test Program 1.2

FILE NAME
TESTCURD.PAS

DESCRIPTION
Demonstrates the CurrDrive procedure.

PAGE NUMBER
12

TestDataEntry

NUMBER
Test Program 3.3

FILE NAME
TESTNTRY.PAS

DESCRIPTION
Illustrates the use of a data-entry loop within a program to speed up entry and display operations. It uses the DataEntry and TestDataEntryScreen procedures.

PAGE NUMBER
106

TestDataEntryScreen

NUMBER
Tool 3.5

FILE NAME
TDES.INC

DESCRIPTION

Produces a data entry screen for use in the demonstration programs Test-DataEntry and UseTemplate.

PAGE NUMBER

106

TestDate

NUMBER

Test Program 4.1

FILE NAME

TESTDATE.PAS

DESCRIPTION

Demonstrates the procedures GetDate, SetDate, GetTime, SetTime, InKey, CalendarDate, ValidDate, ChekDate, and InpDate and function Julian and WeekDayNo.

PAGE NUMBER

145

TestDateTime

NUMBER

Test Program 1.8

FILE NAME

TESTDATI.PAS

DESCRIPTION

Demonstrates the GetDate, SetDate, GetTime, and SetTime procedures.

PAGE NUMBER

38

TestDirectry

NUMBER

Test Program 2.3

FILE NAME

TESTDIR.PAS

DESCRIPTION

Demonstrates the Directry procedure, as well as BeginDirSearch, ContDirSearch, GetDTA, SetDTA, InterpretTime, InterpretDate, ConvertWord, GetFileName, ReadBits, and SetBits.

PAGE NUMBER

73

TestDiskFreeSpc

NUMBER

Test Program 1.6

FILE NAME

TESTFREE.PAS

DESCRIPTION

Demonstrates the DiskFreeSpc procedure.

PAGE NUMBER

27

TestElapsed

NUMBER

Test Program 4.3

FILE NAME

TESTELAP.PAS

DESCRIPTION
Demonstrates the ElapsedTime procedure.

PAGE NUMBER
150

TestExist

NUMBER
Test Program 2.1

FILE NAME
TESTEXST.PAS

DESCRIPTION
Demonstrates the Exist function.

PAGE NUMBER
46

TestFileBytes

NUMBER
Test Program 10.2

FILE NAME
TESTFIBY.PAS

DESCRIPTION
Demonstrates the FileBytes function.

PAGE NUMBER
287

TestFiscal

NUMBER
Test Program 4.2

FILE NAME
TESTFISC.PAS

DESCRIPTION
Demonstrates the Fiscal procedure.

PAGE NUMBER
148

TestGetDirectory

NUMBER
Test Program 2.2

FILE NAME
TESTGETD.PAS

DESCRIPTION
Demonstrates the GetDirectory procedure which, in turn, uses procedures BeginDirSearch, ContDirSearch, GetDTA, SetDTA, and GetFileName.

PAGE NUMBER
61

TestGetError

NUMBER
Test Program 1.4

FILE NAME
TESTGETE.PAS

DESCRIPTION
Demonstrates the GetError procedure.

PAGE NUMBER
19

TestGetVersion

NUMBER
Test Program 1.1

FILE NAME
TESTGETV.PAS

DESCRIPTION
Demonstrates the GetVersion procedure.

PAGE NUMBER
11

TestKbdCtrl

NUMBER
Test Program 3.1

FILE NAME
TESTKBD.PAS

DESCRIPTION
Demonstrates the KbdCtrl procedure.

PAGE NUMBER
80

TestLgChar

NUMBER
Test Program 9.1

FILE NAME
TESTLGCH.PAS

DESCRIPTION
Demonstrates the LgChar procedure.

PAGE NUMBER
254

TestMenus

NUMBER
Test Program 5.1

FILE NAME
TESTMENU.PAS

DESCRIPTION
Demonstrates the CMenu and Menu procedures. The program requires that an ASCII file of menu selections be present and be named MENU-DEMO.MNU. The auxiliary procedures WindowIn, WindowOut, Set-Bits, BitSet, and KbdCtrl are also used.

PAGE NUMBER
169

TestPrLgChar

NUMBER
Test Program 9.2

FILE NAME
TESTPRLG.PAS

DESCRIPTION
Demonstrates the PrLgChar procedure.

PAGE NUMBER
257

TestPrnt

NUMBER
Test Program 10.4

FILE NAME
TESTPRNT.PAS

DESCRIPTION
Demonstrates the SendByte, InitPrnt, and PrintStat functions and the PrinterError procedure.

PAGE NUMBER
296

TestReadKey

NUMBER
Test Program 3.2

FILE NAME
TESTREAD.PAS

DESCRIPTION
Demonstrates the ReadKeyCode procedure.

PAGE NUMBER
91

TestVerify

NUMBER
Test Program 1.5

FILE NAME
TESTVERI.PAS

DESCRIPTION
Demonstrates the GetVerify and SetVerify procedures.

PAGE NUMBER
24

TextRecord

NUMBER

Tool 8.3

FILE NAME

TEXTREC.INC

SYNTAX

TextRecord(FName);

DESCRIPTION

Writes another procedure, which may then be included in a program. This procedure is used in conjunction with other procedures in Chapter 8 for the creation of a screen generator. The procedure written will produce a screen displaying the same characters as those displayed on the screen created with the TextScrn procedure.

PARAMETER

Str255

PAGE NUMBER

220

TryAutoBackup

NUMBER

Test Program 10.6

FILE NAME

TRYAB.PAS

DESCRIPTION

Demonstrates the AutoBackup procedure.

PAGE NUMBER

312

TryBarGraph

NUMBER
Test Program 9.5

FILE NAME
TRYBARGR.PAS

DESCRIPTION
Demonstrates the BarGraph procedure.

PAGE NUMBER
275

TryCursor

NUMBER
Test Program 9.4

FILE NAME
TRYCURS.PAS

DESCRIPTION
Demonstrates the SetCursor procedure.

PAGE NUMBER
269

TryFileSafe

NUMBER
Test Program 10.5

FILE NAME
TRYFS.PAS

DESCRIPTION
Demonstrates the three FileSafe procedures.

PAGE NUMBER
308

.... **TryKillDate**

NUMBER
Test Program 10.7

FILE NAME
TRYKILL.PAS

DESCRIPTION
Demonstrates the KillDate procedure.

PAGE NUMBER
316

.... **UseTemplate**

NUMBER
Test Program 3.4

FILE NAME
USETEMP.PAS

DESCRIPTION
Demonstrates various procedures in Chapter 3 for data input and display.

PAGE NUMBER
123

.... **ValidDate**

NUMBER
Tool 4.5

FILE NAME
VALIDATE.INC

SYNTAX

ValidDate(Month,Day,Year,WeekDay);

DESCRIPTION

Accepts a date and checks to determine that it is indeed a valid date. If the date is not valid, a valid date is returned. The day number of the weekday for the validated date is also returned. For example, if provided with 2/32/87, it will return 3/3/87.

AUXILIARY PROCEDURES

Julian, CalendarDate, WeekDayNo

PARAMETERS

All Integers

PAGE NUMBER

137

WeekDayNo

NUMBER

Tool 4.3

FILE NAME

WEEKDAY.INC

SYNTAX

WeekDay: = WeekDayNo(Date);

DESCRIPTION

Returns an integer number for the day of the week when provided a Julian date from which to calculate it. The number returned corresponds to: 0 = Sunday, 1 = Monday, etc.

PARAMETER

Real

PAGE NUMBER

135

·· ## WindowExample

NUMBER
Test Program 7.1

FILE NAME
WINDOWEX.PAS

DESCRIPTION
Demonstrates the WindowIn, ExWindow, Frame, and WindowOut procedures.

PAGE NUMBER
211

·· ## WindowIn

NUMBER
Tool 7.3

FILE NAME
WINDOWIN.INC

SYNTAX
WindowIn(TopL,TopRow,BotR,BotRow,CursorCol,CursorRow, DataPtr);

DESCRIPTION
Saves the present screen to dynamic RAM beginning at the address returned in the DataPtr parameter, notes the present cursor position in the parameters CursorCol and CursorRow, and returns these values to the program so that the present screen and cursor position can be restored by the WindowOut procedure. A window is then created and cleared at the positions TopL (top-left column), TopRow, BotR (bottom-right column), and BotRow.

PARAMETERS
Integer, Integer, Integer, Integer, Integer, Integer, Pointr

PAGE NUMBER
201

.... ## WindowOut

NUMBER

Tool 7.9

FILE NAME

WINDOOUT.INC

SYNTAX

WindowOut(CursorCol,CursorRow,DataPtr);

DESCRIPTION

Restores the screen and replaces the cursor as it was prior to calling the WindowIn or ExWindow procedure. The parameters CursorCol, CursorRow, and DataPtr were obtained when the WindowIn or ExWindow procedures returned to the program.

PARAMETERS

Integer, Integer, Pointr

PAGE NUMBER

208

.... ## WriteChar

NUMBER

Tool 8.5

FILE NAME

WRITECHR.INC

SYNTAX

WriteChar(ScrAddr,Col,Row,Character,Attribute);

DESCRIPTION

Writes a character directly to video RAM with the screen attribute passed as a parameter. This procedure is used in conjunction with other procedures in Chapter 8 for the creation of a screen generator.

PARAMETERS
All Integers

PAGE NUMBER
234

YesNo

NUMBER
Tool 10.1

FILE NAME
YESNO.INC

SYNTAX
Answer: = YesNo;

DESCRIPTION
A simple function to return a character Y for yes or N for no when it is
called. It is to be used when prompting for a Y/N answer from the user.
The message *(Y/N)* is displayed, and after an answer is input, the function returns to the program with that answer.

PAGE NUMBER
278

INDEX

Selections from The SYBEX Library

LANGUAGES

Introduction to Turbo Pascal (Second Edition)
Douglas S. Stivison
Charles Edwards
268pp. Ref. 414-3
A newly revised and updated version of our bestselling hands-on introduction to Turbo Pascal. Topics range from programming fundamentals to data structures, graphics, sound, and more—all demonstrated in practical sample programs.

Advanced Techniques in Turbo Pascal
Charles C. Edwards
309pp. Ref. 350-3
This collection of system-oriented techniques and sample programs shows how to make the most of IBM PC capabilities using Turbo Pascal. Topics include screens, windows, directory management, the mouse interface, and communications.

Introduction to Turbo BASIC
Douglas Hergert
350pp. Ref. 441-0
A complete tutorial and guide to this now highly professional language: Turbo BASIC, including important Turbo extras such as parameter passing, structured loops, long integers, recursion, and 8087 compatibility for high-speed numerical operation.

Advanced Techniques in Turbo Prolog*
Carl Townsend
300pp. Ref. 428-3
A goldmine of techniques and predicates for control procedures, string operations, list processing, database operations, BIOS-level support, program development, expert systems, natural language processing, and much more.

Introduction to Turbo Prolog
Carl Townsend
315pp. Ref. 359-7
This comprehensive tutorial includes sample applications for expert systems, natural language interfaces, and simulation. Covers every aspect of Prolog: facts, objects and predicates, rules, recursion, databases, and much more.

Introduction to Pascal: Including Turbo Pascal
Rodnay Zaks
464pp. Ref. 319-8
This best-selling tutorial builds complete mastery of Pascal—from basic structured programming concepts, to advanced I/O, data structures, file operations, sets, pointers and lists, and more. Both ISO Standard and Turbo Pascal.

Introduction to Pascal (Including UCSD Pascal)
Rodnay Zaks
420pp. Ref. 066-0
This edition of our best-selling tutorial on Pascal programming gives special attention to the UCSD Pascal implementation for small computers. Covers everything from basic concepts to advanced data structures and more.

The Pascal Handbook
Jacques Tiberghien
383pp. Ref. 053-9

The Pascal programmer's definitive reference, for both micro and mainframe versions of Pascal. A to Z entries, complete with illustrations, cover every Pascal instruction, function, operator and reserved word in detail.

Fifty Pascal Programs
Bruce H. Hunter
338pp. Ref. 110-1
A valuable collection of programs for business, engineering, finance, games, and more, illustrating concepts of structured programming, I/O techniques, transcendental functions, data type creation, sorting and searching, and much more.

Your First BASIC Program
Rodnay Zaks
182pp. Ref. 092-X
This illustrated, step-by-step introduction to computer programming in BASIC will have novices writing complete programs in a matter of hours. Covers everything from first concepts to loops and branches—all in plain language.

Celestial BASIC: Astronomy on Your Computer
Eric Burgess
300pp. Ref. 087-3
A complete home planetarium. This collection of BASIC programs for astronomical calculations enables armchair astronomers to observe and identify on screen the configurations and motions of sun, moon, planets and stars.

Understanding C
Bruce H. Hunter
320pp. Ref. 123-3
A programmer's introduction to C, with special attention to implementations for microcomputers—both CP/M and MS-DOS. Topics include data types, storage management, pointers, random I/O, function libraries, compilers and more.

Mastering C
Craig Bolon
437pp. Ref. 326-0

This in-depth guide stresses planning, testing, efficiency and portability in C applications. Topics include data types, storage classes, arrays, pointers, data structures, control statements, I/O and the C function library.

Data Handling Utilities in C
Robert A. Radcliffe/Thomas J. Raab
519pp. Ref. 304-X
A C library for commercial programmers, with techniques and utilities for data entry, validation, display and storage. Focuses on creating and manipulating custom logical data types: dates, dollars, phone numbers, much more.

ASSEMBLY LANGUAGE

Programming the 8086/8088
James W. Coffron
311pp. Ref. 120-9
A concise introduction to assembly-language programming for 8086/8088-based systems, including the IBM PC. Topics include architecture, memory organization, the complete instruction set, interrupts, I/O, and IBM PC BIOS routines.

Programming the 80286
C. Vieillefond
487pp. Ref. 277-9
In-depth treatment of assembly-level programming for the IBM PC/AT's 80286 processor. Topics include system architecture, memory management, address modes, multitasking and more; plus a complete reference guide to the instruction set.

SYBEX Computer Books
are different.

Here is why . . .

At SYBEX, each book is designed with you in mind. Every manuscript is carefully selected and supervised by our editors, who are themselves computer experts. We publish the best authors, whose technical expertise is matched by an ability to write clearly and to communicate effectively. Programs are thoroughly tested for accuracy by our technical staff. Our computerized production department goes to great lengths to make sure that each book is well-designed.

In the pursuit of timeliness, SYBEX has achieved many publishing firsts. SYBEX was among the first to integrate personal computers used by authors and staff into the publishing process. SYBEX was the first to publish books on the CP/M operating system, microprocessor interfacing techniques, word processing, and many more topics.

Expertise in computers and dedication to the highest quality product have made SYBEX a world leader in computer book publishing. Translated into fourteen languages, SYBEX books have helped millions of people around the world to get the most from their computers. We hope we have helped you, too.

For a complete catalog of our publications:

SYBEX, Inc. 2021 Challenger Drive, #100, Alameda, CA 94501
Tel: (415) 523-8233/(800) 227-2346   Telex: 336311

TURBO PASCAL TOOLBOX
Procedures, Functions, and Programs
Available on Disk

If you would like to use the procedures, functions, and programs in this book but don't want to type them in yourself, you can send for a disk containing these files. To obtain this disk, complete the order form and send it, along with a check or money order for $29.95, to the address shown on the form.

Procedure, function, and program files are furnished on two double-sided, double-density, 360-kilobyte diskettes, formatted for IBM PC compatible computers. One diskette contains files for use with Turbo Pascal versions 4.0 and 5.0, and the other diskette contains files for use with earlier versions.

- -

Affordable Automation
P.O. Box 821338
Houston, TX 77282-1338

Name _____

Company _____

Address _____

City/State/Zip _____

Enclosed is my check or money order for $29.95. Texas residents add 8 percent sales tax. For overseas shipments, add U.S. $3.55. (Make check payable to Affordable Automation.) Please send me a disk containing the *Turbo Pascal Toolbox* files.

SYBEX is not affiliated with Affordable Automation *and assumes no responsibility for any defect in the disk or program.*